NEW PROCLAMATION W9-BCA-558

New Proclamation
Year B 2012

Advent through Holy Week
November 27, 2011—April 8, 2012

Beth Tanner

Paul Galbreath

Melinda A. Quivik

Gordon W. Lathrop

David B. Lott, Editor

Fortress Press

Minneapolis

NEW PROCLAMATION
Year B 2012
Advent through Holy Week
November 27, 2011—April 8, 2012

Illustrations: Joel Nickel, Peggy Adams Parker, Robyn Sand Anderson, Meg Bussey, and Paula Wiggins, © 2010 Augsburg Fortress.
Cover design: Laurie Ingram
Book design: Sharon Martin

Library of Congress Cataloging-in-Publication Data
The Library of Congress has catalogued this series as follows.
New Proclamation: Year B 2012 Advent through Holy Week.
     p. cm.
    Includes bibliographical references.
    ISBN 978-0-8066-9631-7
       1. Church year. I. Moloney, Francis J.
    BV30 .N48 2001
    2511.6dc21 2001023746

Library of Congress Cataloging-in-Publication Data
ISBN 978-0-8006-9771-6

The paper used in this publication meets the minimum requirements of American National Standard for Information Sciences—Permanence of Paper for Printed Library Materials, ANSI Z329.48-1984.

Manufactured in the U.S.A.
15   14   13   12   11   1   2   3   4   5   6   7   8   9   10

Contents

Epiphany—Time after Epiphany / Ordinary Time
Paul Galbreath

Lent
Melinda A. Quivik

Holy Week
Gordon W. Lathrop

Preface

For nearly four decades Fortress Press has offered an ecumenical preaching resource built around the three-year lectionary cycle, a tradition that this latest edition of *New Proclamation* continues. *New Proclamation* is grounded in the belief that a deeper understanding of the biblical pericopes in both their historical and liturgical contexts is the best means to inform and inspire preachers to deliver engaging and effective sermons. For this reason, the most capable North American biblical scholars and homileticians are invited to contribute to *New Proclamation*.

New Proclamation has always distinguished itself from most other lectionary resources by offering brand-new editions each year, each dated according to the church year in which it will first be used and featuring a fresh set of authors. Yet each edition is planned as a timeless resource that preachers will want to keep on their bookshelves as a reference for years to come. In addition, *New Proclamation,* true to its ecumenical scope, has traditionally offered commentary on all of the major lectionary traditions. Now, reflecting changes in practices among the mainline Protestant denominations, those number just two: the *Revised Common Lectionary* (RCL) and the Roman Catholic *Lectionary for Mass* (LFM).

New Proclamation is published in two volumes per year. This first volume covers all the Sunday lections and major festivals from Advent through Easter Vigil and Easter Day. The second volume, which will be published later this year, begins with new commentary on the Easter Vigil and covers the remaining Sunday lections and major festivals through Christ the King Sunday. For those churches that celebrate minor feast days and solemnities, including saints' days, denominational days such as Body and Blood of Christ (Corpus Christi) or Reformation Day, and national days and topical celebrations, a separate volume covering the texts for those days is available: *New Proclamation Commentary on Feasts, Holy Days, and Other Celebrations* (ed. David B. Lott; Fortress Press, 2007).

Longtime users of *New Proclamation* will note the adoption of a fresh look, which ties the series in visually with Augsburg Fortress's popular worship resource *Sundays and Seasons.* We hope that this change not only makes the text more readable and accessible, but also encourages readers to use these fine resources in tandem

with each other. We also invite you to visit this volume's companion Web site, www.
NewProclamation.com, which offers access not only to this book's contents, but also
commentary from earlier editions, up-to-the-minute thoughts on the connection
between texts and current events, user forums, and other resources to help you
develop your sermons and enhance your preaching.

What has not changed with this edition is the high quality of the content
that *New Proclamation* provides to preachers and those interested in studying the
lectionary texts. Each writer offers an introduction to her or his commentary that
provides insights into the background and spiritual significance of that season (or
portion thereof), as well as ideas for planning one's preaching during that time. In
addition, the application of biblical texts to contemporary situations is an important
concern of each contributor. Exegetical work is concise, and thoughts on how the texts
address today's world, congregational issues, and personal situations have a prominent
role.

This latest volume brings together both veterans from previous *New Proclamation*
volumes as well as writers who are making their Fortress Press debuts. A professor of
both Old Testament and preaching, Beth Tanner pushes us beyond easy domestication
of the Advent and Christmas texts to a heartfelt proclamation of good news.
For Epiphany, Paul Galbreath brings his expertise in worship and preaching in
conversation with his particular interest in the formation of Christian communities.
Another worship and preaching specialist, Melinda Quivik, journeys with the
preacher deeply into the texts and practices of Lent. And the esteemed liturgical
scholar Gordon Lathrop once again graces the pages of *New Proclamation* with a
masterful exploration of Holy Week, leading us into a joyful celebration of Easter. All
four breathe new life into the lectionary texts and will help preachers do the same as
they proclaim the gospel within the congregations they serve. We are grateful to each
of these contributors for their insights and their commitment to effective Christian
preaching, and are confident that you will find in this volume ideas, stimulation, and
encouragement for your ministry of proclamation.

David B. Lott

Advent
Beth Tanner

"Another Advent!" is usually uttered in church staff meetings around the middle of September, followed by the inevitable "Where has the year gone?" Soon thereafter begin the plans for all of the services and festivities. For pastors and church staff, Advent also means more meetings, services, and obligations added into an already-packed schedule. It is always a stressful time. This year there is even more to do because 2011 is a year when Christmas Day falls on a Sunday. Decisions must be made in Protestant churches concerning the number and time of services, while the Roman Catholic mass schedule is altered. These changes in our routine add to the stress and strain of the season. There never seems to be enough time to get everything done. It will be a busy Advent indeed.

Truth be told, the congregation itself does not think much differently about this "most wonderful time of the year." Sure, there are nostalgic remembrances of Christmases past with family and hopes for the future, but those thoughts soon give way to thinking of dragging out the ladder so that the lights can go up and the tree can be decorated, all as the hunt for presents gears up. It could be easily titled "the most stressful and busy time of the year"!

This *big* Christmas season is unique to the United States, although its size continues to grow throughout North America and other Westernized areas. This season is the pinnacle of consumer consumption and TV commercials seem to imply the only way to make your family happy is to put a large bow on a new luxury car. Wall Street responds positively or negatively to the daily reports of how much we are spending and sale catalogs flood our mailboxes. It is our responsibility to help the economy by buying, buying, buying. It is the American thing to do and don't think about the cost because that's why we have credit cards.

This may be the American front story, but the dream has come crashing down in the past few years. The economy has turned and both individual members and congregations as a whole are forced to face the economic realities. Economists tell us it may be a decade or more before the unemployment rate drops and housing values return to the level of a decade ago. On any given Sunday, there are parents in the congregation who are wondering how to tell the children there will be few presents this year and children who are praying for their mom or dad to be able to find a job. The hurt is real and the pain is evident. Another group will suffer through the holidays in new sites far from home and feeling alone. For other families, this will be the last Christmas together because one of them has a terminal diagnosis that no amount of spending or partying can alter. Even in a family without major life changes, Christmas is stressful as we balance all of the things to do along with job and family responsibilities. We all long for something that presents cannot buy. We long for something beyond that *big* Christmas experience. We long for peace. We long for a better world that is more substance than show. We long for God. We know the Christmas we see in the ads and on television is not one that will feed the soul or bring us closer to God. We need something else.

Thankfully, Advent is always out of step with our culture's demands and its texts deliver that something else. Advent has nothing to do with growing the economy through shopping. It has nothing to do with overeating and overdrinking. It has nothing to do with the stock market or with political disagreements about what can be placed on the lawn at city hall. It is not involved in the "Merry Christmas" or "Happy Holidays" debate.

Our challenge as preachers is to bring Advent, the real Advent, to full voice, and this is not always easy. It is hard to hear these texts over the roar of commercials and Christmas music. It is even a hard sell in many congregations. Congregations want to sing "O Come All Ye Faithful" and "Joy to the World" on the Sunday after Thanksgiving. In our world, we are encouraged to rush to the manger with no stops along the way. We are told to want the "happily-ever-after" ending of the baby without the long wait for God. The world also wants Christians to leave the baby in the manger instead of taking seriously the grown-up Jesus who is preaching a radical message of love and who is a critic of the religious and political authorities. In short, the culture of Christmas is shaping what we think inside the church about the season. Advent has all but disappeared in the rush to the presents. It is our job each year to bring Advent to our people.

The Advent texts do not bend to the culture and refuse to be domesticated. We as preachers must boldly proclaim these texts and provide solace and hope to those who know the "Christmas dream" is little more than an illusion. We must also proclaim to those who have been influenced by the culture to ignore Advent. These texts tell the story for which we long, even if we have to fight through a haze of secular smoke to get there.

One of the most striking things in this year's texts is the juxtaposition between their message and their context. Isaiah's words of hope do not match the reality of postexilic rebuilding of the country. God's gift of Jesus happens far from Jerusalem and far from the halls of power. God sends a baby instead of a general-king who will remove the Romans. Jesus is the one baptized by that crazy outsider, John. Jesus, who will show us what it means to live, will die at our hands. These and many other ironies are folded into these texts. That is the real story, the biblical story. We are called to preach that gritty story of struggle instead of the sanitized fairy tale that our world has manufactured, for our stories are also gritty and all too real and rarely feel like fairy tales. The real biblical text matches our lives and that is why they resonate with us all of these centuries later.

Our homiletical task is to undomesticate these texts, to unleash them with all of their irony—not just because it is how the stories were formed and saved for us, but mainly because, unbridled, these texts stand as a critique of us and our culture just as God's actions thousands of years ago did the same. Their ironies can help us to set our priorities in order and to reclaim the Christian story during this season of Advent.

November 27, 2011
First Sunday of Advent

First Reading
Isaiah 64:1-9 (RCL)
Isaiah 63:16b-17; 19b; 64:2-7 (LFM)

How can Advent begin with the harsh notes of lament? The Isaiah selection is a communal prayer of confession. It is a prayer that readily acknowledges human frailties and sin. It is also a prayer of longing for restored relationship with God.

Third Isaiah is a book about hope unrealized. The people envisioned a return from exile as a triumphant, restored group. God would wipe away the tears and magically Jerusalem would be restored. The reality of the situation was a jolt. The city and the Temple still lay in ruins. The recovery was not magical; it was hard, slow work. The people were discouraged and lost heart. They thought their struggle was evidence of God's desertion.

This sentiment sounds a familiar note in today's world. I am a Christian, so why is my life so hard? Why is there suffering and greed and sorrow? Why am I still unemployed? Why is the world so broken? Where are God's promises to me? Fortunately, the Bible never shirks away from hard conversations when the relationship between God and human feels broken. Advent marks the beginning of the Christian year, and new beginnings cannot fully begin until old feelings are spoken and tended.

The two readings give this prayer two distinctive shapes. The LFM begins with frankness. Yes, Lord, you are our Redeemer, so why did you make us stray and harden our hearts? Wait a minute, are the people blaming God for their straying? Without a doubt, they are. I did say the Bible is honest. The Bible knows us intimately and we have been blaming God since the creation and that first disobedient act. When caught by God, the answer is quick: "The woman whom you gave to be with me, she gave me fruit from the tree, and I ate" (Gen. 3:12). It is your fault, God, it is her fault. It's somebody else's fault! In Isaiah, the people's next reaction is also predictable, for they are brazen enough not only to blame God, but also to ask God to turn back and fix the situation. They act like children who trust God to love them and fix what they have broken, even after they have wrecked the car. The wish for God to appear follows (vv. 2-4, see below). The LFM reading ends at verse 7, leaving the people still holding their sin and with their iniquities threatening to carry them away. They are left on this first Sunday of Advent waiting for God's intervention to repair their sinful acts.

The RCL begins with the wish that God would "tear open the heavens and come down." In this, it strikes the same tone as the Gospel lesson, hoping for God's dramatic coming into the world. It recalls themes of a powerful God who arrives in a noisy and dramatic way. This powerful God is called on, not to fight an enemy, but because of the people's sin! God's coming into the world is not to destroy, but to restore and heal. The people are lost and overwhelmed by sin and only God can repair what they have broken. This lection ends by expressing the confidence that no matter what has happened God will respond. The people wait here also, but they wait in the belief that God will not remain angry forever.

Psalmody
Psalm 80:1-7, 17-19 (RCL)
Psalm 80:2-3, 15-16, 18-19 (LFM)

The psalm continues the cry of lament. Whether the response begins at verse 1 or 2, the cries are urgent: "Stir up your might!" "Save us!" "Restore us!" The RCL continues to describe the trouble: God is even angry at the people's prayers (v. 4); their food and drink are tears (v. 5); and their enemies laugh (v. 6). What is needed is repeated both in verses 3 and 7: "Let your face shine, that we may be saved." The "shining of the face" is an ancient way of showing favor; just as the faces of the parents shine or light up when the prodigal child returns. We need our God to throw open divine arms and receive us. We need to know our sins have been forgiven and we are restored.

The LFM moves from verses 2-3 with the first refrain to what has happened to the "vine" (v. 15). The vine God brought forth from Egypt (v. 8), reminding all of the long path God and the people have shared. The vine is now struck down by an enemy. The term *enemy* in the psalms needs clarification. This adversary serves not as a combatant but is anything that destroys us and our relationships (vv. 15-16). Most of the lament psalms leave us, the readers, to name the enemy lurking in our lives, whether it is a person or a situation that does not permit us to live abundantly. In the Hebrew, verse 15 is one line longer than in the NRSV, reading, "Support that which your right hand planted; the child you, yourself, caused to grow strong," further stressing the

5

vulnerability of God's people as a child and the intimate connection we share with the one who planted us. The way the LFM reading is shaped changes the intent of the full psalm. It is not the sin of the people from verses 4-7, but the acts of the enemies (vv. 15-16) that are the threat. That is, the threat in the LFM reading is an external one.

The RCL selection shapes the problem as the people's sin. Verse 17 continues to seek the solution of this problem, calling on "God's right hand" to be upon the vine/child whom the one God, God's self, has grown. God is also portrayed in the most powerful of terms: "God of hosts" (or, literally, "armies") in verses 4, 7, and 19, as well as "stir up your might" in verse 2, and "your right hand," all speak of God in the most fearsome terms. We have been taught to fear God's power, but these ancients remind us that we need to call on our powerful God to restore our broken lives. To the ancient folks, God as the Supreme Ruler of the universe is the same one who planted and tended them for generations and God is needed now. The psalm and the Isaiah reading both end with a final plea of the people as they wait for God to respond to their cry.

Both this psalm and the Isaiah text are communal cries to God, asking for the restoration of all of God's people. This universal scope also serves as a reminder on this first day of Advent that God's grace and salvation are not the possession of one person. In this way, it points to God's promise about the coming one, for God so loved the *world*, that God gave God's only Son. The psalm teaches us as individuals to seek the welfare of the world, not just our small corner of it.

Second Reading
1 Corinthians 1:3-9 (RCL, LFM)

The first reading provides the confession and this reading provides the assurance of pardon and grace. An assurance grants forgiveness and it also provides a vision of life as it should be. Paul's greeting offers such a vision. He first gives thanks for God's grace (v. 3). Then he describes a community restored, enriched in speech and knowledge, and as a place where the testimony of Christ is kept and strengthened by our Christian bonds of community. Paul then tells the church it has every spiritual gift that it needs! This is the church at Corinth and, later in the letter, Paul will have much to say about their worship wars and their communion battles (3:1-9, for example). Here he is speaking of the church as it can be only by God's grace; later he will deal with the church that is marred in petty arguments.

Advent is the beginning of the Christian year. With this reading, Paul is offering us a vision for this new year. Our job is to believe Paul's amazing words. Could we, on this Christian New Year's Day, believe our church community has all the resources we need right here in this group of believers? Can we start the year the way Paul starts his letters, believing that through the power of God among us we can do great and magnificent things? Dare we dream for ourselves as much as God dreams for us? As humans, we tend to see what we do not have and all of the things that hold us back.

Paul's thoughts here are not of the church's deficits, but of God's bounty of grace.

Paul's last reminder is also important. We are not called by others, but by Jesus Christ. The church, or even this community, is not our property, just as the world is not. We come only by God's invitation and we are called to work in this place and with these people. Being a community is its own spiritual discipline. It is a discipline because it takes work and commitment. It is a discipline because we are called to be together when it is uncomfortable or even hostile. We are called to grow into loving those we find hard to like. We are called to be Christ-like and see each other through the eyes of our God. Paul calls on us to believe in our community as much as God believes in us and to dare to dream bigger than we have in the past. Pardon from God is step one; a new vision is step two in this Advent season.

Gospel
Mark 13:24-37 (RCL)
Mark 13:33-37 (LFM)

The setting for this text is Jesus' last sayings before he is arrested. Chapter 13 is known as "the little apocalypse." The RCL reading contains three distinctive pericopes: the coming of the Son of Man (vv. 24-27), the lesson of the fig tree (vv. 28-31), and the command to watch (vv. 32-37). The LFM uses only the last of the three.

It is essential that we rightly preach apocalyptic sayings of Jesus, if for no other reason than to counteract their use by some who twist the gospel into a message of hate and condemnation. In Mark, the context of these texts is crucial to their interpretation. Jesus, the one who came as the Prince of Peace, the one who will die instead of raise a hand to his captors, the one whose mission from the Father is to *love* the whole world, speaks these words right before he is unjustly betrayed, tried, and crucified. It is absolutely incongruous with his ministry that his last message be one of threat and damnation. In these texts, there is no statement about the wicked, only the gathering of the elect.[1] Jesus' last words are ones of comfort and assurance and advice on living through the tough times to come as we wait for the second coming.

The context here in Mark is the same seen in the Old Testament apocalyptic texts[2] and the same as set by the psalm. They all express the people's wish for the all-powerful God to come crashing into the world to restore it. Psalm 96 cries out in praise for God to come in all of God's glory and "judge the world with righteousness and the peoples with God's truth!" Instead of greeting Jesus' coming with fear and dread, we are to laugh and leap and welcome it. The coming of God from the clouds is the best news of all! God is coming to shape us into the people and communities we should be, where all are at peace with each other.

The next pericope (RCL) is in the form of a parable and as such requires one to ponder its many meanings. The fig tree has a predictable cycle, year after year, its green leaves signal the coming of summer. It is a familiar sight to Jesus' audience. Then Jesus says, "When you see these things take place, you will know it is near, at the very gates," and it will happen in this generation! Scholars have long speculated on exactly what "these things" refer to without much success or consensus. Read with today's other Scriptures, a possibility emerges. The cycle of the tree is as sure as the seasons and it is repeated each year in a seemingly endless loop of creation. Then how could Jesus be speaking of a one-time event? What is as cyclic as the seasons? There is one cycle repeated again and again in today's texts. When we cry to God, God hears our prayer and restores us to new life. God's love is as sure as the seasons and will last even after the cosmos disappears. This is the cycle we can bet our very salvation on, "for heaven and earth will pass away" but Jesus' words will not. This seasonal sign is the "now" of the "now and not yet." It is what keeps us until the great coming at the end of time. The lesson of the tree then could represent the flashes of grace and forgiveness we see every day. The cycle of God's constant love is the sign that God is always near, keeping us and protecting us from ourselves.

The final lesson is about what humans think they know. There are all kinds of prophets who believe they can read the signs and discover God's eternal timing. Jesus declares that if he does not know, then how could anyone else? This last saying reminds us what is of God and not for human speculation. God's timing is not to be our concern. Jesus is clear and he tells us that we do have a role, that is, to wait and watch and stay awake in the spiritual sense. We are to do what God created us to do and trust in God for the rest. Concentrate on the signs of grace we can see, and do not engage in speculation about what we cannot possibly know. We are to be faithful to the life that God has given us and be content with today while trusting God for tomorrow.

The First Sunday of Advent is about truth telling and teaching. It begins with the cries of the people, lost without their God. People, even though they have strayed, know that God's love will restore them to full life. Paul then reminds us that we are not only restored but gifted by God with all of the tools needed for the tasks of the kingdom. Jesus' words from Mark also tell of God's love for us and how we are to live. Each text also longs for and celebrates the coming of God into the world. God comes for us to offer grace and forgiveness, and that is indeed the best news of all.

Notes

1. Pheme Perkins, "Mark," in *The New Interpreter's Bible Commentary* (Nashville: Abingdon, 1995), 8:692.
2. Sibley Towner, "Exposition of Mark 13:24-32," *Interpretation* 30, no. 3 (1976): 295.

December 4, 2011
Second Sunday of Advent

Revised Common Lectionary (RCL)

Isaiah 40:1-11

Psalm 85:1-2, 8-13

2 Peter 3:8-15a

Mark 1:1-8

Lectionary for Mass (LFM)

Isaiah 40:1-5, 9-11

Psalm 85:9ab + 10, 11-12, 13-14

2 Peter 3:8-14

Mark 1:1-8

First Reading
Isaiah 40:1-11 (RCL)
Isaiah 40:1-5, 9-11 (LFM)

Have you ever felt like God was punishing you? We have all pondered this question. For God's community, the exile and the destruction of God's Temple, the loss of a way of life, and, most importantly, the loss of hope were seen as a punishment from God. They had not been faithful and this was the result. It is not my intention to get wrapped up in the theological question of whether God truly punishes us in this life for our sins. This is how the people of God will frame the exile, whether we agree with their theological perspective or not. The people had sinned. The relationship was broken. The people needed a word from God that would transform their sinful state back to full relationship.

It is from this place that these words sing forth, "Comfort, O comfort, my people!" "[Jerusalem] has served her term, her penalty is paid!" Sometimes these are the only words that can heal the broken spirit. "Comfort, comfort, my people," your God says, and with those two pronouns, "my" and "your," we are again restored to full relationship. This Scripture is, of course, part of Handel's famous *Messiah*. His music sets the right tone for this text. This is not just any reconciliation, for the very creation changes its course to welcome home God and God's people. The world leaps for joy just as the music does. God's coming, God's advent, is a creation-wide party of gigantic proportions.

The second voice (vv. 6-8 in the RCL) takes us back to last week's message and the place of the people and God. The people are grass, they grow and fade, but "the word of our God will stand forever," just as in Mark 13:31. Restored relationship involves us all understanding our place in God's plan. Our function is to remain faithful to our God even if we fade quickly.

The last section is one of pure joy: tell the good tidings, God is coming home! God is coming back to Jerusalem. God is coming in might and in power. God is coming to shepherd God's people, to carry them in the divine arms. God is coming to create peace. The herald here calls forth images of the angels that will sing the tidings in Luke's narrative on the night of Jesus' birth.

God's forgiveness is the reason for this worldwide party. How often do we pause to think of what we are really doing as we sing the Kyrie or the Doxology? Like last week's readings, we are again called to celebrate the very attribute that has allowed this relationship to go forward time after time. Without God's great love manifested in grace and forgiveness there would be no Advent or baby in the manger. This text invites us to dwell on this greatest of gifts and to remember God's forgiveness and to sing praises for it. Advent, or God's coming, is found each and every time we confess and God welcomes us home with open arms.

Psalmody
Psalm 85:1-2, 8-13 (RCL)
Psalm 85:9ab + 10, 11-12, 13-14 (LFM)

The psalm is a good companion for the Isaiah text. The RCL selection begins with verses 1-2, which declare God's forgiveness and favor. This psalm is also a celebration of God's grace and restoration. The excluded section is a plea for God to come and forgive the people (vv. 3-7). Just as with the texts from last week, its focus is on lost relationship and pleas for that relationship to be restored. This two-week focus reminds us of the cyclical nature of the tree and how this cycle of brokenness and forgiveness is the "now" of God's activity in our lives. It is a celebration of the very center of salvation: God's love for us is always greater than God's anger. God may wish to run from the pain we cause, but cannot because of who God is (Jer. 9:1-2).

Verses 8-13 are the celebration in full form and, like the 1 Corinthians text from last week, they speak of a powerful picture of restoration where "steadfast love and faithfulness will meet [and] righteousness and peace will kiss each other." It is the definition of complete bliss where the world is whole and without brokenness. It is a coming together of all of the good attributes of life.

The Christmas season is a time when guilt is often a constant companion. The pressures of this holiday are fierce as we are bombarded with pictures of perfect families surrounding a perfectly prepared table in a perfectly decorated home. None of us achieve that ideal. Failure also seems to come with the season. Here is a reminder of what really matters. Both of these texts tell of the great celebration that comes with

God's grace, forgiveness, and restoration. This second Sunday reminds us of why we are supposed to be celebrating as Christians. It is not about serving the perfect meal or finding the perfect present or being, even for a few hours, the perfect family. It is about grace. Jesus' entry into our world is the greatest example of God's grace. What really matters is living in this complex relationship with God and others and celebrating the things that restore our lives and spirits. It is a celebration of all of God's advents into our lives in both small and large ways in the past, present, and future.

Second Reading
2 Peter 3:8-15a (RCL)
2 Peter 3:8-14 (LFM)

At this time of year time itself seems in short supply. "Too much to do and too little time" is a familiar December mantra. This text from 2 Peter reminds us that it is often best to take the long view of time; to do that will give us needed perspective. This season will indeed pass into the next and so on and so on and so on. God's days are like a thousand human years. The long view of time often adjusts our own clocks.

Of course, the text is not concerned about the lack of time before Christmas morning, but is focused on why the second coming is long delayed. This was a problem, of course, in the early church since expectation for an immediate action by God was a strong belief. We, too, might wonder about the promised second coming. It seems like foolishness to anticipate its long delay some two thousand years later. In my work with college students, they express it bluntly: "It's embarrassing to mention the second coming because so many of my friends use this as an example to explain why God does not exist." This text says the same thing as the one last week: don't worry about it. What should be important is how you live in the present. Just like last week's Gospel reading, we are to prepare by tending to the things God has given us today.

Verse 14 reminds us that Christ should find us at peace—another sage piece of advice in the craziness of our world. To be found at peace is not only the absence of war or violence; from its Hebrew root *shalom*, we know this peace is a completeness of life where one is content in all that one does and in all that one is. We often think that preparing for Christ's return is to be actively doing something, a state of busy activity. That is so typical of our world. It only matters if we are working like crazy, for that is how this world measures our worth. Here we are reminded that we are to strive for peace in our lives, in our work, and in our relationships. The instruction is not what to do, but what one should strive to be.

In this season, we should focus on being at peace, but truth be told, many of us have forgotten how to do it. Our portable iPads and smartphones make sure there is nowhere on the planet where we cannot busy ourselves, doing work that really does not need to be done this minute. Very little in our lives is truly that urgent. Strive to be at peace. Families and the holidays, with the addition of alcohol, often spells disaster. Strive to be at peace. We prepare food for three times the number of people who will eat at our tables, while others search for food. Strive to be at peace. There may be no more important advice in this or any other season. Let's spend our time striving for peace in our own lives and that will then lead to peace in all the earth.

Gospel
Mark 1:1-8 (RCL, LFM)

I confess I love the Gospel of Mark. It is abrupt and often raw in its approach. There is no story of Elizabeth and Mary and the children they carry. To the author of Mark, Jesus' birth is irrelevant. What is important is Jesus' ministry, death, and resurrection. From this book's perspective, the "beginning" (1:1) is the preaching of John. John is seen as the embodiment of the "voice" in Isaiah 40:3. He is the herald that declares the coming of God.

John, in the Gospel of Mark, does not appear to have risen in the tradition to the "John the Baptist" status of Matthew and Luke. He may be a man without a title here (also John 1:15, 19) or he may be known as "John the Baptizer." Either way, his importance is as a herald, not as Jesus' relative or even as an evangelist. He is certainly seen as the ultimate outsider: he is dressed like a sheep herder and eats an odd diet. In this he brings to mind the Old Testament prophets and their outrageous behavior. He is far from the establishment. Yet his message seems to have popular appeal as people flock to him to confess, be forgiven, and baptized. Yet even with his popularity, he is not self-centered but centered on proclaiming the message of another: the one who is more powerful and baptizes with the Spirit.

But the story here seems small. The Isaiah prophecy speaks of God's powerful entry into the world, an entry where mountains are lowered and valleys raised up. It is a crack in the universe, an event that all of the nations will see and will cause them to tremble. Here John is a crazy-looking outsider with a popular following. If Jesus is truly the Christ, the Son of God, you would expect a grand beginning. Donald Juel notes, "The scene is wrong; the career of the promised offspring of David should begin with appropriate splendor; Jesus should be hailed by crowds. As it is, his inauguration occurs in the desert, away from centers of civilization. The attendants are the hordes who come to be baptized by John. There are no cheers, no conversions."[1] Jesus' ministry begins just like his birth narratives, in out-of-the-way places and to the people who are not the "cool" ones. Jesus will remain an outsider and will not move to the center of power until near the time of his death. John and Jesus are understood only in retrospect. Their power is in their humble service and proclamations, not in their social position.

There is one thing that holds these texts together and it is often overlooked: John's apparent popular appeal came from his preaching repentance and the forgiveness of sins. Both Isaiah and the psalm celebrate the same. Forgiveness is a powerful gift. As noted in Isaiah, it floods in to heal the breach the people believed they had caused. Jesus wisely asks the scribes, "Which is easier, to say to the paralytic, 'Your sins are forgiven,' or to say, 'Stand up and take your mat and walk'?" (Mark 2:9). Jesus' point here is that forgiveness is as powerful in a life as physical healing and both only come from God. Therapists know that forgiveness of ourselves and others is the first step to healing. Second Peter tells us to strive to be at peace, and we cannot do that without God's forgiveness of us and our forgiveness of others.

As noted last week, it is an age-old cycle. We transgress the boundaries and disobey God and, instead of destruction, God offers love and peace. God's choice to love instead of to destroy will set the path to the cross long before Jesus reaches Jerusalem or, for that matter, long before there is a David or a nation. God will forgive. We can count on it again and again and again. We are powerless to repair the cracks in our relationship. Only God's grace will allow there to be a future. Last week's lessons focused on our need for confession as a way of beginning the Christian year. It also warned about thinking too little of ourselves and our community (the second reading) or thinking so much of ourselves that we believe we can predict or control God's coming (the Gospel reading).

This week we realize what forgiveness can do for us and how it fosters a life of peace. Jesus begins this amazing ministry in the most unassuming of places. It is not what we expect. It is not a light-and-power show that causes us to stop and take notice even on the busiest of days. God does not barrel into the world with loud pronouncements. God's message of forgiveness is quiet and comes to the brokenhearted. It comes not when we feel powerful and in charge of our lives, but when we feel the most out of control and lost. The good news about Jesus' or God's coming, the ancients had correct. God's coming to earth is a party of enormous proportions. It is the best news of all. We are forgiven and transformed. The grown Jesus will die at our hands while offering us that precious gift. Jesus will remain consistent to the very end and will not return violence with violence. John will announce Jesus out in the wilderness instead of having a herald of Herod proclaim his ministry in the center of Jerusalem.

This second week of Advent we are shown what brings peace to our lives, and that is forgiveness. Wouldn't it be great if this second week of December was not about the sales at the mall but about setting our lives on a more peaceful path full of forgiveness? It is the greatest gift any of us ever receive. Even the great Christmas movies carry that message: *How the Grinch Stole Christmas*, *A Christmas Carol*, *It's A Wonderful Life*—all tell a story where the end only happens when the characters are forgiven for past deeds. The culture calls it "the Christmas Spirit" but we Christians know it is much more than that. It is what our eternal lives are dependent on, and that is the vast grace and forgiveness of our God.

Note

1. Donald Juel, "A Markan Epiphany: Lessons from Mark 1," *Word and World* 8, no. 1 (1988): 81.

December 11, 2011
Third Sunday of Advent

First Reading
Isaiah 61:1-4, 8-11 (RCL)
Isaiah 61:1-2a, 10-11 (LFM)

This text from Isaiah seems clear enough. It is a message of hope. In this text, the prophet is not condemning the people, but bringing good news and comfort. This prophet sends a love letter from God to the people. One would think this would be the greatest news of all. But things are not always what they seem: when Jesus reads these words in Nazareth, his hometown, and then reflects on them, the people get so angry they attempt to throw Jesus off the nearest cliff (Luke 4:16-30)!

Even in its original context of Third Isaiah, this week's reading would have been simply too good to be true. These are "old words," similar to the servant song in Isaiah 42. Here they are given to a people disheartened. The ones who returned to Jerusalem from Babylon expected a grand entrance and an even grander recovery. No such luck would come their way. The task of building Jerusalem back was slow and disheartening. The people wanted to know why their lives were so hard when they were doing God's will. They expected it to be easy. So these words of good news patterned after the description of the servant's mission must have seemed a mockery of their true situation. The reality was not anything like the vision.

The people listening to Jesus that day in Nazareth had an equal problem. They knew the reality of Jesus, Joseph and Mary's boy, who now dared to say that God's word was fulfilled before their eyes. Under the circumstances, it seemed ridiculous. Sometimes news is so good, it seems like a dream or a fantasy.

Look at the text, for it is a big claim for anyone to make. To declare that "the spirit of the Lord God is upon me, because the Lord has anointed me . . . to bring good news to the oppressed, to bind up the brokenhearted, to proclaim liberty to the captives, and release to the prisoners" is a pretty big assertion. It is no wonder that both of these communities could not hear its good news. Both could not see through the day-to-day grind to another reality. Those trying to rebuild their towns and their country's infrastructure could not imagine trading their ashes for garlands. As for "they shall build up the ancient ruins, they shall raise up the former devastations"— that was exactly what they had been trying to do. The struggle was just too difficult. Likewise the people in Nazareth could not imagine that the boy they knew was anointed by God to change the world. After all, he was just a regular guy, hardly a ruler or heir-of-David material. He seemed unlikely to be the one to liberate them from the Romans. Sometimes good news is the hardest to hear and believe in the midst of real life.

As we get older, we become less able to believe in the words we hear. We listen to the politicians' promises to change the world and we balance them against all of those promises that were made and broken in the past. Your son brings his first serious girlfriend home and you are reserved, wondering if she will care for him or break his heart. It is no wonder that we change from bright-eyed children into more cynical adults. Life has a habit of changing us; each broken promise, each heartbreak, each lie, each struggle, each senseless act of violence, all numb us to their hurt and horror and make us more cautious to believe the next time. This is a defense mechanism and its development is important so we can survive in this world. But sometimes we need to extend that trust again, we need to believe. We need to trust that these old words of Isaiah could apply to us. The text calls us to dare to hope, to hope in God's promises even in the face of all that we see. We are called to make a different choice from that of the people in the biblical text. We are called to believe what we cannot see.

Psalmody
Psalm 126 (RCL)

The response to the Isaiah reading is yet another celebration praising the very things that the Isaiah text promises: "The Lord has done great things for us!" Celebrations during the holidays can be difficult and they are difficult precisely because of all of the complicated emotions this time of year can stir up. We all know holidays can be painful for those who are grieving the loss of a loved one, or for the unemployed, or for those far away from family. The pressure to celebrate with friends and family can be overwhelming. The thing about Advent is that these cultural reasons for celebration are not in the lections or the liturgy. There is celebration but, as the psalm declares, it is celebrating God's presence and God's coming into the world. A celebration of the right things can adjust our expectations and tune our hearts to God instead of to impossible expectations. We need to pause here and remember what these poetic words are inviting us to do, for this poetry is always calling forth memories of times past spent with God. We are called here to remember all of the great things God has done in our lives and give thanks for all of them.

The psalm also wishes that those who grieve will "reap with shouts of joy" (v. 5). The holidays rarely bring pure joy and even the memories of past deeds of God bring memories of difficult times in our lives and of persons who have died or are absent. Grief is also part of this season and we as preachers need to name that reality. We all ache for those absent and our lives remain fractured by broken relationships. The psalms have no problem expressing this very real sorrow and neither should we. We are who we are, with all of the brokenness and all of the joy.

Luke 1:46b-55 (RCL alt.)
Luke 1:46-48, 49-50, 53-54 (LFM)

The LFM and alternate RCL responses come from the Magnificat. With this text, the expectation of Christ's coming literally grows each day. Mary sings to her baby and to the world. Her song is one of someone who finds favor. Yet if you do not yet know the end of the story, her song seems as out of place as the good news in Isaiah. Here she is young, pregnant, unmarried. Those from the neighborhood think her song should be one of shame. How dare she sing of blessing and of being one of the children of Abraham. Yet she bravely sings on to her baby and to the world. She senses that good news is about to arrive. She senses change in the air. Her song, like her son's ministry, seems out of place. She is waiting for the arrival of the baby that will change everything.

Second Reading
1 Thessalonians 5:16-24 (RCL, LFM)

These words from probably the first existing piece of Christian literature are used here as an exhortation to a community beloved by Paul. "Rejoice always, pray without ceasing, give thanks in all circumstances" is purely hortatory speech meant to encourage the fledgling community. Rejoicing and celebrating is what this season is all about.

Is that really true? Or does this message seem unnecessarily eager and naïve? Thomas Currie warns, "Paul's words, 'Rejoice always,' sound as impossible to us as not repaying evil for evil, and we are just as likely to turn the former into a happy face as we are to turn the latter into a slogan for self-improvement."[1] This message runs the risk of becoming domesticated and domesticating. It fosters the bad idea that Christians are always happy and should never rock the boat. These words, like the ones of Isaiah and of Mary's song, seem discordant with our lives.

Paul, however, did not live a naïve life. He suffered for this gospel message and he spoke sternly to churches about their disagreements. Later in the passage he will tell the people to "test everything; hold fast to what is good." This is not a Christian faith where one absorbs what others say without question, but an active faith that rejoices and gives thanks even when times are hard. Naïve faith fades away when life becomes difficult. The text, like Isaiah and Mary's song, offers hope in a most difficult time. To others, the faith exhibited by the old prophet, the young woman, and the apostle Paul seemed foolish. Nothing could be further from God's truth. They were able to praise God in the midst of what looks to be abysmal failure.

The season is filled with claims of happiness. In these three texts, we can clear the fog of holiday madness. We see real people with real problems. Like the other readings, these texts strip away the false celebratory nature of the secular holiday and show true celebration and a dependence on God in the most difficult of times. In this way, these texts remind us what true celebration during Advent and Christmas should really be about, no matter what our circumstances.

Gospel
John 1:6-8, 19-28 (RCL, LFM)

The Gospel lesson revisits John the herald of Jesus, and this time he has gained the attention of the authorities. This questioning of John serves as a bookend in this Gospel to the authorities' questioning of Jesus in chapter 18. Both are asked questions about their identity and their ministry. These stories remind us that their lives, too, will be hard. We celebrate Christmas with baby angels and a baby Jesus and a holy family. John and Jesus will not remain children. They will both be questioned and ultimately killed by these authorities. The Gospel story is not a fairy tale, even if modern culture tries to make it one. The Gospel of Matthew even shaped the baby Jesus' story with a shadow of death hanging over it in the form of Herod and his proclamation. The Gospel of John is a bit more subtle, but the authorities appear at the beginning nonetheless.

The announcement of the repentance of sins and the coming of the Messiah is dangerous, especially when the authorities want to control the population so that these crazy rumors do not prompt the people to rise up and cause problems. John and Jesus were an offense to the good people. The questions for John here are designed to trap him. If he said he was the Messiah, he would be guilty of treason. If he claimed to be Elijah, he would be insane. John does not even claim to be a prophet. Just as last week's reading told, he claims to be the voice crying out from Isaiah. In this Gospel, John serves no other function than a voice crying out. He is the herald. This is further illustrated by his answer to the question, "Why do you baptize?" His answer is not a theological treatise on the importance of baptism. Indeed, he does not answer the question, but again focuses on the mission of the one to come.

Is John also implying that Jesus is standing right there, listening in on their exchange? Is John's "among you stands the one" a clue to Jesus' presence? It is possible but not certain. Yet the statement serves to heighten the tension of the event. It is so close, it is among you. Likewise is the mention of the place, Bethany. Scholars have long cautioned that this reference to what is probably Bethabara, a place in the Transjordan region, should not be confused geographically with the Bethany near

Jerusalem where Lazarus and Mary and Martha lived. But a geography lesson is not the point here; the reference, like the enigmatic "among you stands the one," is meant to point toward the importance of this city in Jesus' ministry in the Gospel of John. As with Mary's song to her baby, the signs are becoming clearer with each passing day. The unveiling of God among us, Emmanuel, is approaching.

Yet there are no illusions in these texts. These people will not live charmed lives and, interestingly, humans in the biblical stories *never* live charmed lives. Their struggles, their sins, their doubts are on display for all to read. That is why their stories ring true to us. The people spoken to in the Isaiah text will continue to struggle under the domination of the Persians, then the Greeks, then the Romans; all the while they wait for David's heir to be born and transform their nation into a world power. Paul will write of rejoicing always and still die at the hands of Roman authorities. Mary, the unwed mother, will marry and raise Jesus and then weep at the foot of the cross as her son dies. Others may see the "Son of God" but it is hard for me to believe that Mary could see anything other than her baby boy on that tree. John, the herald, will be silenced and his murder forever enshrined with the metaphor of "serving his head up on a platter." Certainly, that is not a happy ending in a worldly sense.

It is no wonder the miracle is hard to see even as it stands before them. The authorities will never see John and Jesus as anything other than troublemakers. The question this text asks today is, Are we any different? Can we, too, see the magic that God sends in the form of people and places and circumstances that show forth God's everlasting covenant with us?

The cultural Christmas festivities often contain kernels of Advent. Christmas is magic—with reindeer that fly and presents that appear under your tree in the middle of the night. There is magic in the air.

My son is getting to that age. He really knows that there is no magic, but he is determined to hang on to it even harder as it slips through his fingers. He somehow knows that something will change in him when the magic becomes ordinary life. We all want the magic. What we do not understand is that the magic of this proclamation is all around us. We are like the people in Nazareth. We can't believe that the ordinary people we know can be anointed with the Spirit of the Lord to accomplish amazing things. Can the grumpy, smart-mouthed teenager who gets up and shovels the snow from the neighbor's driveway be seen as miraculous? Can those carols sung at the nursing home be understood as more than just a Christmas tradition? Can a note from a friend be seen as God's way of delivering "a mantle of praise instead of a faint spirit"? Can we stop, even in difficult times, and see God's presence in the now and pray for God's coming in our future? These texts challenge us to do just that, to see what others do not and to believe in the magic of God in our everyday and often painful lives.

Note

1. Thomas Currie III, "1 Thessalonians 5:12-24," *Interpretation* 60, no. 4 (2006): 448.

December 18, 2011
Fourth Sunday of Advent

Revised Common Lectionary (RCL)
2 Samuel 7:1-11, 16
Luke 1:46b-55 or Psalm 89:1-4, 19-26
Romans 16:25-27
Luke 1:26-38

Lectionary for Mass (LFM)
2 Samuel 7:1-5, 8b-12, 14a, 16
Psalm 89:2-3, 4-5, 27 + 29
Romans 16:25-27
Luke 1:26-38

First Reading
2 Samuel 7:1-11, 16 (RCL)
2 Samuel 7:1-5, 8b-12, 14a, 16 (LFM)

There are many hero stories about the great King David. This is not one of them. Here David has ceased to fight, for God "had given him rest from all his enemies" (v. 1). Right from the beginning the narrator reminds us of where the king's power lies. He is not the great ruler who will take care of God. God is the one who has taken care of him. Nonetheless, David looks around his McMansion and realizes, "Hey, I have a great house of cedar and God is in a tent. I should build God a house!" Nathan, the local religious authority, agrees. A house for God, how perfect—except God has something else to say to David.

The RCL tells of the whole message God has for David. God begins with a history lesson. God chose the tent and moved with the people as they went from slavery to freedom. God tells David that God never asked for a home other than the tent of the meeting. This section brings up the images of the exodus and the wilderness: God and God's people traveling together toward an unknown future, living together in tents. It is David who chose Jerusalem and it is David who brought the ark there. God was content to live in the old tent with all of its memories even in this new city.

Both lections contain God's next reminder: David, in case you are getting too stuck on yourself, "I took you from the pasture, from following the sheep." The shepherd usually leads the sheep! God is reminding David that he is "not all that." The next verses are all "I" statements about what God has done for David and for God's people. The sum total is to put the king back in his *human* place. God will build David a house (meaning "dynasty" in Hebrew), not the other way around. God will build what no human can, a line of succession. David receives a blessing from God, even while being put in his place.

What in the world does this have to do with Advent? The classical answer is that it is the promise of a dynasty that foreshadows Jesus' birth. Yes, that is one meaning, but could there be another—one that is not so comfortable, one that calls us to a more faithful life? Look around at our houses of cedar, our homes, our churches. We can build anything. We can consume more and more. We can build a place for God, a big beautiful place. But, like David, just because we *can* build a house for God does not necessarily mean that we *should*. In the story of Advent and Christmas, God will have the last laugh. God's Son appears in the world, not in a house of cedar, but in a stable. A barn in out-of-the-way Bethlehem. God chose the stable, not the palace, just as God chose the tent instead of a grand temple. We may try to make God into something impressive, but God has no such needs. God will come into the small places like a stable to announce the good news. As my father would often say, "God does not have to be flashy to be God, for there is no one that God needs to impress." David's building plan was as much about showing off as it was to help God have a house. How often have we thought the same way? Are we serving God or our own egos? The Old Testament text reminds the ancient David and the modern world that God has no such ego needs.

Psalmody
Psalms 89:1-4, 19-26 (RCL alt.)
Psalms 89:2-3, 4-5, 27 + 29 (LFM)

The selected verses of Psalm 89 parallel the 2 Samuel reading celebrating God's steadfast love in covenant form made to David and David's descendants. The selective use of these verses from Psalm 89 is, however, quite ironic. The verses here are pure praise, but in the full context of the psalm these words stand as an accusation against God for abandoning the people during the exile, where these verses are seen as past history and verses 46-51 express the disillusionment with God's silence: "Lord, where is your steadfast love of old, which by your faithfulness you swore to David?" (v. 49).

Waiting can seem that way, when tragedy comes and the heavens are silent. The whole psalm reminds us of the long road God and the people have shared. There are times of celebration and times of doubt and despair. The baby will enter among a broken people still searching for their Davidic king, hundreds of years after the last one was taken to exile in 586 B.C.E. The people hunger for God to show God's power and destroy their enemies. God's answer to that desire will be quite different. The answer, a baby in a manger, seems silly when the Romans control the whole region with a mighty military fist.

Luke 1:46b-55 (RCL)

For commentary on this text, see the Psalmody for the Third Sunday in Advent, p. 16.

Second Reading
Romans 16:25-27 (RCL, LFM)

This text is the final benediction in the book of Romans. After Paul's long treatise and a personal greeting at the beginning of chapter 16, he summarizes the whole of the message in this doxology. The content is the work of God in the whole great unfolding of this love story with humanity. God has revealed what was hidden and even the Gentiles now understand the prophetic writings. To Paul and his community, at least one central function of the prophetic writings was to point to the coming of Jesus into the world. God's truth was hidden there and could only be understood in retrospect. We may see the function of prophetic texts as also much more, for they are also pedagogical and for edification of the people. But for Paul these functions were not as important. Paul is singular in his proclamation of salvation through Jesus Christ. Here, on the fourth Sunday of Advent, Paul is proclaiming that truth to the whole world. The point of reflecting on this passage is that this event of a tiny baby born in an out-of-the-way place will become the one proclaimed by John in the wilderness. Jesus will proclaim the message of God's grace and love for the inner circle of Jerusalem to those who are far away—a message that had every possibility of dying on the lips of the outcasts, but has now made it to the capital of the world, Rome. God, in God's own way, has revealed in God's time the good news that Paul now declares to the world. The baby in the manger is no longer a secret. Jesus' message will not die away for lack of being shared or lack of belief. Paul's letter in Rome proves the wisdom of the Pharisee Gamaliel's proclamation in Acts 5 when he told the Jerusalem council, "If this plan is of human origin, it will fail; but if it is of God, you will not be able to overthrow them—in that case you may even be found fighting against God!" (5:38-39). Advent declares it, Christmas demonstrates it, Easter confirms it, for this has not died away. It is God's truth and it will not, it cannot, be silenced.

Gospel
Luke 1:26-38 (RCL, LFM)

Mary understands what King David does not! The contrast between the two characters is obvious to all who look at them side by side. David has been given everything: peace from his enemies, his own city, the crowns of both Judah and Israel, and a brand-new house of cedar. The actions of David in his later life, after he "arrived," are a sad but predictable tale. He has forgotten God. He is, in my grandmother's words, "too big for his britches"! His arrogance will continue to grow and manifest itself in the attack on Bathsheba and the murder of her husband. David will use his power to harm others for his own benefit.

This is Luke's introduction to Jesus' family tree and it stresses Mary's distance from Jerusalem, the expected place of the Davidic heir. Verse 1 leads with Gabriel being sent to Galilee, the town of Nazareth. The insignificance of the place is hard to overestimate. The town of Nazareth does not appear in the Old Testament, the writings of Josephus, or in early Jewish literature.[1] I can just imagine Luke's audience scrambling for a map. As people who know this story, we have ceased to notice this fact. Nazareth is where Jesus lived and we all know that. Luke's introduction of a backwater town is lost on us. Gabriel, God's own messenger, was being sent to the hinterlands, as far away from the halls of power as Quality, Kentucky, is from Washington, D.C. Even in the selection of this first family, God is choosing to make a certain statement. It is the same message that God sent when Abraham was called from a life of obscurity to be the father of many. It is the same message God sent when God heard the cry of slaves in their oppression and moved to offer them liberation.

And it gets worse: one would expect the angel to find someone important. After all, in the previous story an angel of the Lord appeared to Zechariah in the Temple in Jerusalem in the sanctuary of the Lord. Now we are talking—a priest near to the holy of holies in the middle of the Temple. That is where God is expected to be found. But wait, the angel skips all the elders of the town and goes to a virgin who was engaged to Joseph. Now "virgin" has different theological significance in Roman Catholic traditions than in Protestant, but we can all agree that at the very least this meant that Mary was a young girl, not yet old enough to be married. There was maybe no one in town with less status and power than her. The angel's visit is not just unexpected; it is a scandal. Mary is young and ordinary, living in a tiny place. Her life should have passed completely unnoticed. The angel's appearance guarantees that will not be the case.

The pronouncement itself is certainly one that belongs in the palace, for Mary is with child and the angel declares, "He will be great, and will be called Son of the Most High, and the Lord God will give to him the throne of his ancestor David. He will reign over the house of Jacob forever, and of his kingdom there will be no end." Enveloped in these words are all the promises of the Old Testament. To Abraham, God promises to "make your name great" (Gen. 12:2). This is repeated to David in this morning's Old Testament reading (2 Sam. 7:9), as is the promise of an eternal kingdom (2 Sam. 7:16). The unusual title "Son of the Most High" parallels the adoption motif of 2 Samuel 7:14, "I will be a father to him, and he shall be a son to me." Indeed, this adoption of the king as the son of God is part of the enthronement ceremony (Ps. 2:7) and is a phrase that will reappear at Jesus' baptism.[2] This is royal language given in a very unusual place to an unknown minor. This will be no ordinary baby. Life somehow will never be the same for Mary and her family.

Mary's reaction is one that is different from Sarah's, who when she heard she was to deliver laughed, just as her husband had before her. The news to that old couple was too good to be true. Here Mary expresses her puzzlement without protest. Poor

Gabriel is left to explain the more delicate parts of this conception and he does it with grace. Before Mary can take it all in, he adds the second announcement of Elizabeth's good news. She, too, will bear a child, although the angel does not tell her of that child's importance in the great plan. The angel adds, "For nothing is impossible with God," echoing God's statement to Moses, "Is the Lord's power limited?" (Num. 11:23), and God's declaration to Sarah, "Is anything too wonderful for the Lord?" (Gen. 18:14).

Much, probably too much, has been written of Mary and this text. We all know the story and there is little new to say. What we can do is place it in the context of these four Sundays of readings. Each in their own way speaks of the place of humans and the place of God. Transgressing boundaries is not always bad; indeed, it is our quests for exploration and things never known before that have taken us to the stars and given us important medicines and solutions to hunger. But transgressing the unknown for our own gain or from our own arrogance can and does do harm, to our relationships with others and to the earth and to our God. The message in many of these texts is clear: celebrate God's grace, look with anticipation to God's coming, occupy your time by not looking always in the past or into the future, trust God for that future, do not lose sight of what is of humans and what is of God, tend to your work and relationships in the moment, and strive to be at peace with all. Mary exemplifies all of these characteristics as she accepts the angel's announcement. There is certainly much to worry about and there is a life change to grieve as the world discovers her secret.

This young woman chooses to sing of God's favor and God's blessing. Her song, so out of place in tiny Nazareth, is one of joy. She does not presume to second-guess God as David did. She does not assume she is favored by God and thus has been bestowed with power over others. She follows what Paul will write in the church at Thessalonica, "Rejoice always, pray without ceasing, give thanks in all circumstances." Then she waits for the baby's birth and her unknown future that she puts squarely in God's hands.

Notes

1. Lamonie DeVries, "Nazareth," in *The New Interpreter's Dictionary of the Bible*, ed. Katherine Doob Sakenfeld, et al. (Nashville: Abingdon, 2009), 4:240.
2. Hans-Joachim Kraus, *Psalms 1–59*, A Continental Commentary, trans. Hilton C. Oswald (Minneapolis: Augsburg, 1988), 130–31.

Christmas
Beth Tanner

This year the Christmas season is as brief as the calendar allows because December 25 and January 1 fall on consecutive Sundays. This will usually result in modified scheduling for this season. In Roman Catholic and Episcopal churches, this will mean a slightly altered schedule for the festival masses. Protestant churches will be faced with deciding which of the possible services will be for public worship. This decision is often made by the pastor and local governing body. Typically, there will be at least one Christmas Eve service and a Sunday service on both Christmas and New Year's Day. If there is only one service on these days, there will be two sets of lectionary texts to choose from as the basis of the service.

The texts presented on these days are familiar ones and there are a plethora of materials on these texts, including commentary and narrative reflections. The commentary that follows does not assume that a sermon is the only way to convey the gospel message. The following are reflections on the texts that try to maintain the irony and radical nature of these stories in their ancient context. Over the years and with so much focus on the Christmas story, these texts become ordinary and managed as a part of our cultural story. Yet, in their context, they declare the radical ways that God chooses to alter the world. In addition, many of these texts call not only for a recommitment on the part of Christians, but an altered way of seeing the world and living out lives. We are invited to live as Christ lived, not as a helpless baby, but as an active change agent challenging the status quo. We are also invited to remember that these texts are dangerous, for they proclaim Jesus as the Ruler of the Universe, a Ruler who challenged and is still challenging the human powers of this world. In living out the words of these texts, we are called to extreme praise, critical introspection, and a rededication of our Christian lives. In other words, if we take these texts seriously, this is not a nice domesticated message of a birth, but a story of God's radical love and grace for all of humanity.

December 24 & 25, 2011
Nativity of Our Lord I (RCL) /
Christmas: Mass at Midnight (LFM)

Revised Common Lectionary (RCL)

Isaiah 9:2-7
Psalm 96
Titus 2:11-14
Luke 2:1-14 (15-20)

Lectionary for Mass (LFM)

Mass at Midnight
Isaiah 9:1-6
Psalm 96:1-2a, 2b-3, 11-12, 13
Titus 2:11-14
Luke 2:1-14

At the Vigil Mass
Isaiah 62:1-5
Psalm 89:4-5, 16-17, 27 + 29
Acts 13:16-17, 22-25
Matthew 1:1-25 or 1:18-25

First Reading
Isaiah 9:2-7 (RCL)
Isaiah 9:1-6 (LFM)

The Old Testament lesson is often read as a prediction of the future birth of the Christ child. This text from Isaiah, however, has much more to provide on this night. It declares the new reign of a king and a new chapter in the life of the people. It is probably taken from a coronation hymn or oracle for the Judean king.

Its literary context is the reign of Ahaz during a period of great stress and fear. The Assyrians were intent on empire building. War was imminent. Kings Rezin of Damascus and Pekah of Israel were so afraid of this possibility, they planned to attack Jerusalem to force Ahaz to join a coalition of nations to fight Assyria. It appeared that Judah would fall, either to its northern neighbors or the Assyrians. The young King Ahaz was unsure about the course to take. The prophet Isaiah counseled him to hold firm. God would deliver Judah. Chapter 9 is part of Isaiah's advice to the king, but why did he use a coronation oracle? Was it a reminder to the new king of his role or was it a condemnation of the king's lack of faith in God? Probably both. At one and the same time Isaiah is saying, "This is what you promised and you should trust in God."

The first section (vv. 1-5) is a call to celebrate, for a change is on the way. This rejoicing is equated to two important events: the harvest and the end of a war. This, Isaiah says, is both rolled into one: a celebration of great proportions. In both this period of stress and in the time of the Christ child, the text served as a wish for the end of domination by another and a harvest that is their own.

The second section is the reason for this celebration: "For unto us a child has been born; a son is given to us." This sounds like a birth announcement, but it is probably coronation language.[1] Similar language is used for King David and his dynasty and at the baptism of the adult Jesus (2 Sam. 7:14, Ps. 2:7; Mark 1:9). The proclamation of the anointed king as God's adopted son was an important part of the ceremony and declared God's favor on the king. Another part of the ceremony was to give the king names that honor God. In English Bibles, this naming appears to be titles about the human king: "Wonderful Counselor, Mighty God, Everlasting Father, Prince of Peace." This translation is part of the Christian tradition, but most scholars and the *Tanakh* agree these names should be read as theophanic, honoring God and reading, "One who plans a wonder is the warrior God; the father forever is a commander who brings shalom."[2] In the context of Ahaz, it served to remind the king that it was God who would bring about these things, not humans.

In the context of Christmas Eve night, this text can remind us that the baby born in the manger is not the end of the story. These words of coronation are not used this night. They are bestowed at Jesus' baptism, the beginning of his earthly ministry. This is but the first chapter in the unfolding of the meaning of "Emmanuel." The baby poses no threat, but the grown Christ will shake those halls of power and change the world forever, living up to his royal title.

Psalmody
Psalm 96 (RCL)
Psalm 96:1-2a, 2b-3, 11-12, 13 (LFM)

Tonight is the night to sing praises and Psalm 96 certainly fits the bill. It opens with "Sing to the Lord a new song." Marvin Tate notes, "The 'new song' is to express the realization and acknowledgment that the future belongs to Yahweh,"[3] a fitting parallel with the Isaiah text.

The psalm has three sections, each a call to praise that widens the circle: verses 1-6 are for the faithful to sing to the nations, verses 7-10 call the world to join, and verses 11-12 are a call to the creation.

The reason for the party is God's coming judgment. As noted in Advent, we may have been taught to fear this time, but for the ancients it was the greatest news of all. It was what they had prayed and waited for throughout the years, and we can join in their joy. God is coming to set the world right so all can live in peace. Certainly, the message will be fulfilled this night, even if it does not come from the place or in the ways people expect. Jesus will show what it means to rule with righteousness and justice. On this night, God does come to earth and God brings justice for which the people have longed.

Second Reading
Titus 2:11-14 (RCL, LFM)

Like the Old Testament texts, this reading points beyond the birth of Jesus to the Christ, crucified and risen. It begins by declaring Christ's universal mission. The text also stresses that Christ continues to teach the church how to live, just as he did when he walked the earth. Our work is to understand that his redemption is a gift and we should respond by being Christ's people in the world, striving to do good in his name. We are to work at being what Christ taught us to be.

It is easy to let this night slip into a celebration of a baby born. This text reminds us that on this and all nights there is much more. We are transformed by Christ's gift to us. Christian life is a discipline that requires a commitment of the heart and demands that we seek ways to improve the world as Jesus did. This is not a night of simply watching the baby, but a night for recommitting ourselves to the tasks that we have been given. We look upon the baby, not just as an infant but as Savior of the whole world. We do not own this child, nor do we own the gift. We are called simply to follow all the days of our lives.

Gospel
Luke 2:1-14 (15-20) (RCL)
Luke 2:1-14 (LFM)

Ahhh! I can feel the sigh of relief as I walk into the sanctuary. Finally, the text the congregation has been waiting to hear since the first day of Advent. Finally, no Advent hymns but a full-throated *Joy to the World*! All is right with the world. Preachers, however, never breathe a sigh of relief, for preaching on this night may be one of the greatest challenges to ministry. What is a preacher to do? How can we stay true to the nature of the gospel on this night?

Whether one decides to preach on this night or to gather together readings and other devotional pieces, there is one thing we should not forget and that is the radical nature of this birth. With the candles twinkling and the nativity set almost complete and the beautiful hymns sung by the choir, this night can easily become a celebration that is not grounded in the realities of the this birth and its significance for our lives.

The biblical story in Genesis starts with families, but as Israel and Judah develop as nations, the family story all but disappears. The so-called historical books deal with the stories of kings and their reigns and their acts and their international involvement. As the monarchy and independent status is lost, the messianic hope takes shape. But the hope is one of a Davidic heir who will deliver the country from the hands of the Romans. He is to fight the oppressors and take back the promised land for God's people. He is to be a great hero. Through the years, this vision of a great man grows bigger and bigger.

The angel Gabriel does not go to the halls of power but to tiny Nazareth, to a young woman who was not yet married. Then she and Joseph must make a long journey to another small town, Bethlehem. These places are not the ones inhabited by men of power. The Bible here returns to family matters in the small places of the world. It is no wonder that the grown Jesus will face ridicule from those in Nazareth and by the religious powers in Jerusalem. Someone born nowhere, be it in a housing project or a tiny town, will often never be considered good enough for the halls of power. Jesus' pedigree is just not impressive enough for a king and great hero, so the people scoff.

Small places are often the places God chooses to appear: to Abram in Haran, to slaves in Egypt, to a people on a mountain in the middle of the Sinai peninsula. In addition, God's appearance and God's actions demonstrate again God's radical love. The New Testament opens after a great deal of the story has already been told about God and the people. Again and again, God has offered grace to a stiff-necked people. God's good gifts have been misused again and again. The people are unfaithful. The people cannot "love the Lord with all of their heart, mind, and soul, and their neighbor as themselves." It has taken a powerful God to rein in these obstinate folks when they have gone their own way. Yet, God sends Jesus as a baby into a world that is not safe. Children were the least powerful in this society, completely dependent on others for their care, feeding, and survival. The trust that God places in humanity by sending Jesus as a baby is often overlooked. The precious Son is sent to a bunch of people who could harm or even kill him, and indeed, that is what eventually happens. Yet God loves us enough to do it anyway. God's greatest gift is placed in the hands of ordinary people. One would think this God is crazy. God's Son belongs in a place where he is protected from the evil of this world.

This story, then, tells us much about God. First is God's great trust of humans, even in the face of their continued turning away. Second is the radical way that God chooses to act. Jesus could have been born to the high priest; after all, his cousin was born to a priest in the Temple. God could have placed the birth of this baby in such a way that the whole world would take notice. Instead, the news is delivered by angels to a bunch of shepherds in a field.

At the very least, God could have placed the child in a family that would guarantee his protection. If he were born in the halls of power, it would be easier for him to change the world. But that is not the change God desired. Changing power structures must begin from the inside out and Jesus came to transform first the hearts of people and then for them to transform the world and its structures. To humans it seems like a terribly slow and inefficient way to transform anything. But God's ways are not our ways and this birth is another demonstration of that fact.

The birth story has become comfortable for us, but it was anything but comfortable in its ancient context. It was odd and radical and not what people expected. In its peculiar presentation then, it also shows that God continues to come to the people and offer them love and presence in unexpected places and in unexpected ways.

At the Vigil Mass (LFM)

First Reading: Isaiah 62:1-5. The purpose of the Vigil Mass is to prepare the heart in an intentional way for the upcoming Christmas season. The first reading is an announcement from God to Jerusalem that the exile has come to an end. The good news has finally arrived. The former names "Forsaken" and "Desolate" are to be erased. The new names are "My Delight Is in Her" and "The Land Is Married," indicating the reconciliation between God and the people.

Just as in the more famous Isaiah 40, God's announcement of a change comes to the broken. The response to such news is a celebration of grand proportions. The earth stands in anticipation of the great happening, waiting for the advent of God in the midst of the people. God has come to God's people again and tomorrow will indeed be a new day. The Isaiah text places us in that place of waiting, standing in anticipation for the coming celebration.

Psalmody: Psalm 89:4-5, 16-17, 27 + 29. The psalm tells of God's covenant with David. Indeed, the first 37 verses all focus on that covenant. The covenant is centered on God's steadfast love and faithfulness to David and, by extension, to the people. In its poetic description, it shares many of the same themes as 2 Samuel 7 (see the first reading for the fourth Sunday of Advent, above) and the enthronement rituals. It is this covenant that God made with David and the people that serves as the basis for all that will happen in the future. God has made a promise and God will make good on the promise, even if, as the rest of Psalm 89 tells, it seems like God has abandoned the covenant and the people. The Isaiah text announces the reversal of what Psalm 89 expresses. The Lord's steadfast love of old that by God's faithfulness was sworn to David is still in effect (v. 49). The people will again see the Lord.

Second Reading: Acts 13:16-17, 22-25. The setting for this text is a trip by Paul to Antioch. These trips in Acts represent the spread of the message about Jesus, but at this time it is noted that "they spoke the word to no one except Jews" (11:19). Paul's message is to the Jewish communities that have spread across this part of the world. The text itself is a summary or creed of this early church. The connection with David is still a strong one, as would be expected in Jewish communities. The point here is to connect this Jesus of Nazareth with the expected Messiah. He is David's heir and the rightful King of the Jews. This focus, of course, points well beyond Bethlehem, for the rest of the text focuses on John and his proclamations concerning this Jesus. Christmas is about more than a baby; it is about the Christ who will redeem us. John is the one who makes clear the true purpose of Christ. The message will remain veiled this night and for several years as Jesus grows. Yet it is for this hope that we long. Just as in the other texts, we are called to look beyond even tomorrow's celebration and to the true meaning of Christ in the world.

Gospel: Matthew 1:1-25 or 1:18-25. To skip the genealogy of Jesus is to miss a wonderful opportunity. One would think that this list of names has no homiletical value. But it reflects the whole history of the Bible, along with some of the Bible's most interesting stories. It begins by establishing Jesus' heritage, for he is identified as the son of David and Abraham. The latter ties him to a people, the former to a dynasty.

One would think that this list of descendants is rather boring and, indeed, it is predictable until one reaches Judah, where the unexpected is encountered with the addition of Tamar. Tamar is a woman who goes to great lengths to fulfill the law (Genesis 38). The next set of names continues the line, but they are unknown in the biblical story. Then two more women appear, first Rahab, the mother of Boaz, and Ruth, Boaz's Moabite wife. Rahab may or may not be the Rahab of Judges 2, but Ruth is well-known. Also included is the line, "Solomon is the son of David and the wife of Uriah."

The inclusion of women is unusual, as are the women themselves. Why these women? Scholars have offered a variety of reasons, such as the women are sinners or outsiders. This label implies that the women were of less than stellar character and this simply is not true. Tamar did everything in her power to follow the law and provide her deceased husband with an heir. The Rahab of Judges risked death to save first the spies sent by Moses and they in turn saved her family. Ruth also did what it took to save herself and Naomi. Bathsheba was either married to a Hittite and/or a Hittite herself, and was taken by David's men while she was following Torah law with a ritual bath. Their stories are surprising and shocking and most involve the birth of a child under less than perfect and regular circumstances. These women also share something in common with Mary. The birth of her son will also seem irregular, but is indeed the fulfillment of a promise. These women do what it takes in the circumstances they find themselves in to save the lives of their family and by extension, the family line of Jesus of Nazareth. They are brave and sometimes break the social rules to fulfill their part in the promise.

Next come the kings of Judah, establishing Jesus' royal line. Following the kings are the people in the lineage of Jesus after the exile and destruction of the Temple. Of this group, almost nothing is known. They are just ordinary people who left no trace in any other historical record. Jesus comes from a group that, after the exile, could have easily been forgotten forever. He is both king and commoner. His line has both the great and the scandalous; the insiders born in the line of Abraham and the outsiders born of another heritage. There is no effort by this Gospel to hide the difficult stories or the years of loss or even the skeletons in the family closet. Jesus is part of a long human heritage. He has a fully human genealogy, just as he has a fully divine genealogy.

Notes

1. J. J. M. Roberts, "Whose Child is This? Reflections on the Speaking Voice in Isaiah 9:5," *Harvard Theological Review* 90 (1997): 115–29.
2. John Goldingay, "The Compound Name in Isaiah 9:5(6)," *Catholic Biblical Quarterly* 61 (2006): 243.
3. Marvin Tate, *Psalms 51–100*, Word Bible Commentary 20 (Dallas: Word, 1991), 513.

December 25, 2011
Nativity of Our Lord II (RCL) /
Christmas: Mass at Dawn (LFM)

Revised Common Lectionary (RCL)
Isaiah 62:6-12
Psalm 97
Titus 3:4-7
Luke 2:(1-7) 8-20

Lectionary for Mass (LFM)
Isaiah 62:11-12
Psalm 97:1 + 6, 11-12
Titus 3:4-7
Luke 2:15-20

First Reading
Isaiah 62:6-12 (RCL)
Isaiah 62:11-12 (LFM)

Dawn has come and everything has changed! During the night all of the promises were fulfilled. The Messiah has been born. The Isaiah text is not about the birth but is a proclamation of a new day. God has placed sentinels in Jerusalem to proclaim the end of domination. No more will the fruits of the work of the people go to others to enjoy. God will see to it that the people are free from tyranny. This image of living on your own land at peace brings to mind the promise of the land. The people had been enslaved in their land and it was no longer theirs. They were sharecroppers. Now, in this new day, they are restored, for God has proclaimed it. Clear a path, remove all impediments, pave a road to declare this change. Let the destruction of yesterday disappear.

To commemorate this restoration of land and relationship, God changes the name of the people to "The Holy People, The Redeemed of the Lord." "Redeemed" in Hebrew literally means *to be bought back from debt*. God has paid the people's debt and they are now free to start a new life.

The shepherds who come to the manger do not know that this baby will pay the debts of all. As they wipe the sleep from their eyes, they still do not understand the magnitude of it all. It will take Jesus' full life, death, and resurrection for this declaration to become apparent. God has provided a Redeemer for all people for all time. The baby is a miracle in itself, but this baby's significance for our salvation is what we celebrate this day.

Psalmody
Psalm 97 (RCL)
Psalm 97:1 + 6, 11-12 (LFM)

This is an enthronement psalm celebrating God as the great king. It opens not with human praise, but the praise of the creation. God is settled on the holy throne in the heavenly council. It portrays the great God whose concerns are for the whole universe. God's throne has a foundation of justice and righteousness, making these also the foundations of God's kingdom. To this picture, the creation responds. The thunder booms; the coastlands dance; and the earth trembles before its great God.

It is not until verse 7 that people appear. They have seen God's glory. The ones who worship other gods are shamed as even those gods bow to the great God. There is none greater. Zion and Judah join in the celebration as they hail God's judgments or justices, for in Hebrew these words are one and the same.

The final two verses are all celebration. The people are filled with joy and rejoice and give thanks for God. This, of course, mirrors the announcement by the angels and the rejoicing of the shepherds in Bethlehem as they see the Christ child. There are many things to celebrate in this season: family, friends, and gifts. This psalm reminds us of the source of all of these celebrations—God and God's great gifts to us. We are to be like the shepherds and let our joy overcome us as we dance and sing and offer praise to our God.

Second Reading
Titus 3:4-7 (RCL, LFM)

This is certainly one of those texts that can spark debate among the faithful over the theological issue of justification by faith alone. This, however, is not the time for theological debate. That can wait for Ordinary Time. Just as with the Old Testament texts, this reading should also be seen as celebration, not just of the baby in the manger, but of the full meaning of God Incarnate with us. I fear that many Christians are tempted to leave the baby in the manger, for there Jesus is manageable. The baby Christ makes no demands on us, does not call us to paths of justice, nor questions the culture's values. The adult Jesus will do all of that and more. We are reminded here that Jesus grew and died and is the great God of all. God's grace appeared, bringing salvation to all. Through the Holy Spirit, we are reborn to a life of faith and heirs of eternal life through this tiny one. This is the purpose of the birth, to redeem the world. The baby will not remain manageable, but will bring the radical message of grace to the whole world.

Gospel
Luke 2:(1-7) 8-20 (RCL)
Luke 2:15-20 (LFM)

The focus for this dawn service is the angels and shepherds. The RCL has both the announcement and the visit to the stable, while the LFM has only the visit. Just as last

33

night, the story is so familiar. What can be said about the angels and the shepherds? We have all seen the Christmas pageant many times over. The story is loved but dog-eared from our yearly visits. We have heard it all before.

Yet as this morning's service is celebrated, there are those who are still on watch from last night: our police officers and firefighters, the nurses and doctors that staff the hospitals, all doing noble work. There are others, though, the unseen ones who bundled up last night to work at tollbooths and warehouses and convenience stores, who wanted to attend church and tuck their children into bed. They did not want to work on this night, but work they must to keep their jobs. Many are far from home, away from the families they support in another country. They are homesick, just like those long-ago shepherds. Do they ever see amazing sights? These ones we barely notice. It was to them that angels appeared long ago.

Jerusalem is supposed to be the place where God resides. Yet God shuns the city and instead the announcement comes in the fields to the south when everyone is sleeping, except the ones who must watch while the sheep sleep. That visit, of course, will become the pattern of Jesus who meets the people in the villages and towns and the countrysides. The God of slaves is still a God to the invisible ones, the ones that this morning will pump gas and sell coffee to the few people that trickle in.

Where would the Christ be found this morning? If God is the God of the least of these, then what does that say about us? That may seem too hard to contemplate at dawn, but the baby is calling us to stretch our faith even on Christmas morn. On this morning as we walk out of the building, the neighborhood will be quiet, hushed, just like where the shepherds were found. What can we hear in the silence? What will the Christ say to us in the quiet streets? How will we praise the child and what will we tell of our encounter? The story may be old, but like our favorite stuffed animal that comforted us as a child, it can still comfort. But the story's comfort should never be its only message. The baby in far-away Bethlehem also calls us to see what others do not. Do not be too quick to look to the halls of power and wealth for your salvation. Jesus is over here in the abandoned building without the proper papers. The child, just like God's grace, will not be of the establishment nor will he be domesticated by our human rituals. Jesus will be found in the places we do not notice, and thus we are called this day to be like the shepherds and search for that Christ child.

December 25, 2011
Nativity of Our Lord III (RCL) /
Christmas: Mass During the Day (LFM)

Revised Common Lectionary (RCL)
    Isaiah 52:7-10
    Psalm 98
    Hebrews 1:1-4 (5-12)
    John 1:1-14

Lectionary for Mass (LFM)
    Isaiah 52:7-10
    Psalm 98:2-3a, 3b-4, 5-6
    Hebrews 1:1-6
    John 1:1-18 or 1:2-5, 9-14

First Reading
Isaiah 52:7-10 (RCL, LFM)

We don't often contemplate the absent God, yet this was a serious concern in the postexilic community. The people wondered where God had gone and why God abandoned them, leaving them to fend for themselves as the invaders destroyed their cities. The same cry of abandonment came from the people imprisoned in the Holocaust. Where was God? Why did God not arrive and save the nation, the babies, the world? It is daring theology on this Sunday Christmas morn. Yet without acknowledging the sense of God's absence, we cannot capture the joy of this text. Truth be told, we all know of this absence, even if we do not speak of it openly. This text comes crashing into our lives at the time when God seems nowhere to be found, and it has been that way for a long time. That's how the people felt. From that dark place, the messenger finally arrives bringing words of peace, good news, and salvation. God is returning to us. We are alone no longer.

In today's world, God can seem just as hard to find. There are more people than ever who simply give up on religion, for all they can see is the hate-filled speech of the extremists and God's perceived inactivity in our world. It is easier than ever to slip into unbelief. We must fight to keep our faith alive and that seems wrong. But is it? The Bible gives full voice to the doubts of the people. It does not shy away from the conversation. The word *Israel* means "to strive with God," and that is exactly what the people do, they spar with God. In the lament psalms, they fight with God for their faith.

When did we stop fighting for our faith? I do not mean with guns or with forced conversion of others; I mean to fight with God and ourselves for our own souls. Faith has become easy, expected, and comfortable, and in the process we have lost part of our relationship with God. Even on Christmas morning, we should bring our doubts to full light and present them here, for the only way to deal with our questions is to deal with them in the morning light. To hear the joyous strains of today's readings we need to deal with the dark nights from which they sprang. Then we can hear the messenger announcing peace and good news and salvation, for we will know in our hearts that we have struggled to get to this place of thanksgiving. We can hear the good news not just as some ancient story, but as our very salvation made flesh.

Psalmody
Psalm 98 (RCL)
Psalm 98:1, 2-3a, 3b-4, 5-6 (LFM)

The enthronement psalms continue as the praise of this season and they celebrate God as King, Creator, and Judge of all. We are called to sing a new song, for it is a new day with God and God has done marvelous things. But we are not alone in our song; we are to join with all the earth. Using every instrument we have, we are to make a great deal of noise! Our song should reach to the heavens. On this day that we celebrate the coming of God to live among us and our weekly Sabbath worship, praise should be unleashed as a celebration where little kids twirl and old gentlemen laugh with tears of grateful thanks. In the psalms it gets noisier still as the creation joins in its grateful song. Everything and everyone, just for a moment, shares a time of joy together.

That one idea is so amazing, so thrilling, that it is hard to imagine. All of the languages, all of the instruments, all of the people and the dogs and the cats and the cows together sing to their Creator. The dancing shakes the earth as it laughs in response. These psalms ask us to imagine it and to hold it in our hearts as the event to which we are to strive and wait—wait for the day that God calls all together and judges with righteousness and equity. I hear the party coming to a screeching halt: we are celebrating *what*? God's coming to judge us and set the world right! The idea is so challenging it stops us and makes us think. As persons who live in relative comfort, it is a challenging concept, and there is the rub. Advent and Christmas begin the Christian year but as Christmas ends, so does much of the concern for those in need. Food banks and homeless shelters struggle in the post-Christmas months to keep needed supplies on hand. The season of charity gives way to the long, cold winter. What can we do this year so we might welcome God's coming to bring equity to the world? Do we need to change how we live so others can live? Do we dare be challenged on this Christmas morning? Let us hope so, for worship is never for show and each time we gather we should be challenged to lead stronger and better lives. The psalm calls on us to party for the equality of all. Dare we?

Second Reading
Hebrews 1:1-4 (5-12) (RCL)
Hebrews 1:1-6 (LFM)

As noted in the comments to almost every reading, these words speak not of a baby, but of the great God that lies in this mortal skin. This reading declares Christ's kingship and status as God. This baby, this one who ate with and aided sinners and the unclean is "heir of all things, through whom he also created the worlds." Do not mistake this baby for just a good man who did good deeds. This is the one who sits at the right hand of God. This is the one of whom angels sing. He is of God for he is God.

The optional text continues to speak of Jesus in the same way as the psalm, not as a baby but as the eternal king of the universe. Today, these words seem quaint and nothing but an ancient metaphor. Yet in their setting, these words were dangerous. To declare anyone king other that the emperor was treason. These words had both religious and political ramifications. This baby will become dangerous. It would be hard to say which is more shocking, that Jesus of Nazareth is indeed God or that he is an heir to the throne of David. Both are a threat to the Roman authorities. Jesus, it seems, is in trouble no matter where he goes.

To claim this text as a confession about Jesus is also to claim the radical nature of Jesus' preaching and actions. If we confess that God is indeed the ruler of all there is, then God's law is set above all other things including human law, national loyalty, or denominational creeds. This text calls us to declare our allegiance now, today. So on this Christmas morn, we do not just worship at the manger, but at the throne of our God and our King.

Gospel
John 1:1-14 (RCL)
John 1:1-18 or 1:1-5, 9-14 (LFM)

When I write for Christmas, I try hard to remember that I live in the northern hemisphere and that is not the whole of the world. The fastest-growing areas of Christian faith are in the southern hemisphere. Their Christmas looks much different, for there it is the middle of summer.

But it is hard for me to remember this because so many of our Christmas festivities center on darkness and cold weather, and this has shaped my perceptions of the holiday. Try as I might, Christmas in midsummer is hard for me to grasp. I say this, not as an apology, but to offer others an opportunity to contemplate a different way of celebrating and to realize that our place in the world defines so much of how we think.

Reading or hearing John's prologue is a bit like switching hemispheres. It changes how we think about this day and the event we celebrate. If I ask the children when Jesus was born, they will tell me December 25 or Christmas Day. They are sure. The answers become a bit more varied when I ask them how old Jesus would be on his next birthday. They look puzzled because we are puzzled. Pictures painted through the centuries pop into our heads and Jesus is never old. There are pictures of a baby, a child, a young man, but never an aging Jesus. We carry this image in our heads and they form our reality.

John's Gospel invites us to stretch our views and see beyond our normal horizons. We are called to see the world from God's perspective. The Gospel begins not with a story of Jesus' incarnation on earth but with the beginning, "The Word was with God and the Word was God. He was in the beginning with God." John is making the point that Jesus has always been, just as God has always been. This Jesus is more than meets the eye.

"The Word brings life and life is light of all people." Our heads spin a bit. The sentence is full of meaning. On one level, it means our physical life as in that which makes this body live, breathe, and think. God is the author of that life. Here John is also speaking of life being just as mysterious as light. We cannot produce the sun on command or control it. Both light and life belong to and answer to God. Our very lives depend on the Word for our genesis and continuation. On another level, the Word brings more than physical life. The Word also brings a way of life, or the way we choose to spend those days that we have. The Word comes to show us how to live. That way of life brings light to our lives. We are rescued from the darkness that surrounds us. This passage invites us to contemplate life, both the physical and the metaphysical, as gifts from God.

The Gospel lesson moves forward, telling us that Jesus is the true light and comes for everyone. It is important in this religiously divided world to hear that Christ comes for all, everyone, not just us. Unfortunately, Christmas has become something that divides us, through arguments about what can or cannot be displayed in public places and the question of how to greet each other. It never occurs to us that our Christian decorations or even our calendar are not the norm everywhere. Our vision is skewed by our culture and our position on the planet. We need John's readjustment to remind us that "all" actually means *all*. The light of Christ is like the sunlight falling where it will, not bending to our desires to bring darkness to some and sunshine only to our shores. The parts of the earth now covered in darkness will see sunshine in a few hours. God will go where God will and that is just as sure as the sun coming up and going down, or going around, depending on your perspective.

The beginning of John's Gospel also tells that some will not accept him, a foreshadowing of all that is to come which will culminate in Jesus' death at the hands of the people. Some simply cannot accept that this flesh-and-blood human is truly God. This morning we are asked to believe it again. We are called to see the baby in the manger as the one that was with God at the beginning of it all. We are called to see what others will not and to act accordingly. We are called to set aside our assumptions about the world and see the whole world, both hemispheres and all peoples, and know that Christ comes for all of them, not just us. We are all the same in that regard, for we are all the children of God. The gospel demands we confess Jesus as the God that sees the whole world and loves all people. We are to expand our perspective to see the whole truth of the child sleeping in the stable.

December 30, 2011
The Holy Family of Jesus, Mary, and Joseph (LFM)

Lectionary for Mass (LFM)
Genesis 15:1-6; 21:1-3
Psalm 105:1-2, 3-4, 5-6, 8-9
Hebrews 11:8, 11-12, 17-19
Luke 2:22-40, or 2:22, 39-40

The Feast of the Holy Family of Jesus, Mary, and Joseph is celebrated on December 30 when Christmas falls on a Sunday. The feast is one of modern origin, becoming part of the Roman Catholic calendar in 1921, and is a celebration both of the holy family and our own families as a blessing from God.

First Reading
Genesis 15:1-6; 21:1-3

The opening reading begins with that family the Judeo-Christian and Muslim traditions claim as their genesis. Abram and his wife Sarai are called by God to go to a new land with God's blessing so they will become a great nation. Abram and Sarai obey and travel to this new land, and they wait and they wait for the promise while experiencing all kinds of adventures.

The text opens on a conversation between God and Abram in a vision some time later. Abram has waited and it seems to him that there will be no heir except his foreign servant. Abram, and probably Sarai, are tired of waiting and they are not getting any younger. The promise God made seems to be void and the section ends in doubt, without God's answer.

In the intervening time, much happens. Sarai hatches a plan to have a baby via standard adoption practice in the ancient world. She tells Abram to impregnate her servant and Hagar becomes pregnant. Hagar runs away because of bad treatment and returns, gives birth, and there raises her child, Ishmael. Sarai, however, does not take Ishmael as her own. Again, God continues to promise Abram a child, even giving him and Sarai two new names, Abraham and Sarah. The first act of this newly named Abraham is to fall on his face laughing, saying, "Can a child be born to a man who is a hundred?" Abraham, God's chosen, laughs at God. Next, the Lord appears to Abraham and Sarah and again repeats the promise and this time it is Sarah who laughs. The promise becomes a joke.

The reading continues with the birth of the promised child. Sarah finally gives birth and Abraham names the child Isaac, or "laughter" in Hebrew, because the promise has come true. This family is not without difficulty, however, because they will also send Hagar and Ishmael away. This family has demonstrated both the miracle of grace in the birth of Isaac and utter disrespect in their treatment of Hagar and Ishmael.

What can be learned from this story? Certainly, the baby born to Abraham and Sarah was a miracle child. Yet are not all children miracles? Here with this first family, we see one family protected and cared for, while the other is thrown away. Hagar and her son were a nontraditional family and they were also blessed by God. The humans may have sent them away, but God saw them and saved them from death. We should learn from God here how to act.

We should also learn that this family decision Sarah made seems at first glance to be simply a choice made by a mistress concerning her slave. Yet this household decision made so long ago had world-changing consequences, for it is Ishmael who is seen as the favored son in the Islamic tradition. The way this family made its decisions about how to treat people still has worldwide consequences. This alone points to the importance of family on the future shaping of the world. What may seem to be a private family decision can alter the course of world history.

Psalmody
Psalm 105:1-2, 3-4, 5-6, 8-9

The genre of this psalm is historical poetry, telling the story of the people from Abraham to the settlement. It praises God for all of the ways that God protected and cared for them during that early period. It a psalm of remembering the things God had done for this family as it grew into a nation. It illustrates that God's promise made to Abraham has been fulfilled.

The psalm reminds us to look at the odds against this small, fledgling family. The trip to Canaan was risky enough, traveling to a strange land with no idea what or who they would find there. According to Genesis, their lives were in jeopardy several times. In addition, without an heir, the family would die unnoticed in a far-off land. Looking back, there is much to praise God for in this story.

As the Gospels of Luke and Matthew begin, the holy family is also found traveling and in jeopardy. They have nowhere to stay, are alone for the birth, and, in Matthew's account, they must run to Egypt to hide from Herod's soldiers and their murderous scheme. Both of these tiny family units faced frightening odds and great peril. All could have ended before it had begun.

What of today? As we celebrate this feast, there are hundreds of thousands of tiny families in peril; families all over God's world, both near and far. With the coming of Christ, we have become Christ's kingdom on earth. The welfare of these families is now our responsibility. We can celebrate the ways that God promised to and then did care for these families, but at the same time, we are called to renew our promise to the families of our world. We cannot offer praise to God and ignore our neighbor. Let our praise this day be a call to action for the future.

Second Reading
Hebrews 11:8, 11-12, 17-19

This chapter is one that tells the stories of Old Testament heroes and their faith in God. It serves as an example to Christians of how to live faithful lives even in times of great adversity. The text then serves as both teaching and encouragement for the faithful. But some of its conclusions may be problematic without further reflection.

The selected text focuses on Abraham and Sarah's faith in God. It shows how, as noted above, this couple set out and waited for their promise. In the face of adversity, they continued their faith in God. The text is a celebration of faith and serves as an example for all. We are to strive to be like them and hold to our belief in God's promises. The first verse of the reading celebrates the faith it took to listen to God and set out for a new, unknown place. Abraham and Sarah's faith was stronger than their fear of the unknown.

The next verses tell of the wait and how Abraham and Sarah continued to have faith as they waited for the promised child. It is here that the interpretation of the Genesis story in Hebrews become problematic. As noted above, the Genesis story is not one of absolute faithful and patient waiting for God. Indeed, the humans took the promise into their own hands and the result was both blessing and sorrow for the world. What can one do with the Hebrews text that omits Abraham and Sarah's lack of faith and instead honors them for that very characteristic? The truth seems to be the best choice. We all tell of our heroes in the faith and all of those heroes are human. They all had days of faithful service and days of doubt. Abraham and Sarah's days of doubt had grave consequences, but so do many of ours. Hebrews tells one part of the full Genesis story, just as our stories tell part of the fullness of our lives. Today we can both celebrate their faith and learn from their doubts.

The final section of this reading is the most problematic of all and it is here that there is a clear Christian interpretation placed on an earlier story. The incident is the so-called binding of Isaac. It is said that Abraham showed great faith by following God and sacrificing Isaac. Of course, this has come under question. Is offering your son as a sacrifice really a show of faith, especially when Abraham argued to save the inhabitants of Sodom, whom he did not know? Why did he not do the same for his own son? There are no easy answers, and this text stands as a troubling section of Scripture. With the addition of the new information here in Hebrews about

Abraham's knowledge that God could raise the dead, it appears this section is not about Abraham at all but about God's sacrificial giving of the Son to the world. This section, then, may be more complex than one wants to tackle in a feast-day homily. What we must avoid is a simplistic reading of the text that in any way implies that the sacrificial murder of a child is a sign of faith. This message could be dangerous in the wrong hands and runs the danger of causing harm to the least of God's children.

We can celebrate this family, but we should do so honestly. They are human with all of the faith and doubt that comes with that. We must be careful not to make the persons in the biblical text more perfect than the Bible itself does; we owe that to the preserved tradition and to those we serve.

Gospel
Luke 2:22-40 or 2:22, 39-40

The reading is Jesus' presentation at the Temple. After the birth in Bethlehem, Joseph and Mary traveled to Jerusalem to fulfill the law regarding Jesus' circumcision and presentation. The picture is one of a young family fulfilling its religious responsibilities. Today is the day to focus on this family. What do we really know? Unfortunately, little is definitive. We can surmise that they were young and since the offering Mary provided was the one allowed for the poor, it seems they were of little means. They have traveled long distances and have yet to lay their heads in their own bed in their own home.

It does not take a great stretch to see the same on our own city streets. There are countless new families on those streets. Some even carry the stigma of this family. Maybe there was an unplanned pregnancy and now they are struggling. Maybe, like this family, they are far from home, trying to do the right thing, even if they have no green card or passport. Some who lived in Jerusalem might have seen Joseph and Mary as there to take advantage of others, getting care normally reserved for those paying the town taxes. There is no doubt they were a family teetering on the brink of poverty. If we did not know their whole story, we would not see them as special. Indeed, their story is scandalous with Mary, who will be known as the Holy Mother of God, seen by those around her as a woman who sinned, conceiving a child before she was legally married.

Appearances can be deceiving. We can make judgments too quickly. Too many looked on Jesus and could not believe that what he was teaching was true. They were blinded by their preconceptions of the family, of Jesus' ministry, of his seemingly ordinariness, and of the people he healed and ate with in his travels. They did not look beyond their own assumptions.

Today is a day to celebrate all families. We are thankful for Joseph and Mary who did the right things as they struggled to raise their son. We celebrate because now we know what was not apparent then—that this family is holy. We have seen beyond our assumptions.

This text also involves the blessings of others. First Simeon and then Anna give thanks for and pray for this family and the future of the child. This reminds us of the importance of the support, blessing, and prayers of others that are not part of the family. It takes more than just the three of them to survive the world. We are called to pray for all families and to aid them in any way that we can. We are called to care for our neighbors. We are called like Abraham and Sarah to be a blessing to all of the world.

January 1, 2012
First Sunday of Christmas (RCL)

Revised Common Lectionary (RCL)

Isaiah 61:10—62:3

Psalm 148

Galatians 4:4-7

Luke 2:22-40

First Reading
Isaiah 61:10—62:3

What does the turn from despair to joy look like? In this text, the image is one of dressing as a bridegroom and bride. One can picture the beautiful clothing adorning the happy couple entering a new chapter of their lives. Yet, the clothes God brings are more than regular formalwear. The old clothes are discarded and in their place God provides garments of salvation and robes of righteousness. A possible parallel is the clothes God provides in Genesis 3. The humans do what they were forbidden to do, knowing that the penalty was death, but off they go anyway. When the story is all told, instead of death, God has forgiven them and clothed them. They are literally clothed with God's choice of salvation instead of death. God is doing on this Christmas morning what God has been doing since the beginning of it all: redeeming and saving the humans. Every time the humans destroy their relationship with God and each other, coming to a dead end, God offers another way for healing and a future.

Here this celebration is because God is changing the people's slavery into a bright future where praise and righteousness will spring forth like a garden in spring. The prophet is telling us that just as spring is sure, so are God's salvation and grace. Christ is born and will again and again show us God's love for us. We can celebrate the cyclic nature of it all and the constant promise of God's grace.

God's response seals the restoration. The people are not only forgiven but will become a beacon of glory to all of the other nations. God declares the people a beauty and royal crown, or diadem, in the hand of God. God moves the people from a state of sin to the elevated place of God's treasure and the sign of God's kingdom. God does not just forgive; the restoration is over the top. God restores us in grand fashion and makes us a priestly and royal people.

Psalmody
Psalm 148

Psalm 148 is one of the closing three psalms in the Psalter and it is nothing but pure praise for God. It is a song that calls on all of the realms we know to join together with voice and instruments in that overwhelming song.

The call to praise begins with the outermost parts of the universe, in the heavens with the messengers and hosts (vv. 1-2) and moves to all the celestial bodies—all are called to offer praise. These great bodies celebrate the God that created them and established their courses. Then to the earth and all of its wonders—all that is in the sea and the snow and the rain and the storms join in the chorus. Verse 9 completes the world with mountains and trees and all the animals. Psalm 19 tells that this world which God created "pours forth speech" and "declares knowledge." It is amazing to contemplate this morning on the conversation that goes on between the creation and God. Christmas is so focused on us, on the humans, but it was the creation that announced Christ's birth with a star. The creation offers praise that we do not see or take the time to notice. This psalm invites us to join with that creation in a never-ending song of praise.

At verse 11, the psalm calls on the humans: "Kings of the earth and all peoples, princes and all rulers of the earth! Young men and women alike, old and young together!" All are called to praise: the lofty and the regular, the men and the women, the young and the old. In praise of God, we are united and our differences can disappear. In many ways, what was true then is true now. The things that divide us have to do with what one group thinks God wants or demands. We argue about ordination standards, how to administer communion and baptism, moral questions. But in praise we can all agree that God is great and good. Praise is something today that we can all share, all Christians no matter where or what. Praise is the most universal practice in which we can engage.

Last night, we rang in the New Year via the Western calendar. This morning we join the praise of creation for all of the great things our God is and has done. This is home; this is praise done right. We praise God because we are created to do so.

Second Reading
Galatians 4:4-7

This section of Galatians can be misleading. Read in one light, it seems to condemn the law as a curse. In the verses preceding the focus text, Paul's concern is in the difference between "doing" the law and "fulfilling" the law. To Paul, these are not the same. "Doing" involves all of the required acts, whereas "fulfilling" involves the heart.[1] We know this to be true. It is the difference between going through the motions and dedicating yourself heart and soul to a task. To Paul, the law served a purpose, but that purpose can get turned upside down. Christ came to show the way we are to live. Christ comes to make us heirs, children instead of slaves. The law was temporary to Paul, holding the people together until the advent of Christ. The spirit of Christ in our hearts transforms us, Jew and Gentile alike, into equal heirs via the promise God made to Abraham.

Like many other Pauline texts, this one can generate debate about the nature of the law and the purpose of Christ's mission to the world. Yet in this season of Christmas, the point is not to argue about theology, but to read this text in light of the first two lessons and see it as a call to celebration. We have been made heirs of God through Christ. The story is as old as the exodus. God hears the cries of enslavement and acts to free the people to a new life of liberation. The birth we are celebrating has changed our lives forever. We are heirs to the kingdom.

Gospel
Luke 2:22-40

On this Sunday of Christmas, we continue to celebrate the coming of the Christ child into the world with Jesus' presentation in the Temple. This small family has done a lot of traveling. Joseph and Mary travel from Nazareth to Bethlehem where the child is born. The child is then taken to Jerusalem on his eighth day (2:21). The parents of Jesus are doing exactly what parents were supposed to do. Each trip was required by the laws of the land: the first for the Roman census, the second to fulfill their religious obligations. Joseph and Mary are stand-up parents who are doing their best to start off their family in the prescribed way.

Fred Strickert helps us see the irony of this trip to the Temple, not for the family, but for Jesus' ministry: "a closer examination of the text brings to light a stark contrast between the old reality and the world into which Jesus was born and the new reality of his life and ministry. This is a story about an inclusive gospel in an exclusive world."[2] The Temple in Jerusalem was an exclusive place. All except Jews were excluded. There were also gender and class distinctions. The sacrifice brought is not on behalf of the child, but for the mother as purification after childbirth (Lev. 12:1-8). Mary follows the provision for a poor mother. She does not have the resources to bring a sheep so she brings two birds and she is excluded from all but the women's court at the Temple. The point is, the place of Jesus' presentation is one that is exclusive, classist, and sexist. This is not meant to be antisemitic in any way. Our churches, over the centuries and even today, practice their own exclusions. Jesus comes even today to our exclusive communities. God does not wait for us to do better, but enters our broken world.

The irony continues in the two persons that the young family meets. The first is Simeon, who is introduced without a title but is said to be righteous and devout. One would expect the blessing of the child to come from a priest, but that is not to be. Simeon blesses the child and tells of Jesus' universal message to all as "a light for revelation to the Gentiles and for the glory of your people Israel." He sees what others would not and declares inclusion of the whole world in this place of exclusion. The second person to praise the child is Anna, a prophet who lives in the Temple. She is of great age and, like Simeon, tells of Jesus' future ministry of redemption. A woman doing a man's job, she blesses this child. These two represent all of those without title that Jesus will meet, love, heal, and transform. This is not a family that the Temple authorities usher in with great fanfare. They are not important enough for special treatment, yet these two souls provide that special treatment.

The irony in this story is great. Jesus' parents take him to the Temple to do exactly what was supposed to be done. They are good people doing what good people do. Jesus has a mission to shake up that world, just as he comes to shake ours. It is not a question of Temple authorities being mean or exclusive, for they, as the religious leaders of the day, thought they were doing the right thing. The same light that shines on these ancient practices shines on us. What practices do we have that Jesus comes this time to change? Where are we shutting people out? The first two readings speak of offering praises to God, praises given by everyone and everything together without division, in harmony. Do we cut off that praise with our divisions? Are our rules of conduct restrictive? Jesus comes to us anyway, just as Jesus came in his time. Our job this day and every day is to join with all of creation and all of God's people to offer praise to our God for all of God's benefits.

Notes

1. Daniel Boyarin, "Was Paul an 'Anti-Semite'? A Reading of Galatians 3–4," *Union Seminary Quarterly Review* 47, no. 1–2 (1993): 49–50.
2. Fred Strickert, "The Presentation of Jesus: The Gospel of Inclusion. Luke 2:22-40," *Currents in Theology and Mission* 22, no. 1 (1995): 33.

January 1, 2012
Holy Name of Jesus (RCL) /
Mary, Mother of God (LFM)

Revised Common Lectionary (RCL)
Numbers 6:22-27
Psalm 8
Galatians 4:4-7 or Phillipians 2:5-11
Luke 2:15-21

Lectionary for Mass (LFM)
Numbers 6:22-27
Psalm 67:2-3, 5, 6 + 8
Galatians 4:4-7
Luke 2:16-21

These are the texts for the two services celebrated on January 1. In the Episcopal and Lutheran traditions, this day is the Holy Name of Jesus celebration. In this year's calendar, this day also falls on the first Sunday of Christmas, thus there are two sets of readings for this day in the Revised Common Lectionary. January 1 is, in the Roman Catholic tradition, the Solemnity of Mary, Mother of God, and is the only set of readings for this day in 2012.

First Reading
Numbers 6:22-27 (RCL, LFM)

In 1979 in a burial cave beneath the Church of Saint Andrew in Jerusalem, archaeologist Gabriel Barkay discovered a curious artifact. On further inspection, it appeared to be a piece of thin metal rolled into a cylinder. The artifact was studied and dated to the seventh century B.C.E., or the time of Jeremiah, before the Babylonian exile. Engraved in fine script on this silver scroll are these verses, known as the Priestly Benediction.[1] The scroll was worn as a protective amulet as a blessing for ancient believers. The blessing is familiar because it is often used as a benediction in Christian worship. The blessing itself is three lines, giving wishes for one's life. Its words are to be contemplated and used as they were by the ancients as a blessing that we carry with us.

"The Lord bless you and keep you" in the Hebrew means to "give strength to" and "to keep, guard, or watch." The next line, "The Lord make his face to shine upon you," is an ancient expression of favor. In our vernacular, we would say, "His eyes light up when she walks into the room." It reminds us of our closest relationships, husbands and wives, parents and children. What a wonderful thought that God's face lights up at the sight of us! It shows we are loved. Added to that is for God to be gracious, to show us grace in times of trouble and even when we pull away.

The final line contains a wonderful image; "to lift up one's face or countenance" in the ancient world means "to look another in the eye." Imagine for just a moment standing toe to toe with God and having God look you in the eye, another image of intimacy. From a human perspective, it also is frightening, so frightening that the ancients thought if they looked on God directly they would die (Exod. 33:20). Yet we are also told that Abraham stood in such a position before the Lord (Gen. 18:22). It is frightening because it is so intimate, to look straight into the eyes of God with all of one's life exposed. Yet it is this very connection with our Creator that we long for, to be really seen and known by God.

The final blessing is for God to give peace, or *shalom*. This is a word that is often underestimated today for it is so much more than the absence of war; it is a state of completeness in all aspects of our lives, of happiness and fulfillment and the achievement of our full humanity. It can only happen in the presence of God, when we have been blessed by our Creator, God, with love and grace. It is a blessing that fits well on a day when we celebrate the naming of Jesus in the Temple and Mary as the Mother of God, both of whom teach us what it means to stand face to face with God.

Psalmody
Psalm 8 (RCL)

This psalm is a celebration of the human in God's created order. The first and last verses are identical and form an envelope. This structure places human action within the universal scope of God's rule.

Verse 2 is problematic, as the multiple English translations of this verse demonstrate. Its meaning is probably something like "the babbling of babies is more powerful than God's enemies, placing them where they belong from God's perspective."

Verses 3 through 8 speak of the humans. It begins with the small feeling we have when we contemplate the vastness of the universe by looking at the night sky. In this vast context, the psalm asks why God would even consider humans or visit them. In Hebrew, that last word can mean either "care for" or "visit," but in the context of Christmas, "to visit" seems the appropriate choice. The answer moves one from insignificance to the center in a moment: "Yet you have made them a little lower than God, and crowned them with glory and honor!" Some translations follow the Latin translation and use "angels" for "God," but the Hebrew is clear. Humans are made a bit lower than God and God has crowned them with glory and honor. On any Sunday, this should make our spirits soar. Today, in the context of this Sunday, Jesus comes to earth to show us the full content of what this verse means.

This next section should be read carefully because, just like the life of Jesus, it teaches us something about power. The verses look innocuous enough, telling of all of the things that we, humans, have dominion over. But when one thinks about it, we do not have dominion over the animals in our homes, not to mention the birds of the air and the fish in the sea. Granted, we do have the power to destroy these animals, but we have little power to control them. This psalm, then, challenges our ideas of dominion and what we might think that means. People thought Jesus came to save them from the Romans but, indeed, he came to save them from themselves. Likewise, "dominion" here is not a show of pure power. In the Hebrew, the text is confusing; the verb means "one was caused to rule." In clearer terms, the human is caused by God to rule, noting that it is by God's direction, not our own, that humans are to rule. The next word is not really "over," as in to rule over the works of God's hands. It more often means "to rule with" or "to rule among." From this perspective, we begin to understand more clearly our Christian vocation. We are to partner with the creation to which God has also given a task. We are not to take over with brute force, but to learn from Christ's example what it means to be king of the universe.

This psalm in the Christmas season reminds us that Jesus teaches us how to live and this way of living is not the same way as our world is run. It is the very definition of what it means to be fully human and is fitting for this day when we celebrate the giving of a human name to Jesus.

Psalm 67:2-3, 5, 6 + 8 (LFM)

The psalm serves as a parallel to the priestly blessing from Numbers. The wish for blessing this time comes not from a priest, but from the people themselves. Yet the wishes are virtually the same. The psalm, however, adds to the blessing the reasons why God should grant their wish. The reason is not the people, but to show God's rule and saving power to the world. In this, it also serves as a link to the Magnificat, for Mary's song expresses the same sentiment with "My soul magnifies the Lord." People are here to show forth God's glory. The psalm moves to praise, for all nations will be glad because of God's governance of the people. God will indeed guide the nations and bring justice to all. Praise rings all around the world as the peoples give thanks for all of God's great benefits.

Second Reading
Galatians 4:4-7 (RCL, LFM)

For commentary on this text, see the second reading for the First Sunday of Christmas, p. 45.

Philippians 2:5-11 (RCL alt.)

On this day when we celebrate the presentation and naming of Jesus, the so-called Christ hymn from Philippians is certainly an appropriate choice. One should take caution, however, not to become entangled in the arguments about its origin and original purpose or the dogmatic questions about the nature of Christ. With the other readings for today, the stress is on what Jesus teaches us about being fully human and thus is a celebration of his incarnation. Indeed, this context is probably the one meant in Paul's letter. Ronald Allen notes the text was used by Paul as an example of what it means "to look not at your own interests but to the interests of others" (2:4).[2] The point of the hymn is to praise Christ and it also serves an example for us to follow.

The first part of the text focuses on the gift of Christ's incarnation and his refusal to exploit his position as God. Instead, he humbled himself to the point of death for our sake. Like Psalm 8, it is a lesson about how we are to live and use power. We are to never exploit our positions for our own gain, but use them to support and aid others.

The second section is very fitting for this Holy Name of Jesus day, for it is pure praise of that name. His name is above every name and at that name every knee in heaven and earth should bow. This certainly presents a different picture than the one in Luke when young Mary and Joseph take the baby to the Temple. There is praise, but only from Simeon and Anna who hardly represent the whole world. That irony is part of the lesson about how Christ teaches us to humble ourselves for others. We may be fortunate enough to have a name that garners the attention of the world, and the temptation is to use that name for our own benefit. Jesus teaches us the importance of using power for others, instead of using power over them.

Gospel
Luke 2:15-21 (RCL)
Luke 2:16-21 (LFM)

The Gospel text is the first birth announcement followed by his naming. The text is certainly familiar and that makes it difficult to hear. Placed with these other texts, its focus is the blessing of Jesus' coming to the world. The angels offer an announcement to shepherds. A grand announcement is given in a small place. This also continues the ironic message of these birth narratives. A grand, almost inconceivably grand, act is given to shepherds who are probably young men of meager circumstance.

As noted earlier, the story, told year after year, loses its irony for we become accustomed to the angels singing in the sky. So much so, we sing "Hark! The herald angels sing, Glory to the newborn king" without a thought to its incongruity. Well, let me tell you, angels flying through the sky is not an ordinary sight at Christmas or any other time of the year! God surprises the world and I am not sure if it is the fact of the angels themselves or the fact that they appear in the middle of nowhere that is more shocking. These shepherds tell others of what happened (Luke 2:18) and all who hear "were amazed." Yet I wonder, What was their amazement? Did they believe the story or did they think the town better hire different shepherds? The shepherds are in the same category with the women returning from the tomb in the Gospel of Mark. Their news is simply too wonderful to believe. Maybe, just maybe, if the angels had appeared over Jerusalem so that serious and stable men of high reputation saw them, then we might start to believe it. God went to all the trouble to send the angels to a group of guys that sleep in a field. But appear the angels do, to the ordinary and the regular. The angels sing to the people Jesus comes to save. God is consistent from the rescue from Egypt to the appearance of the angels, for God sees and hears the nobodies of the world and attends to them.

Mary ponders all of these things in her heart. We know so little about this young girl turned young mother. What we know most is of her presence as the God bearer, as a quiet presence as Jesus grows and at the foot of the cross. She appears quiet and reserved. What we do know is that she accepted her situation with a song of thanksgiving and she tries to be a good parent. She welcomes the shepherds to her makeshift birthing bed. She sees her son grow and die on a cross. In the biblical tradition, she is faithful and silent. She is ordinary and she never seems to use her son to increase her position.

The final verse is also ordinary. The child is eight days old so it is time for his circumcision and naming. No fanfare, no angels to escort the family to the Temple. Just a regular couple doing a regular thing. The contrast of this verse with the Christ hymn, where at the mention of his name every knee in heaven and earth shall bow down, is clear. Jesus does not come crashing into the world in a way that makes everyone stand up and take notice. Jesus comes into the world as just another baby born in Judah, a regular baby with regular parents who is welcomed to the world by angels singing: a fully ordinary-appearing, extraordinary human and fully God; our gift, our salvation, today and tomorrow and all the days of our lives.

Notes

1. As is typical in cases of archaeological discoveries, there is scholarly disagreement about how closely these scrolls match the biblical text and the date of the creation of the scrolls, but the above is considered the current consensus on the matter. See Gabriel Barkay, et al., "The Challenges of Ketef Hinnom: Using Advanced Technologies to Reclaim the Earliest Biblical Texts and Their Context," *Near Eastern Archaeology* 66, no. 4 (2003): 162–71.
2. Ronald Allen, "Philippians 2:1-11," *Interpretation* 61, no. 1 (2007): 73.

Epiphany—Time after Epiphany / Ordinary Time
Moving Toward Transfiguration

Paul Galbreath

The word *epiphany* means "to show or make manifest." In Scripture, the stories associated with Epiphany portray Jesus' appearance as God's chosen one to those around him. Mary and Joseph huddle around their newborn child in the hope and promise that this child will fulfill the promises and prophecies that they have heard. (Those congregations who celebrate the feast of the Holy Family and the Solemnity of Mary may consider ways that the layering of these stories provides a diverse witness to the incarnation.) The shepherds who come to visit the child cast their eyes upon the infant and kneel around the manger in wonder and awe. The magi who travel from the East to visit the manger and look upon the baby Jesus take in the vision of this child as one who is anointed to announce the reign of God. These traditional images of Epiphany depict the season as one in which the Word shines its light upon those who gather around it. As the biblical characters gather around the Word made flesh, the promise of the Christ child is shown to them. So, too, as communities of faith gather around these sacred stories, the claims of Scripture are made manifest to us. Together we enter into Epiphany—this time when the testimonies of those who first encountered the Christ child make their claims on our lives.

There is another side to Epiphany, though. The biblical witnesses that we read speak primarily in terms of the journey to Bethlehem and the encounter of those who travel to visit baby Jesus. We are left wondering how this experience transformed their lives. What happened to them after their visit to the Christ child? How did this manifestation of the divine disrupt their routines and how did they live out of this encounter? Christian churches (ecclesial bodies) have different ways of counting the Sundays in this season. Some communities number each Sunday after the Epiphany. Each Sunday is marked in light of the great manifestation to the magi. Each new text in this season becomes an additional testimony that is added to the witnesses of those travelers from the East who followed the star until it rested over the manger in Bethlehem. Over the course of these Sundays "after the Epiphany" the church assembles a cloud of witnesses whose voices echo the hope and promise that this Christ child will indeed bring good will to all people. This time from the

Epiphany to the Transfiguration looks at each week in light of the Epiphany and challenges us to mark our calendars as well as our lives in light of the appearance of the divine Christ child in our lives. There is another way of counting these Sundays after Epiphany. After the high point of Epiphany, some communities enter an early period of Ordinary Time. From this perspective, the drama of Epiphany yields to the daily demands on our lives. While Epiphany remains a marker of our encounter with the divine, we return to the ordinary tasks that fill our lives. Here, the Sundays in Ordinary Time press us to see how even the ordinary can be filled with the divine.

These slightly different ways of counting after the celebration of Epiphany point to the primary challenge of celebrating Epiphany: How are we changed by the testimonies of those who have encountered God through the birth of this child? While we may not be able to fill in the details of how the first visitors reacted after their encounter with the divine, we can take note of the ways that the Spirit takes shape in our lives in light of God's manifestation to us. Thus, this birth narrative that we hear each Christmas season becomes our own birth story as we remember our baptism and give thanks for the Spirit that carries us to new birth.

These weeks following Epiphany offer a chance for us to listen to the witness of Scripture and to examine our own lives to see where we are growing as disciples of Jesus Christ. Whether we count these days in light of the Epiphany or whether we mark the days as a return to Ordinary Time, the goal of this time is to find ways in which our lives begin to resemble the witnesses to God's presence in our world. During these weeks, preachers have the opportunity to present ways that these texts come to life in our own communities of faith. Hence, the story of the incarnation becomes a series of incarnational moments as we encounter God at work in our lives. This transition from long ago to the present is a crucial one for preachers to grasp. The preacher adds her or his voice as a witness to the ongoing work of the Spirit who brings the gift of new life and who nurtures us to maturity.

The goal of these weeks is for us to encounter Christ so that we may more clearly manifest God's presence to those around us. The celebration of Epiphany and the journey through the Scriptures each Sunday thereafter serve as a mirror for us to see ways in which these events can be seen in the life of our faith communities and in our own lives. Through careful listening, faithful modeling, and actively responding to the needs of those around us who hunger for hope, peace, and justice, we become manifestations of God's redemptive presence and we become transfigured into the image of Christ.

The journey to discover the Christ child that we celebrate each Epiphany becomes our own travel story in which we remember where we encountered the gospel and how it came to birth in our own life. Year after year, as we hear these texts, we respond by examining our own lives to see how the Spirit is manifest in our congregations. As we gather around this Word and as we celebrate this good news with the gifts of bread and wine, we move toward the transfiguration of our lives as God's light shines upon us and through us.

January 6, 2012*
Epiphany of Our Lord

The lectionary readings for Epiphany provide a set of complementary texts that sketch out major themes for celebrating this day. Central motifs include Jesus' birth as a fulfillment of the promises of Scripture, the role of outsiders in recognizing God's presence in our midst, a cast of witnesses who offer testimonies, and the role of faithful discipleship in times of suffering and persecution. Preachers will want to select from these themes and discover ways to portray them in light of the needs and issues of their own congregations.

Gospel
Matthew 2:1-12 (RCL, LFM)

While the Gospel of Matthew is generally considered to be written to a primary audience of Christians from a Jewish background, our text for Epiphany establishes an early theological claim regarding the role of Gentiles and outsiders in the Gospel story. Matthew's extended genealogy and birth narrative in chapter 1 establishes a major motif by presenting Jesus as one who comes from David's lineage. At the same time, the genealogical list in Matthew 1 weaves in a series of outsiders who play important parts in this gathered history of God's redemptive plan. The religious royalty of Abraham, Isaac, and Jacob is balanced by the inclusion of Rahab and Ruth. Together this ancestral list provides the framework for the theological claim of Jesus as one who comes in fulfillment of the Jewish history and as one whose lineage balances the surprising inclusion of unlikely characters. This family tree includes all sorts of branches.

55

* Some denominational calendars allow this festival to be transferred to the previous Sunday, January 1.

Today's reading from Matthew 2 builds on this prominent theme in Matthew's Gospel. Matthew is quick to develop parallels between Jesus' birth and the lives of key figures in the Hebrew Bible. The focus on Bethlehem as the birthplace of this "king of the Jews" draws on the narrative of Bethlehem as David's hometown and the place where he was anointed king. From the beginning of the Gospel, Matthew makes a messianic claim that this child comes as one who will fulfill the hopes and expectations of those who long for God to send a new leader. Matthew also uses the language of Jesus as the king of the Jews as a point of contrast to King Herod who resides in Jerusalem. This imagery of kingship will recur throughout the Gospel and culminate in the conflict that leads to Jesus' crucifixion at the hands of the powerful political and religious leaders in Jerusalem. Matthew's Gospel goes full circle in portraying Jesus as the one who is born to be the king of the Jews (2:2) and the one who dies under the sign "This is Jesus, the King of the Jews" (27:37).

Matthew typically develops the narrative as a fulfillment of Old Testament prophecy. Many scholars see a connection between the magi and the oracle of Balaam (who also came from the East) in Numbers 24:17-19, where a future leader is envisioned as a star coming out of Jacob.[1] Jesus' birth as fulfillment of prophecy is further buttressed by the insertion of words from Micah 5:2 and 2 Samuel 5:2 (in Matt. 2:6), which are ironically placed on the lips of the chief priests and scribes. Daniel Harrington interprets Matthew 2 as a parallel to the Moses narrative—with slaughter of innocents and flight to Egypt.[2] Moses is saved in a miraculous way when the pharaoh wants to kill the Hebrew male children.

In the midst of this story of fulfillment and royal lineage, Matthew offers the contrasting witness of the magi as the outsiders who journey from the distant East. Throughout the Gospel, outsiders will play key roles in pointing to Jesus as the one who comes from God. In today's text, the magi deliver the good news to the central corridors of power in Jerusalem. King Herod, who is threatened by the birth of a potential rival, and all the chief priests and scribes (v. 4), whose knowledge of Scripture leads them to Bethlehem of Judea, will not be able to acknowledge Jesus as the Messiah. Instead, these Gentiles who have traveled from afar seeking signs from the sky are the ones who are able to first discern what God is doing.

Preachers enable listeners to recognize ourselves in these portraits. As baptized followers of Jesus, we share in the royal lineage as beloved sons and daughters of God. At the same time, we are outsiders to this story. A challenge here is for the preacher to open the text in a way that underscores the dual nature of this inside-outside role. How does the church as an institution remain open to the voices and testimonies of outsiders who come from different places and backgrounds? In the mirror of Scripture, we can discover ourselves playing multiple characters in this text. At times, we are cast in the roles of political and religious leaders who want to cling to our own sources of power and deny places around the table for those who look, talk, and act differently from what we expect. At other times, we may find that our witness to the

Gospel casts us as countercultural and marginalizes us from the dominant centers of power in our own time.

In this place where we live as both insiders and outsiders, the text offers us clues about how to respond to the presence of Christ. Matthew provides contrasting images in our reading today. Herod is portrayed as curious to learn more about the birth of this new king in order that he, too, can pay homage to Jesus (v. 8). Yet, it is left to the magi, these Gentile outsiders, to model an authentic response to the Word made flesh. In the house of David, the magi fall to their knees and offer gifts of gold, frankincense, and myrrh (v. 11). For Matthew, the imagery of falling down as a sign of worship demonstrates the appropriate response to Christ's presence. The magi in Bethlehem, the disciples on the mountain at the transfiguration (17:6), and the disciples who gather around the risen Christ to receive the great commission (28:17) model this posture of falling down before the splendor of Christ as infant, as transfigured teacher, and as risen Christ.

Matthew underscores the actions of the magi as the ones who demonstrate an authentic response to the good news. Herod feigns homage even while he secretly plots to kill this threat to his power. Immediately following our reading, Joseph, Mary, and Jesus will flee in light of the suffering and persecution that Herod brings to bear. The earlier hearers of this text were likely confronted with the challenge to keep the faith despite threats of persecution. Today's listeners may struggle to allow our desire to pay homage to Christ to come to grips with the radical claims of the Gospel to stand alongside the poor, forgotten, neglected, and marginalized. Increasingly, Western Christianity's own pilgrimage from the centers of cultural power to the margins of society provides an opportunity for us to embody our allegiance to Christ. Identifying with the magi as outsiders allows us to respond to God's call as well as to offer the many gifts that we bring. The text includes a final word of warning in the form of the magi's vision telling them to travel away from the centers of power in Jerusalem and to continue their journey by a different path. Here, the church is challenged not to attempt to recast itself as the dominant cultural voice, but to trust that God's light will lead us in new directions. As the Spirit calls us to recognize Christ's presence, we respond with gratitude, offering ourselves and our belongings in thanksgiving for God's grace. We rise up, trusting in God's Spirit to guide us on a new journey into God's future.

First Reading
Isaiah 60:1-6 (RCL, LFM)

The lectionary treats the reading from Isaiah and the psalm (see below) as corroborating witnesses to the theological claims that Matthew presents in the Gospel. These opening words from Third Isaiah speak of a future hope that the faithful will rise to see the light of a new day breaking through the darkness that envelops them. The prophet's vision of a new future that God is bringing to the people recognizes Israel's worship as central in marking the place where Yahweh's light will shine upon the people.[3] Two aspects are particularly noteworthy. First, the faithful are encouraged to rise up to experience the glory of the Lord as it comes upon us. This call to worship is a contrast from our passive attachment to pews where we quietly sit to look upon worship services and the entertainment-driven model of worship where professional musicians and motivational speakers offer inspirational and moral advice for our edification. In contrast, worship renewal in light of this text is a call for active engagement with our bodies as we rise up in the hope and promise of encountering God's light and glory.

Second, this hope of a new day is accompanied by the vision of a great host of outsiders streaming toward the light that shines upon Zion. These strangers cradle in their arms the sons and daughters of those who have gathered to worship God. Thus, a family reunion occurs in the most unlikely way. Those outside the family tree have gathered up the relatives and are bringing them with them as they seek together to bask in the light of God's grace. Caravans will travel from distant lands and offer the gifts of gold and frankincense. Here, the notions of Yahweh as God and king are closely tied together. The text underscores that the primary purpose of this gathering is the proclamation of God's glorious deeds of salvation.

While the images of shining light associated with the star of Bethlehem and the gifts of gold and frankincense offered by those who have followed the light provide the obvious links to the Gospel reading, preachers will benefit from paying close attention to the role of the outsiders who in response to the light of God's glory bring healing and reconciliation to the community. Thus, while congregations are urged to look up to experience the light that shines upon us, we are also urged to look beyond our doors in expectation that we will encounter reunion and wholeness through the gifts that those beyond our circles bring us. Similarly, the text portrays the hope that even in the midst of exile, separation, and suffering God will bring a group of people together in ways that defy our imaginations. The line between family and stranger blurs as we bask in the light that surrounds us.

Psalmody
Psalm 72:1-7, 10-14 (RCL)
Psalm 72:1-2, 7-8, 10-11, 12-13 (LFM)

The psalm of the day shares with the Isaiah reading an obvious link to the Gospel text, namely the kings of Sheba and Seba who offer gifts and prostrate themselves before God (vv. 10-11). Here again, the theme of outsiders who journey to pay tribute and offer worship to God provides a unitive message throughout these diverse texts. This psalm, which is identified with King Solomon and recognized by scholars as one of the royal psalms, may have served as part of the coronation ceremonies for Israel's king.[4] The idealized rhetoric of the text has caused some interpreters to identify it less with a specific monarch and more with the hopes invested in new leaders (and increasingly among readers with the desire for a messiah who will bring God's reign). Preachers can develop the references to Solomon as another of the extended group of witnesses throughout these texts who point to the glory of God. King Solomon is joined by the royalty from around the world who respond to God's majesty and offer gifts of thanksgiving. In Song of Songs, Solomon is associated with myrrh and frankincense (3:6; 4:6), which provides a striking parallel to the magi's gifts in the Gospel. Here, the descriptions of Solomon and foreign kings serve to prefigure the story of the magi who fall prostrate before the baby Jesus and offer their gifts to pay homage to the Christ child. Together the testimony and actions of all these characters in the various biblical narratives provide a set of witnesses that point to faithful ways to respond to God's presence.

However, there remains a risk in pushing these texts into an overly historical and literal direction. Their shared use of the language of vision and hope in God's future deliverance provides an antidote to the temptation to press them into strict conformity with one another. Instead, they offer a diverse tapestry of distant voices that point toward God's promise to bring deliverance and salvation that extends beyond our narrow expectations. The psalm connects this vision explicitly to the plight of the poor and needy (vv. 12-13). The outside-in imagery that we have seen throughout these texts (with outsiders bringing good news and reunion to the community) gains another important layer. The purpose of this reunion and restoration of God's community is not insular and self-serving. Instead, the community's response of falling down before the glory of God is linked to its response to hear with God the cries of suffering, poor, and marginalized people who live around us. As the psalmist notes, "God takes pity on the poor and needy, and saves the lives of the needy." We are invited into God's redemptive activity in the world. Here the gifts that we offer in thanksgiving for God's grace are put directly to use to alleviate the pain and suffering of those who are in need.

Second Reading
Ephesians 3:1-12 (RCL)
Ephesians 3:2-3a, 5-6 (LFM)

The epistle lesson offers a different tone in support of the lectionary texts of the day. The text takes the tone of a logical presentation by a lawyer in the courtroom who seeks to convince a jury of the soundness of the reasoning in his case. The apostle Paul presents his case as an additional witness to the good news of God's light that shines through the one who comes to bring God's reign. Similar to the other readings, Paul develops this point in terms of the inclusion of outsiders (Gentiles) in God's plan. What is striking about this approach is that Paul begins with the Jewish language of Jesus as Messiah that is quickly expanded through this gospel where "the Gentiles are co-heirs, members of the same body, and co-partners in the promise in Christ Jesus" (v. 6). Once again, the imagery of reunion and reconciliation in response to God's presence underscores a primary theme.

Hints of other themes that we have explored in the lectionary readings for the day shimmer beneath the surface. Scripture as that which is fulfilled in the life of Jesus is linked with the secret (mystery) that becomes known to those who respond to the gospel. Paul, as a prisoner (v. 1) and servant (v. 7) of the gospel alludes to the role of suffering included in the life of faith. Yet Paul points beyond any suffering to the faithful companionship of God and the community gathered to worship who accompany and sustain him on his journey.

Focal Points for Preaching

The annual celebration of Epiphany is often associated with images from children's pageants with the camels and the three wise men and the singing of "We Three Kings of Orient Are." Preachers on this day have the opportunity to expand the imaginations of listeners who have oversentimentalized, disregarded, or become placated by these traditional components. Epiphany offers a radical vision of unexpected people, places, and ways to encounter God's grace. From beyond our sanctuary walls and closed doors, new hope, new light, and new family march to meet us, to challenge us, and to offer us new ways to encounter God's redemptive grace.

Opening up these texts anew offers us the chance to reorient our lives and our priorities in order that we may experience the light and hope that dawn from the East and participate in the reign of God that is inextricably linked to the cries and plight of the poor and needy. In light of this, our celebration of Epiphany offers us the possibility of a new spiritual beginning as our lives take on the sign of new light and life. Marking this occasion as a beginning point in the life of the community allows the celebration of Epiphany to move from that of a distant memory from once upon a time to a shared commitment for this community to take on the characteristics of those who pay authentic homage to Christ's presence. The light of Christ that shines upon us becomes a part of us as we move out into the world to welcome stranger and friend on the journey toward God's new reign.

Notes

1. Robert Gundry also recognizes allusions to Isa. 60:1-3 and Daniel 2. Whether or not the preacher decides to reference these texts that may lie underneath (or behind) the Matthew text, the primary point is to note ways that the testimony of the Gospel writer is layered upon the witness of other testimonies to God's presence in our world. See Robert Gundry, *Matthew: A Commentary on His Literary and Theological Art* (Grand Rapids: Eerdmans, 1992), 27. See also Raymond Brown, *The Birth of the Messiah* (New York: Doubleday, 1979), where he writes: "In other words, the wicked king sought to use the foreign magus to destroy his enemy, but the magus actually honored his enemy. Obviously this is very close to the story of Herod and the magi" (194).
2. Daniel J. Harrington, S.J., *The Gospel of Matthew*, Sacra Pagina 1 (Collegeville, Minn.: Liturgical, 1991), 48–49.
3. Claus Westermann, *Isaiah 40–66*, Old Testament Library (Philadelphia: Westminster, 1977), 356.
4. Mitchell Dahood, *Psalms II, 51–100*, Anchor Bible (Garden City, N.Y.: Doubleday, 1968), 179.

January 8, 2012
Baptism of Our Lord / First Sunday after Epiphany / First Sunday in Ordinary Time

Revised Common Lectionary (RCL)
Genesis 1:1-5
Psalm 29
Acts 19:1-7
Mark 1:4-11

Lectionary for Mass (LFM)
Isaiah 55:1-11
Isaiah 12:2-3, 4bcd, 5-6
1 John 5:1-9
Mark 1:7-11

The light that guides us to the Christ child is the light that we celebrate in our baptism as beloved children of God. Scripture is not read in a vacuum during worship. The liturgical context creates imaginative links between the texts and the lives of those in the congregation. This is particularly true on days like the Baptism of the Lord where a wide variety of liturgical options (e.g., will members of the community participate in a renewal of their baptismal vows?) color the way that listeners interpret the text. The feast of the Baptism of the Lord allows us to relive this occasion in light of the defining story of Jesus' baptism in the Jordan River. The diversity of texts used by congregations articulate the primary link of the Spirit's presence with the act of baptism (both in Jesus' baptism and in those who are baptized in his name).

Gospel
Mark 1:4-11 (RCL)
Mark 1:7-11 (LFM)

Mark's Gospel starts with Jesus' baptism—there is no nativity scene or Christmas Eve story. For Mark, the story of Jesus' birth begins here in the Jordan River. Out of this seminal experience, his teaching, healing, and feeding ministry begins.

The scene of Jesus' baptism opens with John the Baptist out in the wilderness. Already, Mark is contrasting the emergence of this renewal movement from the fringes of society as opposed to Jerusalem where the religious and political leaders reside (note the similarity here to the Gospel reading for Epiphany Sunday). Mark develops this contrast in a new way by showing an exodus from Jerusalem to the wilderness where "the whole Judean countryside and all the people of Jerusalem" are journeying to hear John's message (v. 5). This contrast foreshadows the conflict that will develop throughout Mark's Gospel and ultimately leads to Jesus' arrest and crucifixion as one who is seen as a threat to powerful special interests in Jerusalem.

The location of the wilderness as site of religious pilgrimage aligns with the descriptions of John the Baptist. John is presented in the garb of the prophet Elijah. Clothed in camel's hair and a leather belt, John wears the signature wardrobe of Elijah (2 Kgs. 1:8), John's rhetoric parallels Elijah's blistering condemnation of the powerful leaders. The crowds of people who travel out to hear this message bask in the messianic fervor that longs for the return of Elijah as a sign of God's deliverance.

It is part religious revival and part circus spectacle, and evidently everyone wants to participate. John presents his role as one who prepares the way by calling the people to confess their sins and be baptized in the Jordan River in preparation for the coming of the Messiah. John limits his action to a baptism with water, whereas the Messiah will baptize with the Holy Spirit.

Jesus joins with the crowd that gathers in the wilderness and is baptized in the Jordan River—the same river where Elijah and Elisha met to pass the prophetic mantle. It is also the same Jordan River that Moses looked out across in order to see the promised land. It is the river that the children of Israel would cross through on their journey of discipleship.

While the Old Testament stories of the Jordan River picture the water opening up so that the people can cross through, the story of Jesus' baptism is one of the water closing over him while the sky appears to have ripped open and the Spirit descends. Here in the waters of baptism, Jesus receives a divine blessing. Here, in the waters of baptism, Jesus' ministry begins.

The Gospel's portrait of Jesus' baptism as well as the baptismal rites of the church treat the narrative of Jesus' baptism as one of the defining reasons for the adoption of baptism as a central rite of the church. This is true despite the fact that John's baptism for the repentance of sin is presented differently from that of later Christian practices (see comments on the second reading from Acts 19, below). While Christian baptismal practice developed into patterns that are significantly different from John the Baptist's call for Jewish renewal, Jesus' baptism remains central to the development of liturgical practices in the church. On this point, Mark's Gospel provides a helpful frame in the way that we as listeners are pulled into the text and encouraged to identify with the one who comes to baptize us with the Holy Spirit. Jesus' baptism culminates with a divine seal of approval as the heavens are torn apart and the Spirit descends like a dove and a voice from heaven announces, "You are my Son, the Beloved; with you I am well pleased" (v. 11). Each of these descriptive elements will return at crucial moments in the Gospel narrative. For those who mark this liturgical time by its movement from Epiphany to Transfiguration, these elements gain particular importance as they are featured in the description of the transfiguration in Mark 9.

The new cathedral in Managua, Nicaragua, offers an architectural vision of this passage in its baptismal space. One enters the front corner of the vast sanctuary and discovers a rock with a rough-hewn opening to hold water. The dark room is illuminated solely by a skylight directly above the baptismal rock, literally a hole in the ceiling through which the sun shines on the baptismal area. One of the rough concrete walls is painted with a large mural presenting baptism as a dreamlike sequence. On the left side of the wall, John the Baptist stands knee-deep in a large stream of water with his right hand stretched out, pointing off in the distance to Jesus, who is entering the water. On the right side of the mural, a larger portrait of the risen Christ, still partially submerged in the water, depicts him with wounded hand upraised and blessing all who enter the space. A disciple kneels in adoration at his side, and Christ's hand is placed on the head of the disciple to bestow a blessing. In the middle of the mural, a naked adult in a fetal position with arms crossed in the sign of a cross is pushed completely beneath the water by one who stands in the stream to perform the baptism, while the shimmering gown of the risen Christ floats in waves through the rippling water and extends toward the one being baptized as another form of blessing.

This remarkable portrait places each baptism that takes place here within the movement of the biblical narrative. The architecture itself provides a theological commentary on the act of baptism. Standing near a rock from which the water comes, illumined by the light from above (shining through a hole in the roof), dwarfed by a mural of the Christ's baptism and resurrection, the baptismal candidate is drawn into the Gospel narratives. She becomes a recipient of the water that springs from the rock in the exodus narrative. The heavens are opened above her, and she is declared a beloved child of God. Her body assumes the place in the mural of the one submerged beneath the Jordan River alongside Jesus who comes to be baptized and the risen Christ who rises up out of the water.

While the baptismal spaces in our sanctuaries may not present this portrait in such a dramatic way, one of the central tasks of preaching on this text (and related ones) is to persuade the listeners to view and interpret our own baptisms in light of this narrative. The church presents the act of baptism in ways that are directly related to the Gospel accounts of Jesus' baptism: the call to repentance and the forgiveness of sin, the use of water as an act of renewal and reorientation, the public witness of baptism, the gift of the Spirit, and the declaration that we, too, are beloved sons and daughters of God—these are all derived from this central narrative. The preacher who opens our imaginations to relive this text also opens our imaginations to interpret our own baptismal stories in light of the gospel. As we ponder the rich imagery of this text, we discover layer upon layer of biblical allusions that lie behind the narrative as well as details and symbols that the Gospel writers use throughout their narratives. Prompting the listener to explore further the threads of this text encourages not only the development of biblical literacy, but can also help readers to discern ways that our lives take on the shape and form of Christ.[1]

First Reading
Genesis 1:1-5 (RCL)

The inclusion of this reading from the opening verses of the Torah provides a narrative link to two important themes in celebrating the Baptism of the Lord. First, the use of Genesis 1 alongside the account of Jesus' baptism links this version of the creation story with an understanding of baptism as a new creation. God's movement across the water begins the process of creation. As God speaks, light emerges from the darkness (which provides an echo of themes from the celebration of Epiphany last week). Second, the wind (*ruach*) that sweeps across the face of the waters and breathes life into the universe provides the inspiration for the interpretation of the Spirit's presence in the waters of baptism so that the baptized will receive the gift of new life. Both the text and the baptismal liturgy present this act of creation as the work of God who speaks new life into being. The theme of creation and new creation was further developed by early church fathers who spoke of the Sunday gathering of baptized Christians as the eighth day. This way of counting understood the wholeness of the seven days of creation (from the Genesis narratives) to come to full circle when Christians gather to celebrate Christ's resurrection as a sign of new creation.

Isaiah 55:1-11 (LFM)

This reading from Second Isaiah looks back to the covenant with David as well as looks forward to a new covenant with Israel. The text begins with a series of commands (come and buy, come and eat) and concludes with words of assurance that this word of promise will not return empty (v. 11). In between, poetic words of hope invite the hearers to partake in a feast that God sets before us. The invitation is issued in the voice of Wisdom who points to the gathering as that which will lead to a new way of life.[2] While the prophetic utterance lacks particularity, it soars in rhetorical grandeur. The text shifts the expectation away from the political realm toward the hope that God will form a new Israel. This expectation comes with an invitation to prepare by turning away from evil and turning toward the mercy of God.

When read alongside the Gospel, the text takes on vivid sacramental themes that invite the listeners to the baptismal water and to the communion table as places where we encounter God's grace in the new covenant established in Christ. While these associations provide vivid imagery, preachers should take care to avoid language that negates God's faithful promise to Israel's covenant or that substitutes today's church for Israel. Instead, the text offers a prophetic challenge to our communities of faith to turn from evil and to turn toward God.

Psalmody
Psalm 29 (RCL)

The psalm echoes the images from the Genesis reading with shared allusions to the Spirit hovering over the waters (v. 3). Scholars believe that this psalm relies on primordial Canaanite myths in order to present an alternative theological claim that it is Yahweh who brings creation to life. In this world, the Lord's voice carries the power to animate the waters and to break and shatter the cedars. Robert Alter notes the association of great cedar trees with the pride of loftiness.[3] The psalmist weaves together God's power in creation with God's presence in new creation, where even the destruction of trees and the flood give way to new life.

Central themes in the baptismal rite of most ecclesial bodies are replete in this psalm. When worship includes the sacrament of baptism or a congregational renewal of the baptismal covenant, then the language and images of this text will find additional resonance with the baptismal prayers and rituals. God's word as that which animates and sanctifies the water that the church uses to baptize those who follow in the way of Jesus is central to the integral connection between proclamation and baptism. Similarly, word and water as those which have destructive power as well as carry the promise of new creation are imbedded in the baptismal imagery of the one who through this water dies to the old and is raised to newness of life.

Isaiah 12:2-3, 4bcd, 5-6 (LFM)

This song of deliverance and thanksgiving expresses a confidence that God will bring salvation to the people. In a congregation where I once served, we sang Marty Haugen's setting of this text each time we celebrated the sacrament of baptism. There the text provided the marching music as we gathered around the baptismal water to share the promise of new life that the Spirit was bringing to us. The language of salvation runs prominently through this text as Isaiah portrays the faithfulness of God as the one who will provide salvation. While the use of this text alongside the celebration of baptism relies on literal notions of baptismal water, the text plays poetically and metaphorically with the imagery of water as that which is drawn from the wells of salvation (v. 3). In either case, the outcome leads to praise for God for the wonderful deeds that bring new life to us.

Second Reading
Acts 19:1-7 (RCL)

The text develops a central notion of Christian baptism that associates the reception of the Holy Spirit with baptism in the name of the Lord Jesus (v. 5). At stake is a recognition of different baptismal practices and interpretations of baptism. The absence of the Spirit in the lives of these disciples prompts Paul to question them about the form of baptism. John's baptism as one of repentance is contrasted with baptism in the name of Jesus which leads to the reception of the Holy Spirit. The inclusion of this reading reinforces a central motif of the Spirit's presence over the waters of creation and its descent on Jesus as he is baptized in the water of the Jordan River. Deeper problems reside beneath the surface of this text, however. The preacher is left to wrestle with the problem of why John's baptism was sufficient for Jesus and inadequate for this set of disciples in Ephesus. Recent research on early baptismal practices in the church points to the use of diverse language, images, and practices in different locations.[4] This reading from Acts shows the shifting nature of early Christian practice as it moves toward clarifying core components of the church's theology and liturgy. When the text is read alongside the church's present baptismal liturgy, it reinforces the importance of the church that gathers around the water to call upon the Spirit to bring new life in and through the act of baptism.

1 John 5:1-9 (LFM)

This text takes the baptismal language and framework that is celebrated on this feast day and wraps an important exhortation around it. Central images of water, blood, and Spirit point to the experience of new life by those have been born of God as believers in Jesus Christ. The epistle's author links the gift of new life that comes from God with the promise of victory over the tribulations and suffering of this world. At the same time, though, this exhortation is lived out in the spirit of obedience as we love God and one another (note the way this text develops the commandment to love God and our brothers and sisters in 4:21). Those baptized into this new life take on a shared commitment to this new commandment that Jesus gives his disciples, that is, the law of love (John 15:12: "This is my commandment, that you love one another as I have loved you."). Preachers have the opportunity to interpret this text in ways that fill out the baptismal lives of the congregation with a shared Christian ethic. Here, the text points to a deeper understanding of baptismal life as a lifelong journey of faith by those who respond to the call of Christ.

Focal Points for Preaching

The richness of this set of diverse texts provides the preacher with nearly unlimited options. Not everything can or needs to be dealt with, but it will aid the listeners for the sermon to weave together the texts alongside the liturgical context of the assembly. Central to the celebration of this occasion is the church's memory of Jesus' baptism, the presence of the Spirit who brings new creation and new life to us, and the opportunity to interpret our own lives ritually and symbolically in light of the gospel. Since water is featured prominently throughout these texts, both the liturgy and the sermon should emphasize and embody the church's use of water in our baptismal rites. One final note: as water becomes an increasingly precious and restricted commodity, it will be critical for the church to develop an ecological ethic that addresses the use of water not only inside our sanctuaries, but assumes responsibility for the protection, purity, and availability of water for all people as part of a Christian practice and stewardship in caring for God's gift of creation.

Notes

1. Portions of this section are adapted from *Leading through the Water* by Paul Galbreath, with permission from the Alban Institute. Copyright © 2011 by The Alban Institute, Inc., Herndon, Va. All rights reserved.

2. Claus Westermann, *Isaiah 40–66*, Old Testament Library (Philadelphia: Westminster, 1977), 281. Westermann notes the similarities to other Wisdom texts, particularly Prov. 9:11.

3. Robert Alter, *The Book of Psalms* (New York: Norton, 2007), 99 n.5.

4. See Bryan Spinks, *Early and Medieval Rituals and Theologies of Baptism: From the New Testament to the Council of Trent* (Aldershot, UK: Ashgate, 2006).

January 15, 2012
Second Sunday after Epiphany /
Second Sunday in Ordinary Time

Revised Common Lectionary (RCL)	Lectionary for Mass (LFM)
1 Samuel 3:1-10 (11-20)	1 Samuel 3:3b-10, 19
Psalm 139:1-6, 18-20	Psalm 40:2 + 4, 7-8a, 8b-9, 10
1 Corinthians 6:12-20	1 Corinthians 6:13c-15a, 17-20
John 1:43-51	John 1:35-42

Call and response: discipleship and testimony are primary motifs in the readings for this week. The preacher speaks a word from the gospel and the congregation offers an affirmative response. The ensuing dialogue lifts the rhetoric to new heights and together the community experiences the Spirit infusing their lives with a desire to follow Christ. This simple pattern is filled out in our readings this week, which describe ways of hearing and responding to God's call as well as the ethical demands of living in light of it. As we journey in light of the Epiphany, these themes help fill out our role as followers of Jesus Christ.

Gospel
John 1:35-42 (LFM)

There is power in repetition. The Gospel reading employs this technique by building on John the Baptist's initial testimony regarding Jesus as the "Lamb of God who takes away the sin of the world" (v. 29). John immediately recognizes Jesus the "Son of God" (v. 34).[1] Today's reading begins with John's repeated announcement that Jesus is the Lamb of God. For the Gospel writer, this language carries layers of nuances with it. On the one hand, the descriptive language builds on the imagery of the suffering servant in Second Isaiah. Here the text refers back to the prophetic description of a servant who will come to bear the sins of many.[2] The text also looks ahead to John's use of the Lamb of God as paschal imagery. John's Gospel carefully constructs the Passion-week narrative so that Jesus' crucifixion coincides with the preparation of the Passover lamb (see John 19:14ff.). Thus, John's description of Jesus as the

Lamb of God at the beginning of today's reading carries weighty significance. The announcement prompts the disciples to turn and follow Jesus.

The disciples' initial encounter with Jesus results in an invitation to spend the day with him. For Andrew, this initial visit was so compelling that he immediately went searching for his brother Simon. Andrew's testimony proved vital—"We have found the Messiah!" (v. 41)—and he brought his brother to meet Jesus. Jesus announces that Simon now has a new name (or nickname) as Peter (the Rock). The significance of individuals receiving new names is of long-standing importance in the Hebrew Scriptures (e.g., Abram as Abraham[3]). The practice remains important in some cultural settings today where one receives a Christian name at the time of baptism as a way of marking the event as an occasion of new birth.

Preachers will want to develop the way that this text underscores the importance of naming as well as its description of the crucial role that testimony plays in the furthering of the gospel. Both the naming of Jesus as the Lamb of God and the naming of Simon as Peter are important. Here, the preacher can point to the way that our own nicknames often provide insight into central characteristics of our lives. While the designation of Simon as the Rock lacks the explanation in the Matthean version (see Matt. 16:16-18 where Jesus names Peter as the Rock upon which the church will be built), it became historically significant in the interpretation of Peter's role as a prime leader in the growth of the early church. These developments, though, are dependent upon the evangelical witness of one brother to another. John's testimony prompts Andrew's curiosity and Andrew's conviction leads Simon to meet Jesus. This chain of witnesses to Jesus as the Christ models a basic pattern of Christian testimony. In his description of preaching, Tom Long underscores the way that the preacher comes from the midst of the congregation to offer his/her own witness to the transformative nature of the gospel. From this perspective, the sermon comes not from above and not as a word of expertise, but as a testimony of a fellow traveler on the road of discipleship.[4] The words of the preacher seek to prompt the listeners to share their experience of the good news of the gospel with their neighbors. The preacher, then, understands his or her own testimony about the claims and truth of the text as a way of modeling God's call on his or her own life. In this respect, the sermon seeks to inspire this form of truth telling by members of the congregation. The preacher's word of witness serves to prompt others in the community to identify ways that God's call comes to them. From this perspective, preaching offers a personal voice and a first word, rather than a last word. Sermons seek to open up the text in order that we can identify ourselves in the responses of Andrew and Simon Peter.

John 1:43-51 (RCL)

As in the previous pericope (see above), the testimony of one person to another leads to an encounter with Jesus. Philip searches out Nathanael and declares that Jesus is the one who fulfills the Mosaic law and the prophets. The imagery here carries messianic significance as Jesus is presented as the one who carries the heroic roles of Moses and Elijah. These two legendary figures in Jewish faith serve as representative of the significance of both the Law and the Prophets. The narratives of Jesus' transfiguration on the mountain include the appearance of Moses and Elijah alongside Jesus. Here, in the beginning of his Gospel, John describes Jesus as one whom is held in as same high regard as these heroic leaders.

Today's listeners of the text will need help to decipher the obscure references that are imbedded in the verbal exchange between Jesus and Nathanael. First, there is Jesus' curious observation as he looks upon Nathanael that "here is truly an Israelite in whom there is no deceit" (v. 47).[5] While biblical scholars have offered a wide variety of interpretive options, one possibility is that Nathanael's title (as a genuine Israelite without guile) is intended as a reference to Jacob. The book of Genesis tells the story of the renaming of Jacob as Israel and of his interactions with Laban and Esau where he is presented as a deceitful man (cf. Gen. 27:35).[6] Odder still is the series of exchanges between Jesus and Nathanael that center around Nathanael's presence under a fig tree. Scholars have offered a variety of creative interpretations on the subject. According to Raymond Brown, Jewish tradition held that "some rabbis taught or studied under a fig tree," while other rabbis "compared the Law to the fig tree."[7] While these interpretive details are speculative, the description of Nathanael suggests that he serves as a representative of Israel who is persuaded by his encounter with Jesus to follow him.

Our passage concludes with continued attention to the revelatory nature of names, as Nathanael's confession of faith in Jesus adds to the list: Son of God and King of Israel. These messianic titles draw on the tradition of King David as the great leader of Israel and point to the hope that Jesus is the one who is bringing God's reign to Israel. Here, an encounter with Jesus leads to a growing identification of Jesus as the Christ. Preachers will want to identify ways in which our encounters with the gospel prompt us to recognize God's redemptive work in our lives and in the world.

First Reading
1 Samuel 3:3b-10, 19 (LFM)
1 Samuel 3:1-10 (11-20) (RCL)

In a time when God's word was rare and God's vision infrequent, Samuel struggles to identify the voice that calls to him in the night. The narrative describes a dormant stage in the life of the religious institution. In spite of Eli and Samuel's presence in the Temple, their tending to the lamp, their passing on the tradition of the elders, it is a time of religious decline. Even in a text that offers a word of new hope about the call and rise of a new leader, this good news is wrapped around the demise of the old. There is no straight line in worship renewal between Eli and Samuel. While Eli has prepared, nurtured, and mentored Samuel for his new role, God's call to Samuel includes a denunciation of Eli and his family.

While this story is often sentimentalized around the aspects of Samuel's call from God in the night, it is a sobering tale of the way that the birth of the new is wrapped around the death of the old. Preachers will wrestle with ways to speak both of these words faithfully in contexts where the structures of the institutional church remain on life support in the hope that new leaders will resuscitate them and return the church to its prominent place in culture and society. Note that the text does not present an outright rejection of the institutional structure. Instead, in the midst of the setting, Samuel receives a call that God is not absent, but about to bring about transformative change in the Temple and in Israel. It is left to Eli (who in the narrative structure is about to exit stage left) to provide a last word of encouragement and direction to Samuel in order for God's call to be rightly discerned. Samuel's willingness to hear and respond to this call ("Speak, for thy servant hears" [RSV]) and his deliverance of this difficult word to his teacher models a faithful response. Even in his decline, Eli mirrors faithfulness in the way that he receives a word of condemnation in a spirit of reliance upon God ("It is the Lord; let him do what seems good to him"). Samuel's response to God's call is portrayed as steps on his faith journey as he grows and responds to God's word. His faithfulness is recognized by those around him who see in him the signs and qualities of one of God's prophets.

Interpreting this text in light of the Gospel reading(s) of Jesus' call of the disciples can lead to a preoccupation with different approaches to call (from overly spiritualized, private experiences to ecclesiastically driven, bureaucratic ones). One of the advantages of reading multiple call stories is for the preacher to note the different ways that these calls are heard and interpreted. It is equally important to allow the texts to highlight an ongoing tension between the old and the new in each of these call stories. Samuel's training at the hands of Eli prepares him for a new leadership role. Similarly, the Gospel accounts point to the decisive role of John the Baptist and his followers (as participants in a first-century Jewish reform movement) in the early days of Jesus' public ministry. Whether your congregation reads of Andrew bringing Simon Peter or of Philip bringing Nathanael to see Jesus, the dynamic remains the same. The call to discipleship requires both a preparation for leadership as well as a willingness to respond to the new work that God is doing in the world.

Psalmody
Psalm 40:2 + 4, 7-8a, 8b-9, 10 (LFM)

The psalm expresses praise and thanksgiving as the psalmist reflects on God's deliverance in the time of suffering. God is the one who lifts us out of the pit and places us on solid ground. In light of this, the psalmist responds with a willingness to answer God's initiative. "Here I am . . . I delight to do your will" (vv. 7, 8). Alongside the readings of the day, the psalmist models a faithful response to God's merciful action. Preachers can help the listeners reflect on times in the community's life and in their own lives where God's deliverance provides assurance in the midst of turmoil and difficulty. Responding to God's call to new forms of service may grow out of the reliance on God's word to take root in our lives. Here, the example of Samuel's growth and maturity in the word of God pairs up nicely with the psalmist's reflection on divine deliverance that leads to an increasing desire to grow into God's word.

Psalm 139:1-6, 18-20 (RCL)

The inclusion of this psalm links the call to discipleship with the process of examination and discernment. The psalmist invites Yahweh to examine his life in the hope that God will provide deliverance from the charges brought against him. Mitchell Dahood describes this as "a psalm of innocence by a religious leader who was accused of idol worship."[8] On the one hand, the psalmist places his trust in God who already sees and knows all. This utter dependence on God to bring relief from judgment provides an example of faithful reliance on God in times of trial. On the other hand, the text carries the tone of one who is so convinced of his piety that he takes the occasion to plead his case before God. Preachers need to deal carefully with this text in order for the listeners to identify appropriate ways to respond. While it certainly seems appropriate to encourage faithful members to call upon God in times of adversity, the danger remains for the psalm to be co-opted as a defense mechanism by those who are unwilling to respond to God's call to move in a new direction. In this case, our infatuation and addiction to the old ways (that may provide us comfort) prompt our sense of self-righteousness. When these lectionary texts are held in tension together, they make clear that God's call is often a disruptive one that brings change as well as assurance.

Second Reading
1 Corinthians 6:12-20 (RCL)
1 Corinthians 6:13c-15a, 17-20 (LFM)

Given the intensely personal nature of the call narratives in today's readings, the epistle lesson provides an important corrective to the dangers of privatized and individualistic notions of Christian call. The apostle Paul writes to the church in Corinth to deal with conflict that has emerged around sexual practices in the community. Some Christians in Corinth interpreted their freedom from the demands of the law to allow them to adopt an ethic of cultural norms from those who advocated for absolute freedom. Richard Hays summarizes such an approach drawn from the Stoics in this way: "The enlightened wise person is free to do anything he or she chooses."[9] For these new Gentile Christians, the removal of the demands of the Jewish law reinforces the temptation to define their freedom as a right to do whatever they want to do. Note, however, that in the logic of such an interpretation individuals have self-determined that they are the wise ones.

Paul offers a rhetorical argument to counter such interpretations. While the radical freedom extended in God's grace in Jesus Christ does provide a logical starting point that can lead to libertine arguments, Paul rebuts such an approach for its failure to recognize the interdependence of the community as the body of Christ. As members of the body of Christ, Christians are invited to ethics of mutual respect where our actions encourage respect for God's good gift of creation. Paul recognizes the significance of our bodies as temples of the Holy Spirit (v. 19). Our actions then require both the consideration of our bodies as God's home as well as the broader notions of the community of faith as a center of mutual respect and encouragement for practices that encourage and build up the community as signs of God's grace in the world. Dietrich Bonhoeffer once observed that the church exists as a place for the body of Christ to be present in the world. Our response to God's call to discipleship then leads us to careful discernment about the ways that our actions make room for Christ's presence in our lives and in our world.

Since sexual ethics remains a hot-button issue in most congregations, this text will likely be heard as reinforcing the presuppositions the listener already holds. When the text is read alongside our other readings of the day, however, it becomes less of a lesson about sexual ethics in ancient Corinth and more of a lesson about the importance of critical attention to community discernment and practice in light of Christ's call to follow him. Preachers can help listeners grapple with this tension by pointing to the ways that the dynamics of the debate in Corinth model a movement beyond personal preferences and privatized spirituality. Instead, Paul invites us to bring our experience of God's call into the messy light of the day where, through the difficult practices of compassionate listening and mutual affirmation, we gain a clearer perspective of how to live out this call together.

Focal Points for Preaching

The rich array of the texts for this day display a variety of expressions of God's call and ways that biblical characters respond to this call. The texts also point to ways that God's call surprises us and disrupts our expectations about where God may be leading us. In the process, we are encouraged to look for the Spirit's work in each other's lives as we testify to God's faithfulness and as we strive to discover ways to live out God's call faithfully.

Notes

1. Raymond Brown, *The Gospel According to John (I–XII)*, Anchor Bible 29 (Garden City, N.Y.: Doubleday, 1966), 55.
2. Ibid., 60. Brown even notes the Aramaic correlation between "lamb" and "servant."
3. Check out Gen. 17:5 and 32:8 according to ibid., 80.
4. Thomas G. Long, *The Witness of Preaching*, 2d ed. (Louisville: Westminster John Knox, 2005), 15.
5. Brown, *The Gospel According to John (I–XII)*, 81.
6. M. de Goedt, quoted in ibid., 87.
7. Ibid., 83.
8. Mitchell Dahood, *Psalms II, 51–100*, Anchor Bible (Garden City, N.Y.: Doubleday, 1968), 284.
9. Richard B. Hays, *First Corinthians*, Interpretation: A Bible Commentary for Teaching and Preaching (Louisville: John Knox, 1997), 101.

January 22, 2012
Third Sunday after Epiphany /
Third Sunday in Ordinary Time

Revised Common Lectionary (RCL)
Jonah 3:1-5, 10
Psalm 62:5-12
1 Corinthians 7:29-31
Mark 1:14-20

Lectionary for Mass (LFM)
Jonah 3:1-5, 10
Psalm 25:4-5, 6-7, 8-9
1 Corinthians 7:29-31
Mark 1:14-20

Calling, calling, calling. The readings about the call to follow God carry a sense of urgency. As we track this theme through these weeks after Epiphany, it is helpful to listen for the steady, repetitive way in which this sound can be heard drumming through the Scripture and through our own lives. This rhythmic beat of God's relentless pursuit of us breaks apart the notions of a vengeful God looking to punish us for our sins. Instead, even in our disobedience, God's mercy and invitation reaches out to offer us new life. As we respond, we join in the divine initiative to expand the good news of God's grace that brings healing and redemption to our world.

Gospel
Mark 1:14-20 (RCL, LFM)

Are you ready for a major announcement? In the rapid-fire way that is typical of Mark's Gospel, our reading today begins with two major news stories. First, we learn of the arrest of John the Baptist. In modern terms, the news appears almost like a crawl line at the bottom of the television screen regarding a breaking news item. Details will be provided later, but not until chapter 6. Mark uses this style like a theater director to move John off stage and turn the audience's attention to Jesus. No sooner have we learned of John's arrest than we learn that Jesus appears in Galilee to preach the gospel, the good news that God's reign is here. Jesus assumes the prophetic mantle of John the Baptist. Note the transition from John's message of preparation to Jesus' declaration that the time is here. Both messages contain the call to repentance as an act of preparation for participating in God's reign. Mark's

Gospel begins with a rapid staccato pace to Jesus' public ministry: baptism as birth announcement, the temptation in the wilderness (which Mark outlines in two verses), and this brief summary statement that the time has come. This is kairos time, a time of anticipation, promise, and fulfillment. Kairos time is an "appointed time" that grows out of the eschatological vision of judgment and new beginning.[1] Kairos time is a way of speaking about a new beginning that comes only with the end of the old ways. Preachers face the temptation of extending the hope and promise of a new way without alluding to the pain and cost of leaving the old behind. Here, the lectionary helps us identify the shape of the gospel story as it comes to birth and is immediately threatened by King Herod (see the texts for Epiphany Sunday, above) and ultimately is hung to die on a hill outside of Jerusalem. The Christ story is the good news of God's salvation from the birth of Jesus to his resurrection. It is a story that offers new life to the listeners, but also challenges us to place our trust in the one who brings this new way of life.

Once again, the geography of the Gospels provides an important contrast. Jesus' public announcement occurs in Galilee. Away from the cosmopolitan centers of power in Jerusalem, Jesus opens his campaign near his hometown of Nazareth. Galilee is a northern territory filled with Gentiles and populated by poor people. It is separated from Jerusalem by Samaria.[2] Thus, the first public announcement comes far away from the religious and political centers of power.

What does this time of fulfillment look like in Mark's Gospel? It appears in a rather mundane way. Jesus wanders by the seashore and invites a few fishermen to follow him. The rhetoric here shows a shift from catching fish to going after people in order to build a movement that can challenge the current power structures. Who is there to hear and respond to this declaration? Mark describes the onset of Jesus' ministry as a process of searching for followers. The call to the first four disciples is outlined in our reading today. Jesus actively seeks out and invites people to follow him. The invitation to Simon, Andrew, James, and John is extended along the shore of the Sea of Galilee. These fishermen leave their work and family behind to join Jesus in a new work that is beginning in the most unlikely of places.

Preachers face the challenge of addressing the fishing metaphor ("Follow me and I will make you fish for people") both to those who have grown accustomed to hearing this language and to those who may hear it for the first time. The imagery likely references Jeremiah 16 where the prophet speaks of a coming day in which God will bring Israel back together. Yahweh concludes, "I am now sending for many fishermen . . . and they shall catch them" (Jer. 16:16). Jesus' invitation to discipleship enacts Yahweh's invitation to participate in Israel's deliverance. The imagery, however, involves difficult and sometimes painful work. In spite of Sunday school songs and sentimental portraits to which we have become accustomed, the disciples are offered a challenging job to engage actively in the movement to share the news that God's reign is at hand. This message of change will challenge the status quo and lead to conflict.

Even the notion of pursuing and catching people as fishers suggests the work will be long, messy, and painful for all those who are involved in it. Mark underscores the cost of such an enterprise by describing how these first disciples left everything, their nets, their boats, and their families in order to follow Jesus on an unknown journey into the future.

In light of the call stories of the early disciples from this text as well as last Sunday's reading from John, preachers may want to invite members of the congregation to reflect on the diverse ways that we experience God's call to Christian discipleship in our lives. Here, the preacher may use his/her own call narrative as illustrative. Care should be taken, however, to underscore the central notion of call as that of immersion into the life of discipleship, a call that is extended to all people. Note as well that the biblical notions of this call show a ripple effect. The calls to which we respond prompt us to act in ways that foster a sense of call in those around us. It may be helpful to trace what we as individuals and as a community need to leave behind in order to follow Jesus' invitation. The call to discipleship carries a cost of letting go of treasured things, leaving behind our notions of self-reliance, and accepting a willingness to move forward together into the unknown. Many congregations struggle with the desire to return to the good old days when the church played a prominent role in the culture. This nostalgia for the way things used to be prompts some to resist change. At the same time, the nostalgia taps into a yearning to experience life that may be attached to earlier notions of call. Honoring the past and the ways that God's call is understood in our lives may be a helpful way of identifying how to listen for a new call that will lead us forward into the future.

The mystic Meister Eckhart spoke of the metaphor of God as fisherman in pursuit of us: "God lies in wait for us with nothing so much as love, and love is like a fisherman's hook: without it he could never catch a fish, but once the hook is taken the fisherman is sure of the fish. Even though the fish twists higher and yon, the fisherman is sure of him." In spite of our struggle to yield to God's call, Jesus' invitation to follow him echoes in our hearts and souls. We find ourselves slowly yielding to the possibility of grace and forgiveness as well as to the lure to discover a new direction for our lives. Eckhart concludes: "When one has found this way, he looks for no other. To hang on this hook is to be so completely captured that feet and hands, and mouth and eyes, the heart, and all a man is and has, become God's own. . . . Whatever he does, who is caught by this hook, love does it, and love alone . . ."[3]

First Reading
Jonah 3:1-5, 10 (RCL, LFM)

As the sole lectionary reading from the book of Jonah (apart from an inclusion in the Lutheran readings for the Easter Vigil), today's selection requires the preacher to provide a larger context for the brief selection of verses. While many listeners are likely to remember the outline of the Jonah narrative from their time in Sunday school (or even its appearance in film and literature), the scandalous nature of the claims of this book escape the imagination of most hearers of today's highly edited reading. As a prophetic text, Jonah presents the portrait of discipleship in terms of faithful and unfaithful responses to God's call. Jonah runs from God's call to go to Nineveh. The significance of Nineveh as location for the proclamation of God's message should not be overlooked. Nineveh is the capital of the Assyrian empire, a site that the prophet Jonah sees as unlikely for the declaration of God's word. Jonah would rather flee in the opposite direction than preach God's word to this Gentile community.

Today's reading represents a second chance for Jonah to respond to God's call. After running in the opposite direction and floundering at sea, God calls Jonah again to preach a message of repentance and redemption to the people of Nineveh. Thus, the previous unfaithfulness of Jonah in refusing God's call is set alongside the unfaithfulness of Nineveh. This is a story of second chances and Jonah's gift of a second chance to respond faithfully to God's call leads to the second chance of the Ninevites to hear and respond to the call to repent, turn around, and respond to God's word. Christian readers of this text may glimpse a resurrection story in the call to new life that follows the proclamation of God's word as Jonah walks around the city preaching for three days. As the hearers of this text turn from their wickedness, God embraces and welcomes this group of foreigners into God's redemptive plan. As a text of radical inclusion, preachers may want to press the question of where God is calling us to go and preach God's word. By analogy, the story of Jonah leads us far beyond the safe confines of our sanctuaries into neighborhoods we usually ignore. The call to faithful discipleship takes us out of our comfort zones in order to experience the redemptive work of God in places and with people who we normally would not expect to be included in God's salvation. Discipleship breaks open the safe categories and expectations that we create and which constrict the gospel. The surprise that God's love and grace includes us is extended in the ways that God's call presses us in new directions to experience God's passionate love for all of creation.

Psalmody
Psalm 62:5-12 (RCL)

In the midst of uncertainty and travail, the psalmist declares his hope in God. The psalm mirrors the movement of the gospel as the psalmist moves from a sense of call that God is the source of help and protection to a declaration to those around him that everyone should place their trust in God (v. 8). The psalm takes the form of a dialogue by showing the movement within the psalmist from despair to certainty followed by a ripple movement from the psalmist to the congregation around him. It takes the shape of testimony as the psalmist recalls his own sense of despair before recalling the mercy of God that moves him from desolation to trust that God will deliver him. In his witness to the congregation, the psalmist reminds his listeners that power and money will not bring them the comfort that they desire. Only God provides the grace that is extended to everyone and will deliver us from our predicaments. The linkage of power and grace is a particularly significant way of identifying Yahweh as one who is trustworthy and will provide for us even as this grace leads us to a new way of life. Faith and righteousness walk hand in hand as the psalmist declares his trust in God.

Psalm 25:4-5, 6-7, 8-9 (LFM)

This psalm is a journey psalm. It describes the life of faith in terms of a travel narrative as one grows and matures in faith. From the time of youthful indiscretion, it moves toward occasions of learning and instruction in the path of faith. Read alongside the Gospel reading, the psalm is suggestive of the invitation to discipleship as a first step in a lifelong journey. As the psalmist reflects on his life, he asks God's forgiveness for youthful transgressions before noting ways in which his faith has deepened over the years of his life. Preachers may see here an opportunity for the testimonies of discipleship to portray faith as a crooked journey full of bumps and detours along the way. At the same time, as we look back on our lives, the psalmist encourages us to recognize God's providence on our journeys and the occasions in which we experience God's lovingkindness and faithfulness (v. 10).

Second Reading
1 Corinthians 7:29-31 (RCL, LFM)

This brief reading is likely to raise more questions than it resolves. At the center of this unusual relationship advice is an emphatic message of the importance of responding to God's call given the shortness of time. While this emphasis on the eschatological demands of the gospel as a time of decision is a powerful and important one, the unusual tone of this reading with its denial of family life will be bewildering to most contemporary readers. Preachers will need to provide a theological context in order to help the listeners interpret this text and its claim on our lives. Throughout the history of the church, interpreters have provided different options. Some scholars emphasize Paul's mistaken notions about Jesus' imminent return as that which prompted this commentary on ignoring one's wife or forgoing times of mourning, rejoicing, or investing. While such an approach may provide an explanation for Paul's argument, it still does little to connect the text to contemporary concerns. It may help to see this snippet in its broader context as Paul addresses a series of ethical questions and concerns of the church in Corinth. At stake in these concerns is the unity of the Christian community and its witness to Jesus Christ. Thus, Paul continually places the highest priority on the gospel's claim on our lives. Rather than an outright rejection of marriage, grieving, and property, Paul rhetorically underscores the temporal nature of these parts of our lives in favor of the eternal claims of the gospel. In this in-between time, as we deal with the daily joys and sorrows of our lives, the text encourages us to adopt a broader perspective as we wait for God's reign to bring a new heaven and new earth. When read alongside our other lectionary texts, the epistle presents a dramatic word about the importance of responding to God's call in spite of the other demands and distractions around us. While there may indeed be other chances (as the tale of Jonah suggests), we should not overlook the significance of this moment and this invitation that comes as a gift of God.

Focal Points for Preaching

How will we respond in these days after the manifestation (epiphany) of God's grace? Today's readings offer a variety of images of the ways that we may answer God's call. Like the first disciples in the Gospels, we may immediately leave everything behind in order to follow Jesus (although even here the Gospels show the disciples' ongoing struggle to understand and live out this call). Others may see our lives in the drama of Jonah as ones who run away from God's call only to find ourselves lost and moving in the wrong direction. The opportunity of a second chance to respond may push us into places where we never saw ourselves. Still others experience the pull of God's call over against the demands of family life and economic realities. In all these experiences, Scripture affirms that God's call is a relentless pursuit of humanity in order for us to experience the forgiveness, hope, love, and grace that God offers to all people.

Notes

1. C. S. Mann, *Mark*, Anchor Bible 27 (Garden City, N.Y.: Doubleday, 1986), 205. Mann notes Old Testament references that fill out this understanding in Ezek. 7:12; Dan. 12:4, 9; and Zeph. 1:12.
2. Ched Myers, *Binding the Strong Man: A Political Reading of Mark's Story of Jesus* (Maryknoll, N.Y.: Orbis, 1990), 128.
3. Meister Eckhart, in David James Duncan, *The River Why* (San Francisco: Sierra Club, 1983), 279.

January 29, 2012
Fourth Sunday after Epiphany /
Fourth Sunday in Ordinary Time

Revised Common Lectionary (RCL)	**Lectionary for Mass (LFM)**
Deuteronomy 18:15-20	Deuteronomy 18:15-20
Psalm 111	Psalm 95:1-2, 6-7a, 7b-9
1 Corinthians 8:1-13	1 Corinthians 7:32-35
Mark 1:21-28	Mark 1:21-28

At first glance, preachers may be put off by this rather disparate set of texts. From Jesus' initial appearance in the synagogue commencing his public ministry to Moses' recognition of the role of prophets to Paul's discussion of ethical conflicts in the church in Corinth, the texts wander through issues that draw from the particular contexts of followers of God in times gone by. This is not simply a series of history lessons of how people of faith have survived in difficult times. The liturgical calendar provides a context as we seek to discover ways in this in-between time that God's word can take root and become incarnate in our communities and our lives. At stake in this process is the need for us to make room for the prophetic word of God as it comes to us and challenges our habits, customs, and practices.

Gospel
Mark 1:21-28 (RCL, LFM)

After the calling and gathering of disciples along the Sea of Galilee, the scene shifts quickly to Capernaum, a nearby urban center on the north shore of the sea. On the Sabbath, Jesus enters the synagogue where he proceeds to teach. The congregation is amazed by his teaching. Mark notes the development of an immediate tension. Jesus teaches as one with authority and not as one of the scribes (v. 22). Here, Jesus is portrayed as a prophetic figure over against the regular scribal task of interpreting the law.

Jesus' entrance into the sacred space to proclaim God's reign prompts a confrontation with a man with an unclean spirit. In Mark's Gospel, the demon-possessed, ill, and outsiders are those who recognize Jesus as God's messenger. In this episode, Jesus' teaching prompts the man with the unclean spirit to speak truth aloud: Jesus is the Holy One of God (v. 24). The exorcism in the synagogue on the Sabbath foreshadows a controversy over the proper religious actions by faithful Jews on the day of rest. Jesus will be accused of breaking the law by engaging in a series of Sabbath exorcisms and healing. Furthermore, his contact with the demon-possessed and sick continually violates the purity codes that separate the holy and righteous from the unclean.

Contemporary readers of this text are often puzzled by the strange images of demonic possession and exorcisms. Interpreters often attempt to provide rational explanations in terms of first-century healing and medicinal practices or offer metaphorical and symbolical literary images. Rather than attempt to explain this text to listeners, it is more helpful to examine what is at stake in this text for Mark (and for us). From the very beginning of Jesus' public ministry, Mark wants his audience to recognize that this will be a cosmic struggle. Jesus' declaration that God's reign is near is immediately met by resistance. While the congregation in Capernaum may show signs of curiosity, the message is heard and recognized by the man with the unclean spirit as one that challenges the status quo: "What have you to do with us, Jesus of Nazareth?" (v. 24). Biblical scholars differ on their interpretations of the use of the plural "us" by the man who cries out. Some regard it as a reference to the congregation, with the man speaking in solidarity with the congregation. C. S. Mann suggests that its usage parallels typical expressions in encounters between Old Testament prophets and their audience.[1] In contrast, Ched Myers argues that in the sacred space of the synagogue, the demon expresses the point of view of the scribal establishment.[2] However one may decipher the details of this passage, it is clear that for Mark this initial exchange represents the struggle between Jesus' ministry of healing and reconciliation and the established practices of religious communities and authorities.

The cry of the man with the unclean spirit is a recognition that Jesus as God's Holy One is a threat to the ways things have always been done. "Have you come to destroy us?" the demon-possessed man calls out (v. 24). The exorcism is an act of destruction, a spiritual housecleaning in the most unlikely of places. The synagogue, as symbolic sacred center of the community, will not be the same. Jesus brings not only a new teaching, but a new way of acting that commands authority.

Several aspects of this narrative may help the preacher illumine the text for an audience of modern and postmodern listeners. First, it is helpful to note the role of religious assembly as a place of both authority and conflict. While churches may no longer stand at the center of culture, they remain significant places of exchange where the possibility remains for truth telling and discovery. Second, the inclusion of the man with an unclean spirit in the synagogue setting suggests the importance of the church's ministry to the unclean, outsiders, and the estranged. Third, there will be conflict when the gospel is proclaimed. The good news that Jesus declares includes a call to repentance (v. 15) and an invitation to follow him into an unknown future. The requirements of discipleship are changing our ways and learning to depend on God. Both of these challenge the myths of self-reliance and success that are popular in Western culture. Thus, the call to follow Jesus will inevitably lead to conflict in congregations whose primary concern is maintaining the status quo.

Finally, the church is invited into this narrative in order that we may engage in the cosmic struggle that lies at the center of the gospel. Following Jesus is about challenging power structures that exclude and marginalize people. Taking up this work requires a willingness to speak and act out against the powers and principalities of our day and age. Let me offer one small example: in the wake of the tragedy of 9/11, the congregation where I served decided to open the doors of our building and welcome people into the sanctuary where they could gather to pray, grieve, and meditate. Each morning, we unlocked the doors so that neighbors and strangers could come in. Voices of opposition were quickly raised: a homeless person might steal something or it was unsafe for the day care center that was housed in our building. The simple act of opening the doors of the church was perceived as a threat to maintaining our property and protecting our belongings. Change and openness challenged the security and sanctity of our property. In the end, the church doors were locked again. As a congregation, we could not find a way to extend the hospitality to the stranger and outcast who would likely disrupt our patterns and expectations. This is but one small example of the daily battles that pastors and congregations face as they seek to move the church from the way things have always been done to an understanding of church as a center that welcomes people to explore ways to hear and respond to the gospel.

While many leaders avoid conflict, it is helpful to note that Mark outlines the conflict in this setting in order to show how the conflict in the synagogue advances the spread of the gospel. This first public episode in Capernaum prompts the participants to recognize Jesus as one who brings a new teaching—with authority (v. 27). It is an authority that is demonstrated by Jesus' act of exorcism. The power of evil is on the run when it faces up to Jesus! This is the good news in word and action. It is a word and work that amazes, excites, and astounds all who are present to witness it. This event is so powerful that the participants quickly spread the word about Jesus throughout Galilee. How can our events that proclaim and enact the gospel spread the good news of the gospel in our neighborhoods? Likewise, how can the conflict in our congregations prompt reflection and action that make room for the gospel to take root in our communities?

First Reading
Deuteronomy 18:15-20 (RCL, LFM)

In contrast to the magicians and soothsayers of neighboring countries, God promises to provide Israel with prophets who will deliver God's word to them when people have gone astray. These prophets will come "from among your own people" as the successors to Moses. Jeffrey Tigay notes the importance of this text in the way that it allows Moses to introduce the coming role of prophets in Israel in contrast to the development of prophecy as a parallel to prophetic figures in neighboring religions.[3] With the future rise of monarchs to rule over Israel, the prophet's role was to oversee the fulfillment of the covenant responsibilities. The seriousness of the prophet's utterance is underscored in the text by the call for obedience to the prophet who announces God's message. It is also highlighted by the threat to the prophet who speaks a word outside of God's name.

In light of the gospel reading, the text is open to different interpretations. Clearly, the lectionary sees these words of Deuteronomy as a distant reference to Jesus' proclamation of the gospel. In this case, Jesus embodies the prophetic role as he teaches in the synagogue in Capernaum. As one who calls the Jewish people to repentance and to a renewal of the covenant relationship with Yahweh, Jesus takes on the mantle of Moses and the prophets (this imagery is consistently reinforced throughout the Gospels; for instance, note the baptismal description as well as the transfiguration narrative).

In another sense, the text comes as a word of warning to all of us who rise to preach. As a prophetic act, preaching announces God's word. While this proclamation comes in our own vernacular, it carries with it the dangerous power and responsibility of faithful articulation of God's message of repentance and grace. To distort this message is to risk placing ourselves among the unfaithful prophets who risk God's judgment. Preachers have the awesome task of challenging tightly held cultural assumptions in order to make room for God's word to be heard in new ways. In doing this, the preacher does not stand over and against the community (as one in a special place), but rises up from the midst of the community as one who is equally dependent on God's grace.

Psalmody
Psalm 111 (RCL)

This psalm of praise (and Psalm 112) takes the form of an acrostic. It recounts the work of Yahweh as each line begins with a different letter of the Hebrew alphabet. The creation of this form of poetry may have been as a mnemonic device or as a form of completeness in its testimony to God's faithfulness. Its inclusion in the lectionary suggests ways that our verses give witness to God's presence in our world. Here the words of the prophet that testify to God's faithfulness give rise to the memory of God's steadfast mercy that sustains us. Preachers may want to use the psalm text to press the question of how our lives illumine God's grace and love. Texts of remembering like this psalm, as well as works whose beauty prompt us to read the text in a new way (e.g., the Book of Kells or, more recently, the St. John's Bible), provide ways of illustrating how texts move and shape us into becoming instruments of praise. Ultimately, the goal is that our own lives become texts of praise.

Psalm 95:1-2, 6-7a, 7b-9 (LFM)

The call to worship God is connected with the experience of God's redemptive work in our lives. It is also linked to the responsibility to heed the prophetic word of God that addresses us. Here the psalmist draws on the wayward example of the children of Israel in Meribah and Massah who murmured against God during their time of wandering in the wilderness (Exodus 17). Preachers can use the psalm to present a contrast of responses as we remember God's acts. Do we find ourselves filled with gratitude for the grace that we receive or do we identify with those who murmur and complain that God has abandoned us? For congregations in transition, this text carries a powerful imagery about our reliance on God in spite of uncertainty and difficult circumstances. The act of remembering God's faithfulness and expressing thanksgiving prompts us to develop a spirit of gratitude.

Second Reading
1 Corinthians 8:1-13 (RCL)

After offering advice regarding sexual ethics, Paul turns his attention to questions about the appropriateness of eating food that had been offered to idols. Nearly all meat available for purchase was part of the sacrificial system in the numerous temples throughout Corinth. Christians were divided in their practices. Some argued that since the idols had no power, there was no harm in eating food that had been in the temples. Others believed that the food had been contaminated by being a part of the temple system and should be avoided in order for Christians to maintain a witness in contrast to the alternative religious systems. The dilemma over whether to eat temple food was further complicated by the Jewish prohibition of participation on grounds of its association with idols as well as uncertainty as to its kosher status.[4] Jewish Christians would likely continue to avoid contact with the food markets associated with many religious temples. In contrast, Gentile Christians might continue patterns of eating this food and saw little harm in it. Paul's solution to the conflict is to hold the community to a higher ethical standard in order that community solidarity and concern for one's brother and sister override individual preferences. While Paul argues that the meat is not contaminated by idols (since only God has true power), the ethic of love and care for one's neighbor takes precedence. Richard Hays concludes, "Rather than asserting rights and privileges, we are to shape our actions toward edification of our brothers and sisters in the community of faith. In so doing, we will be following the example of Christ . . ."[5]

Alongside the other lectionary readings, this passage invites communities to examine our daily actions in order that they may correspond to the proclamation of God's reign. The goal is not to create a kind of legal conformity to moral codes, but to build up a community that lives out the gospel in love and concern for those around us.

I Corinthians 7:32-35 (LFM)

The lesson continues Paul's ethical commentary to the church in Corinth. Paul seeks to remove any distractions that cause members of the congregation to turn their focus from following Christ. Paul addresses the challenges of engaged couples in the life of the community. In this time of transition, should they go ahead and marry or not? Regardless of their decision, Paul counsels them to adopt a certain sense of detachment. Such a perspective is distinguished from the Stoic appeal to apathy based on building up one's own strength. In contrast, Christian relationships seek to maintain primary focus on the dedication to following Christ. Paul does not forbid marriage to these couples in Corinth, but places the attention on maintaining a sense of vigilant expectation of God's appearance in the world.

Preachers are left again to wrestle with interpreting this strange text in a vastly different cultural and theological climate. Here, the notion of vocation as a sense of divine calling to respond to the gospel may provide a helpful framework for speaking of sexuality, marriage, and celibacy. For example, how do our relationships provide witnesses to the gospel to those around us? Is God's redemptive love evident in the relationships that are central in our lives? When heard alongside the readings from Deuteronomy and Mark, this ethical exhortation may provoke us to examine the ways that our own lives can provide a prophetic witness to God's presence in our lives.

Focal Points for Preaching

How will our assemblies make room for the disruptive presence of God's word, which continues to come to challenge the norms and assumptions that we hold? The preacher prods the congregation to remember ways in which God's word has been heard and embodied in earlier times. Perhaps it was the community's witness to civil rights, its inclusion of mentally disabled persons, its feeding program for the homeless, or its stand against an unjust war. Here, the preacher mines the memories of members of the congregation in order to prompt conversation about ways to provide a faithful, prophetic witness that responds to issues in our day and time. Thus, the particularities of the past (both in terms of the text and in terms of the lives of our communities) become examples of the struggle for congregations to make room for the proclamation of the gospel. The willingness to hear God's word in new and fresh ways, even when it challenges our cherished ideas, and to live out our calls in the context of a community of brothers and sisters points to the ongoing challenge of life in the body of Christ.

Notes

1. C. S. Mann, *Mark*, Anchor Bible 27 (Garden City, N.Y.: Doubleday, 1986), 212. Mann cites the exchanges in Judges 11:12 and 1 Kings 17:18 as examples of the questions: "Why do you interfere with us?"
2. Ched Myers, *Binding the Strong Man: A Political Reading of Mark's Story of Jesus* (Maryknoll, N.Y.: Orbis, 1990), 143.

3. Jeffrey H. Tigay, *The JPS Torah Commentary: Deuteronomy* (Philadelphia: Jewish Publication Society, 1996), 176.

4. C. K. Barrett, *The First Epistle to the Corinthians* (New York: Harper & Row, 1968), 188. Barrett also notes that the Jewish requirement of a tithe on the food would not have been met.

5. Richard B. Hays, *First Corinthians*, Interpretation: A Bible Commentary for Teaching and Preaching (Louisville: John Knox, 1997), 145.

February 5, 2012
Fifth Sunday after Epiphany /
Fifth Sunday in Ordinary Time

Revised Common Lectionary (RCL)
Isaiah 40:21-31
Psalm 147:1-11, 20c
1 Corinthians 9:16-23
Mark 1:29-39

Lectionary for Mass (LFM)
Job 7:1-4, 6-7
Psalm 147:1-2, 3-4, 5-6
1 Corinthians 9:16-19, 22-23
Mark 1:29-39

The lectionary readings provide insight into the demands of ministry in our lives, communities, and the world. The Gospel lesson as proclamation and action responds to the needs of the human condition and the plight of the earth. The call to discipleship that is grounded in our baptism is one of service that brings healing and challenges the presence of evil. The demands of such a calling are set alongside the need for prayer and renewal, a vision of ministry as acts of participation in God's redemptive work (rather than enlarged notions of our own self-importance), and a willingness to live in solidarity with those around us. During this extended period of liturgical time as we move between Epiphany and Lent, the texts provide images of the shape, content, and challenge of ministry as followers of Jesus Christ.

Gospel
Mark 1:29-39 (RCL, LFM)

Following the exorcism in the synagogue on the Sabbath, Mark portrays a healing in a home among the opening actions of Jesus' public ministry. Jesus' declaration that God's reign is at hand is accompanied by two dramatic actions. Last week's reading highlighted the public exorcism of the man with the unclean spirit while today's reading underscores a healing in the semipublic space of Simon Peter's home in Capernaum. Jesus leaves the crowds at the synagogue to visit the home of Simon and Andrew. There, he is immediately informed of the illness of Simon's mother-in-law. Mark offers no details of the healing, but simply describes Jesus as taking her by the hand and raising her up. Her fever disappears and she begins to serve them (*diakonia* is the Greek word).

Some scholars see in the reference to the house (*oikos*) a message of healing and hope to the Markan community as they gather in house churches. At the very least, the contrast between synagogue and house as the initial centers of Jesus' ministry indicates that the movement begins from within cultural and societal centers. The synagogue as the local center of Jewish religious life and the household as the economic and social center of family life are transformed by the presence of Jesus who disrupts the order and expectations. It is also significant that the initial recipients of Jesus' healing are a demoniac and a woman, both considered outsiders in the hierarchical order of the day.

The healing of Simon's mother-in-law appears as a minor motif with little fanfare or description. However, it functions as a call story in which the woman who is healed rises up to serve those around her. While some feminists have objected to the way that the text has been used to reinforce a patriarchal placement of women serving in the home, Mark's goal here is to describe how faithful service can take on ordinary means. Within today's culture of success and heroic response, this small episode can provide an example of vocation that is important for congregations to hear. The point here is not to reinforce society's gender roles, but to show that responding to Jesus' healing touch may take many forms (some simple and others grandiose). As a portrait of service, this (nameless) woman is among the first of the disciples. Throughout the Gospel, Mark provides examples of faithful women disciples.[1] Preachers may choose to develop images of discipleship from the lives of members of our congregation that are often unrecognized or modest in scope. Yet, in many ways, the witness of the church remains dependent on these simple acts of faithfulness. For example, Ann Potter was a member of a congregation where I served as pastor. For decades, every Sunday, Ann made hundreds of cups of coffee for the fellowship time following the worship service. While she may not have spoken of it as a form of ministry, it was an act of service that extended hospitality to all.

The Gospel reading shows an intrinsic connection between proclamation and action. To proclaim the reign of God is also to work for the healing of those who are sick and marginalized by society. A simple act of healing Simon's mother-in-law dramatically increases Jesus' growing fame as crowds gather outside the doors of the house. Here again, Mark plays with the notions of open space as Jesus moves from inside the house into the crowd to heal the sick and cast out demons. Preachers may choose to explore the way that healing begins within the synagogue and house and then extends into the neighborhoods. The movement is suggestive of the need of Christian communities to encounter Christ's healing in our own lives and extend it to those around us. The movement outward to those in need of healing and exorcism shows Jesus' act of compassion as the proclamation of the good news of God's reign.

Today's reading also provides an example of the need for balance between prayer and action. Overwhelmed by the crowds seeking healing, Jesus retreats to a deserted place to pray. The ongoing demands of public ministry require regular occasions of contemplation and isolation in order to continue to respond to those in need. As the church engages in ministries of healing and compassion in a broken world, we need to maintain regular patterns of daily prayer.

Lest we miss the point, Mark stresses again that the proclamation of the gospel in word and action is an engagement in conflict with the powers and principalities that oppose God's reign. Jesus heads out to visit other towns in Galilee for the express purpose of preaching in the synagogues and casting out demons (v. 39). Here, the emphasis is that the word of good news will prompt the exchange and conflict with evil that will need to be addressed. Our work in proclaiming the gospel in word and deed inevitably leads us into conflict. Discipleship involves struggle against the power of evil in the midst of social structures that call us away from the demand of the gospel to love God with all of our heart, mind, and soul and to love our neighbor as ourselves. Our culture stresses the need to get ahead at all costs, to accumulate and hoard belongings, to look out for number one. In contrast, the gospel stresses Jesus' ministry that begins in the small towns of Galilee and leads those who experience God's healing into serving those around them.

Most baptismal rites in denominational worship books include a version of the questions of renunciation that are asked of candidates coming for baptism. The recovery of these questions from the baptismal practices in the early centuries of the church stresses the process of conversion as a turning from sin and evil to Christ. The minister asks the baptismal candidate: "Do you renounce all evil, and powers in the world which defy God's righteousness and love?"[2] Some liturgies in the early church involved the candidate physically turning toward the rising sun while answering the question. The significance of these questions is to portray Christian faith as an engagement in a lifelong struggle for God's righteousness and love to take root in our lives, our communities, and our world. Mark's Gospel demonstrates Jesus' public ministry growing out of his baptism in the Jordan River as a campaign against the evil that distracts us. It is an evil that is not simply out there, but one that we confront within our own religious communities and households. The work of promoting God's righteousness and love that reaches out to the marginalized, forgotten, and ignored will run into conflict with the constant pressure within our Christian communities for success, bigger buildings, balanced budgets, and growing endowments. When we accept society's benchmarks for effective ministry, we turn away from the messy, demanding, difficult portrait of Jesus' ministry in Mark's Gospel. Jesus' example of proclamation, healing ministry, and confronting evil in its manifestations is balanced by times of prayer and meditation. Christian ministry in today's settings requires us to live out our baptisms in ways that parallel the model of ministry that Mark offers us in today's reading.

First Reading
Isaiah 40:21-31 (RCL)

The RCL pairs a section of Deutero–Isaiah's call for God's comfort with the Gospel reading. The images provide a stark contrast to the descriptions of Jesus' engagement in public ministry in Capernaum. The Isaiah text provides a hopeful tapestry of God's sovereignty in the midst of difficult situations. The transitory nature of the power structures of princes and rulers is contrasted with the lasting dimensions of the Creator who is pictured as enthroned above the earth. From this divine perspective, God remains in charge of both the heavens and the earth, bringing down corrupt rulers. God's power and strength maintain the order of the universe that is evidenced by a careful examination of the heavens and stars. The prophet invites us to look beyond our own weariness and frailties and place our trust in God who is the source of life. Our fatigue and discouragement at apparent injustices that persist is contrasted with God's commitment to give power to the faint and strengthen the powerless (v. 29). God, as source of hope and renewal, is trustworthy in leading us into God's future.

When set alongside the Gospel's call for action and engagement in ministries of healing, wholeness, and reconciliation, the reading from Isaiah provides a helpful perspective. One can read the vision of Isaiah 40 as a way of filling out our prayer lives. The emphasis here is that God's reign is not ultimately dependent on our tireless work. Instead, our service draws its strength from this vision of God's sovereignty. In spite of failures and setbacks in our ministry, we gain energy for our work as we place our hope in the one who brings us renewal.

Job 7:1-4, 6-7 (LFM)

In contrast to the images of discipleship from the Gospel lesson, the reading from Job describes the travails and difficulties of daily life. Job's words are in the form of a lament about the harsh realities of life. This passage is a portion of Job's address to God about his feelings of emptiness and misery at the conditions under which he suffers. No resolution to this cry to God is provided.

This is a difficult text for Christians in our cultural setting to hear. While we may find comfort in a sense of solidarity with one who expresses anguish over the difficulties of life, we have grown accustomed to faith as providing some form of solution to the pain and injustices we face. Lingering with uncertainty and allowing space for lamentation may be gifts that the church has to offer in a culture that wants instant results.

Another way to hear this text is to allow Job's voice to express the pain and suffering of those around us whom we usually silence or ignore. Job's words become those of the homeless, abused, and forgotten who call out to God for relief from the painful conditions under which they suffer. Alongside the Gospel lesson's call to service, this text prepares us to hear the voices of brothers and sisters in our communities who struggle with injustice and who daily suffer. Preachers can address this text as a listening exercise that speaks not only of our own pain, but of the anguish of those in our communities who long for comfort, healing, and companionship.

Psalmody
Psalm 147:1-11, 20c (RCL)
Psalm 147:1-2, 3-4, 5-6 (LFM)

The psalm provides a helpful link between the images of the Gospel reading and the contrasting portraits of the Old Testament texts. The psalmist shares the emphasis on God's sovereignty as the Creator and Sustainer of the earth. Yahweh is the one who tends to the earth, providing rain, nurturing the grass and grain that feed cattle and crows (v. 9). Thus, the psalmist adds his voice of praise to that of all creation for the goodness of God who sustains the universe.

In addition, the psalm provides a link to the healing narrative of the Gospel reading. Yahweh is the healer of the brokenhearted and binder of their wounds (v. 2). Here, the psalm follows Job's lamentation with a word of comfort or reinforces Isaiah's vision of comfort with an added testimony. Care should be taken in not allowing the hope of healing and comfort to eliminate the voices of suffering and the painful groans of the earth as it suffers from pollution, neglect, and human consumption. Instead, the psalmist invites us into God's healing work as those who tend to the brokenhearted, bind up wounds, and work for clean air, fertile soil, and healthy rivers and streams so that they, too, may be signs of God's glory.

Second Reading
1 Corinthians 9:16-23 (RCL)
1 Corinthians 9:16-19, 22-23 (LFM)

Why proclaim the gospel in word and action? Paul addresses the question in his letter to the church in Corinth. The call to proclamation at the heart of the vocational identity of the baptized is to a life of solidarity that God's longing for the wholeness of all people and all creation may come to fulfillment. Here Paul denies motivation based on any kind of reward system. In stark contrast to those who advocate forms of the prosperity gospel, Paul simply recognizes a calling (commission) to share the transformative grace of Jesus that he has experienced. He does this for the sake of the gospel and in doing so shares in its blessings (not as a reward system, but as a partaker in the divine life that sustains the gospel message). Rather than assert his own rights to freedom from the law, Paul empathizes with those around him by adopting practices that reflect the concerns of others in order that the gospel is seen and heard with clarity. In commenting on the passage, Cyril of Jerusalem observes that Paul follows in the path of Christ as a pattern of empathy: "Everywhere the Savior becomes 'all things to all men.' To the hungry, bread; to the thirsty, water; to the dead, resurrection; to the sick, a physician; to sinners, redemption."[3]

91

The text comes as an invitation to set aside our rights, preferences, and prejudices in light of the larger goal of sharing the gospel. While there may be an "I" in ministry, Paul asserts that ministry is not about ourselves, our own agendas, or benefits that we may obtain. Instead, ministry is about the process of being formed into the likeness of Christ who knows our suffering and pain. In a culture that thrives on entertainment, this portrait of ministry as one of self-giving will appear as radical and countercultural. Difficult and challenging as it may be, contemporary listeners long for a vision of life beyond the isolated, small worlds in which we often live. Paul's message to the Corinthians may prompt us to reexamine our congregation's ministry, our church budget, and our own individual commitments to determine if they adequately represent the gospel's commission to solidarity with our neighbors.

Focal Points for Preaching

The church as a community of the baptized is called together into ministries of service and compassion. This vision of incarnational ministry is grounded in the example of Jesus Christ. The work of ministry confronts the evil and suffering that remain present in the church, community, society, and throughout the earth. With a vision of God's desire for healing and wholeness, Christians participate in the redemptive work of Christ who comes to heal the sick, bind up the brokenhearted, release the captive, bring sight to the blind, and declare the coming reign of God. From the reservoir of prayer and contemplation, we place our trust in God as Creator and Sustainer and participate in God's ongoing work of healing and salvation.

Notes

1. Lamar Williamson Jr., *Mark*, Interpretation: A Bible Commentary for Teaching and Preaching (Atlanta: John Knox, 1983), 55. Williamson lists the following examples: the poor widow, the woman with the ointment, the women at the cross, and the women at the tomb.
2. "The Sacrament of Baptism," in *Book of Common Worship* (Louisville: Westminster John Knox, 1993), 407. Worship books from different ecclesial bodies have various wording, including renouncing Satan and all his works.
3. Cyril of Jerusalem, in *1–2 Corinthians*, Ancient Christian Commentary on Scripture, New Testament VII, ed. Gerald Bray (Downers Grove, Ill.: InterVarsity, 1999), 86–87.

February 12, 2012
Sixth Sunday after Epiphany /
Sixth Sunday in Ordinary Time

Revised Common Lectionary (RCL)	Lectionary for Mass (LFM)
2 Kings 5:1-14	Leviticus 13:1-2, 44-46
Psalm 30	Psalm 32:1-2, 5, 11
1 Corinthians 9:24-27	1 Corinthians 10:31—11:1
Mark 1:40-45	Mark 1:40-45

Imitating Christ. At the center of today's reading, Mark offers us a portrait of what it means to follow Jesus. Jesus' disregard for religious rules that place people into the categories of insiders and outsiders echoes through the other readings for the day, whether it is the healing of Naaman, an officer in a foreign army, or in Paul's advice to the church in Corinth to live like Christ in order to witness to God's grace to those around us.

Gospel
Mark 1:40-45 (RCL, LFM)

With the story of the healing of the leper, Mark begins a major theme that will run throughout the Gospel. The cleansing story presents a major attack on the purity code of Jesus' day. The Levitical code that lay behind this narrative is discussed in the section on Leviticus 13 (see below). From its earliest days, Jesus' public ministry attacks the social and religious isolation of people from the community. Today's reading begins with the leper coming to Jesus and pleading for healing. The leper recognizes Jesus' ability to heal him from his disease and to restore him to wholeness in the community.

Jesus' response to the request is marked by several significant characteristics. First, Ched Myers notes, is Mark's use of the words "to declare clean." The story is not simply a healing story. The cleansing refers to the removal of the purity codes and stigma that were placed upon the man.[1] Second, Jesus expresses indignation (sometimes translated as "pity") at a system that pushes aside people in need.[2] Third, note the description of Jesus' action toward the man with leprosy: he stretches out his hand and touches him (v. 41). Contemporary listeners miss the shocking drama of such a move. In touching the leper, Jesus places himself not only at risk of contracting the disease, he also immediately becomes ritually unclean through physical contact with a man who is considered a social outcast. The narrative offers a form of transference: the leper receives healing from Jesus while Jesus becomes ritually unclean in the process. The action is followed by Jesus' instructions for the man to go to the priests as a form of witness against the injustices of a social and religious system that moves those who are suffering outside the social, economic, and religious boundaries of society. Myers underscores the point that Jesus' instruction need not be interpreted as a corroboration of the Levitical code, but as a form of assault on the code's injustice.[3] Thus, the point of the healing is to press the issue of injustice with religious leaders who uphold laws in ways that violate God's mercy for those who are sick and weak. Jesus sends the man to the priest in order that he may provide witness over and against a system that has isolated him from contact with members of his community.

The ensuing public testimony of the man who is healed adds to Jesus' growing fame. As the news spreads, Jesus is unable to enter into towns and he finds crowds growing around him. Note here again the point that the crowds' interactions with Jesus continue to perpetuate the violation of the purity codes. By touching the leper, Jesus is ritually unclean and all who come into contact with him share in this condition. Whether or not the leper presents himself to the priest and makes the required offering for reinstatement in the community, the broader narrative presses the issue that Jesus' ministry will continually attack, violate, and expose the injustice of systems that separate and alienate people.

While ancient purity codes may sound like an odd topic for preachers to address, parallels abound in the social, religious, and economic systems in which we live. In recent times, those who suffered with AIDS often met with a similar sense of isolation and anxiety that mere human contact would cause the disease to spread. Homeless people who struggle with addiction and mental illness often are deemed invisible, if not disposable, in cities that push them aside in favor of commerce and development. Undocumented workers struggle to earn a livable wage in jobs that many of us would never even consider while constantly living under fear of imprisonment and deportation. The underlying principles of greed in today's modern forms of capitalism have created their own purity codes that define those who are successful and who are welcome in the marketplaces today and isolate those who are deemed as outsiders and are pushed to the margins of society.

Today's Gospel lesson is clear about whom Jesus sides with when we divide people into categories of clean and unclean, worthy and unworthy, successful and unsuccessful. Jesus embraces outsiders. Jesus' identity with the outcasts presents a portrait of ministry to those who profess to follow in his path. The church as the body of Christ is called to the ministry of healing, the prophetic witness of exposing injustice, and the messy work of accompanying those who find themselves in deserted places. This gospel stands in stark contrast to churches whose identity is built around the creation of successful programs, the growth and management of endowment programs, or an interpretation of the gospel as a modern self-help manual. Instead, Jesus' ministry from its earliest days is an attack on religious systems that fail to address the spiritual, physical, social, and economic needs of those who are poor, hurting, and isolated.

If all of this sounds like a recipe for unpopularity, the Gospel lesson concludes with an interesting twist. Jesus is besieged by people who want to hear and experience the reign of God. While transforming our congregations from centers of power and influence to stations of hospitality and healing will undoubtedly be a difficult challenge for many of us, solidarity with those who are in need will bring its own form of growth. This may present problems for the budget balancers and bean counters among us, but it provides a clear vision of ministry as identification with those who are not at the center of today's society. Outsiders unite! God's reign is reaching out to embrace you when the church extends Christ's welcome to all people.

First Reading
2 Kings 5:1-14 (RCL)

The gospel often takes the form of mimesis or imitation. Jesus' healing of the leper in Mark's Gospel provides a parallel to the famous story of Naaman's healing in 2 Kings. Naaman is presented as a powerful military leader of a foreign army who becomes afflicted by leprosy. The narrative itself is layered with significant reference points: a successful outsider gets advice from an Israelite slave girl; the king of a foreign country sends financial properties to the king of Israel as a way to pay for services to be rendered; Naaman turns to Elisha, the prophet for help; the prescription for healing involves the Jordan River; and the method of dipping involves the repetition of seven times (is this a reference to creation and thus new creation or a veiled reference to the conquering of Jericho?). The richness of the narrative details provides for a wide variety of interpretive options. The primary point in the narrative remains the possibility for all people (including dignitaries and outsiders) to experience God's healing. Alongside this shocking claim comes the description of the healing taking place in an unlikely setting. Naaman anticipates providing a magical act of healing (perhaps in exchange for the goods provided) and is shocked to simply receive instructions to head down to the Jordan River. While Naaman viewed the Jordan as inferior to the more impressive rivers in Damascus, Aban, and Pharpar, the Jordan holds symbolic significance as the crossing site of the children of Israel into the promised land of milk and honey. Thus, one can read this text as a kind of conversion experience of Naaman's reluctant faithfulness to follow God's direction and pass through the waters of the Jordan to the banks of the other side. Christian interpreters have often found the story to provide a proto-baptismal image of cleansing and healing.

Leviticus 13:1-2, 44-46 (LFM)

The inclusion of the reading from Leviticus provides a helpful historical backdrop to the Gospel reading. The description presents an ancient form of examination, identification, and treatment for those dealing with a wide range of serious skin diseases. Those who suffered from diseases were to report to a priest for the determination of a treatment plan. Those who suffered from acute symptoms would be quarantined for a period of time in order to determine the seriousness and infectious state of the disease. Those who showed no signs of healing were declared unclean and might be permanently banished. In ancient societies with limited medicinal procedures, the threat of exposure to terminal diseases was significant. Thus, the development of codes and procedures for how to respond to those who contact an acute illness is understandable.

It is important to note that the use of this reading from Leviticus in the context of Christian worship is to provide an explanatory, historical footnote to the account of Jesus' healing of the leper in Mark's Gospel. It is not a validation of ancient practices that continues to maintain a divine status. One can raise legitimate questions about the practice of liturgical responses to readings like this one. The lector intones, "This is the Word of the Lord." And the people respond: "Thanks be to God." Care must be taken within these practices not to reinforce notions of divine punishment for those who suffer from illness and disease. Nor should this text be understood to legitimate the isolation of the marginalized from our communities of faith. Today's Christians will not find any part of the Levitical code of ancient Israel to provide a moral or spiritual basis for the exclusion of members from our communities. We do not have the right to pick and choose certain portions of the Levitical code while ignoring vast segments of it. Instead, the Levitical code provides historical and cultural insight into ways that ancient Israel struggled to define its own community in light of the covenant extended to them by God.

Psalmody
Psalm 30 (RCL)

The Revised Common Lectionary pairs the 2 Kings text with this psalm due to its emphasis on healing and regeneration. The psalmist offers praise to God for deliverance. God hears the cries of the psalmist and heals him (v. 3). As a result, the psalmist moves from a time of mourning to a time of dancing; a time of lament to occasions of rejoicing. With its emphasis on the transformation that takes place as God brings healing, the text provides an opportunity for communities and individuals to look at times and occasions of healing in their own lives and to celebrate the places where God's Spirit continues to bring wholeness into our lives. Preachers may want to connect the themes of these texts with occasions in the lives of congregations that have moved from brokenness and despair to reconciliation and restoration. Looking back provides an opportunity to recognize and give thanks for God's grace in our lives.

Psalm 32:1-2, 5, 11 (LFM)

Psalm 32 presents the experience of healing in terms of deliverance from sin. Alongside the Leviticus reading where leprosy is defined as a form of God's judgment to justify the exclusion of one from the community,[4] the psalm presents the act of healing as primarily addressing the forgiveness of sin. The psalmist confesses his sin to God and receives God's pardon for his iniquity. He encourages those around him to participate in the act of confession and to seek God's mercy. The psalm represents a response to the experience of divine healing. The early church father Athanasius once remarked, "When you see people being baptized and ransomed out of a generation that is perishing, and you are in wonder at the lovingkindness of God toward the human race, then sing to them Psalm 32."[5] Here, the preacher may want to raise questions about the presence of sin and injustice in our communities and in our lives in order to seek God's healing and forgiveness.

Second Reading
1 Corinthians 9:24-27 (RCL)

The selection of this famous pericope with its metaphor of Christian faith as a marathon race emphasizes Christian discipleship as an act of daily discipline and training. Just as one does not show up and run a marathon without putting in miles and miles of training, so, too, Christian faith and life involves the continuous practices of welcoming the stranger, caring for the neglected, practicing hospitality, and embracing the sick and estranged. Alongside the other lectionary readings, this text offers a call to the ongoing commitment of Christians to embody the gospel of Christ in our daily lives. This should not be interpreted as a call to individualism or competition, but to the development of spiritual disciplines within our lives as part of our participation in the body of Christ. In his commentary on the passage, Richard Hays notes that Paul's use of self-control is not for the sake of becoming self-reliant or super-Christians. Instead, Paul is encouraging those who become strong in faith to give up their rights "for the sake of others in the community."[6] Note also the text's emphasis on avoiding running aimlessly, but to run with a sense of purpose. The text cautions us against the notions of busyness that often preoccupy our time and ministry and urges us to focus our discipleship on practices of compassion that present Christ to those around us.

1 Corinthians 10:31—11:1 (LFM)

The epistle reading stresses the primary task of disciples as that of following in the footsteps of Christ. To that end, Paul encourages those in Corinth to examine his own life and recognize the signs of Christ in it. Paul's embodiment of Christ among them reflects his commitment to imitate Christ. Christians serve as witnesses to one another in the way that we incarnate Christ in our daily lives. Because of the importance of this as the central task of faith, Paul urges those in Corinth to examine their actions to make sure that all that they do brings glory to God. Paul connects this practice with the advice to avoid offending others regardless of their status or of your own rights and instead seek the benefit of those around you in order that others may recognize Christ's light within your life. Hays writes, "For Paul, such imitation means one thing only: shaping our lives in accordance with the pattern of Jesus' self-sacrificing love."[7] Ministry as the giving of one's self for the betterment and building up of the community follows the incarnational model of Jesus' ministry.

Focal Points for Preaching

The lectionary texts provide portraits of imitating Christ that stand in opposition to many popular interpretations based on the slogan: What would Jesus do (WWJD)? In many places, WWJD has become a way to justify our ongoing participation in systems that are not only corrupt but are opposed to the values of God's reign (for example, simply note the banality of the advertising campaign around Jesus' choice of automobile purchases). The gospel contrasts these individualistic images by presenting Jesus' ministry as an outright attack on social and religious systems that perpetuate the estrangement of certain groups of people (regardless of whether or not this is based on claims of divine decree). The proclamation and enactment of God's reign breaks down these barriers. Those who follow Jesus take on the task of unmasking idols and exposing injustices in our religious communities and in the world around us. Imitating Christ means that our lives bear witness against any system which reinforces categories that separate, diminish, or alienate people. Instead, as followers of Christ, the church witnesses to the light of Christ present in all people and throughout all creation. Tending this light in our lives and in the world around us is a way for us to work toward the healing that God longs to bring to our world.

Notes

1. Ched Myers, *Binding the Strong Man: A Political Reading of Mark's Story of Jesus* (Maryknoll, N.Y.: Orbis, 1990), 153.
2. C. S. Mann, *Mark*, Anchor Bible 27 (Garden City, N.Y.: Doubleday, 1986), 219.
3. Myers, *Binding the Strong Man*, 153.
4. See the analysis in Jacob Milgrom, *Leviticus 1–16*, Anchor Bible (Garden City, N.Y.: Doubleday, 1991), 805ff.
5. Athanasius, in *Psalms 1–50*, Ancient Christian Commentary on Scripture, Old Testament VII, ed. Craig A. Blaising and Carmen S. Hardin (Downers Grove, Ill.: InterVarsity, 2008), 236.
6. Richard B. Hays, *First Corinthians*, Interpretation: A Bible Commentary for Teaching and Preaching (Louisville: John Knox, 1997), 156.
7. Ibid., 181. Hays offers the examples of Dietrich Bonhoeffer, Martin Luther King Jr., and Archbishop Oscar Romero.

February 19, 2012
Transfiguration of Our Lord /
Last Sunday after Epiphany (RCL)
Seventh Sunday in Ordinary Time (LFM)

Revised Common Lectionary (RCL)	Lectionary for Mass (LFM)
2 Kings 2:1-12	Isaiah 43:18-19, 21-22, 24b-25
Psalm 50:1-6	Psalm 41:2-3, 4-5, 13-14
2 Corinthians 4:3-6	2 Corinthians 1:18-22
Mark 9:2-9	Mark 2:1-12

How is it that what we do in church relates to the deep pain, longing, and needs of the world for healing and reconciliation? Liturgical scholars have often suggested that liturgy prepares us for mission and service in the world. In an essay on ritual practice, Michael Aune notes the claim by some that the word and the meal prepare us to share what we receive with the poor. Aune then adds insightfully, "This sounds fine, but most likely once the liturgy has ended, we go downstairs to the coffee hour instead."[1] To put it another way, we church people have a tendency to get stuck inside the walls of the church. Today's readings challenge us to engage in ministry with the poor by coming down from mountaintop experiences to meet the pain and suffering of the world or by opening up space for those searching for healing and wholeness.

Gospel
Mark 9:2-9 (RCL)

The transfiguration scene in Mark lies at the midpoint of his Gospel. It functions as a narrative high point between Jesus' baptism (which acts as Jesus' birth story for Mark) and Jesus' crucifixion in Jerusalem. The scene on the mountaintop deftly weaves together major images from Hebrew Scripture: Moses and Elijah, the representatives of the Law and the Prophets, appear on the mountain alongside Jesus. Their appearance on the mountaintop draws on biblical themes of their ongoing communion with God: at the end of his life Moses ascended the mountain while Elijah was transported in his chariot into the heavens.

The text links the mountaintop experience to the divine voice at Jesus' baptism. The voice from the heavens that accompanies Jesus' baptism with the words, "You are my Son, the Beloved; with you I am well pleased" (Mark 1:11), echoes again with the similar words, "This is my son, the Beloved; listen to him." The disciples see Jesus clothed in dazzling white, an image associated with God as judge wearing new white garments in the book of Daniel (7:9) as well as an image in the early church of the new robes wrapped around the newly baptized. Preachers can develop this imagery in terms of preparation for the coming season of Lent (and its accompanying narrative of Jesus' journey to Jerusalem).

From today's transfiguration account, Mark traces Jesus' journey as he moves back down the mountain to the cross in Jerusalem. Throughout this long journey, Jesus' ministry of compassion is undergirded by the sense of vocational identity that is portrayed in both the baptismal and transfiguration narratives. Both accounts offer a divine blessing ("This is my beloved son"), which is used in the baptismal rites of the church for all who profess faith in Jesus. This sign of baptismal identity as a child of God is wrapped around Jesus as swaddling clothes that will surround him through the difficult days ahead.

In the early centuries of the church's existence, if you showed an interest in Christianity, then you underwent a kind of preliminary examination, called a *scrutiny*. The test consisted of one question: Are you willing to help out those who are in need? If you were, then you went through a time of preparation for baptism (in some places it lasted for a couple of years). During this time, the primary purpose was to work on caring for your neighbors—not just the people around you whom you liked, but the widows, orphans, imprisoned, and strangers from different countries. These folks who otherwise were neglected were the focus of attention. In fact, Christians became known as the people who took food and clothes to those who were otherwise usually ignored. The test for readiness for baptism was to spend your time and energy caring for the forgotten. When you made enough progress on this journey, then you were brought before the congregation and stood up in front of everyone and one of the regulars in the congregation stood beside you and testified on your behalf. "I have been watching [name] . . . and I have noticed how he spends time caring for the sick and poor and I see signs of growth in his life." Once you made it that far, then there was a crash course during Lent to prepare you for the big event of your baptism at Easter. You learned the Lord's Prayer and the Apostles' Creed. Then, on the eve of Easter at the Vigil service, those who were going to be baptized gathered and were taken to the water and there they were baptized in the name of the Father, and the Son, and the Holy Spirit. When they came up out of the pool of water, they were wrapped in new white clothes—their baptismal gowns. Afterward, everyone gathered around a table to share a meal, a celebration, a feast of bread and wine and sometimes of milk and honey. This bread and this cup, that we still share together today, became the weekly occasion for baptized Christians to come together, to renew their baptismal vows, to encourage one another, and to continue to go out to feed and clothe their neighbors.

This vision of ministry draws from Jesus' ministry to the sick, poor, and needy. This self-sacrificial giving takes its strength from the divine blessing pronounced on Jesus at his baptism and again at the transfiguration. This same blessing is pronounced upon each of us at our baptism and heard again in moments of spiritual renewal. Preachers can encourage congregations to prepare for Lent by living out of these occasions of divine blessing.

Mark 2:1-12 (LFM)

Jesus' return to Capernaum is marked by the arrival of crowds in the home where he stays. His teaching is interrupted by a paralytic man who is carried by four of his friends. When they are unable to make their way through the crowds that surround the house, they proceed to remove the roof and lower him through it in order that Jesus may heal him. As in the previous episode of the healing of the leper, Mark crafts the healing story of the paralytic man to portray the nascent conflict between the onset of Jesus' public ministry and its opposition by portions of the scribes.

On one level, Mark describes the confrontation in terms of an economic conflict. Jesus' public ministry is among the poor who flock to him in crowds. As we have noted in previous passages in Mark's Gospel, it is the outsiders, women, and outcasts who cry out to Jesus to bring healing and wholeness. Jesus' proclamation of God's coming reign is precisely on behalf of those longing for God's salvation. This message and its accompanying actions place Jesus in immediate opposition to the religious leaders who seek to maintain structures of power and authority that reinforce the status quo. Today's reading portrays this opposition as it shows the crowds who gather around a typical, modest home with an earthen roof. The narrative offers descriptive terms that allude to the conditions of poverty: the crowd (a term often associated with those who are poor), the roof that is easily torn away, and the paralytic man's stretcher or mattress.[2] Furthermore, the healing of the man is accompanied by Jesus' declaration, "Son, your sins are forgiven." Ched Myers argues that this forgiveness of sins is not simply a reference to a spiritual condition, but is primarily an outright attack on a hierarchical debt code that has restricted the man from full participation within social, economic, political, and religious structures of his day.[3] Hence, the text describes the immediate response from some of the scribes who are present. They object to Jesus' declaration of forgiveness on the grounds that Jesus lacks the authority to restore the man to a place of wholeness in the community. Mark establishes a crucial point here: like the healing of the leper, this healing threatens to overturn the entire system on which the religious establishment is built. For the scribes in attendance to recognize Jesus' authority is for them to relinquish their own authority. Jesus responds to their charge of blasphemy by using apocalyptic imagery from the book of Daniel: Jesus acts with authority as the Son of Man. Daniel 7 portrays this as one who will come with

God's authority. In responding in this way, Jesus adopts popular messianic imagery to describe himself and the emergence of this populist movement. It is little wonder that this exchange with the scribes leads to the crowd's expression of amazement as well as a coming investigation by religious and government officials (Mark 3).

Preaching on this text is more than a matter of reporting about ancient Middle Eastern power struggles or even offering inspirational examples of past healings. Preaching requires placing the gospel message of liberation into present-day contexts. As religious leaders, we preachers find ourselves cast in the position of the scribes, as ones who often bring prescribed expectations about how and where God is active in our world. Today's reading challenges our own preconceptions about the importance of the rules and regulations that we have created in the church that define God's presence and actions as working through particular conduits. The healing of the paralytic man serves as a metaphor for the church to open up to those in need around us. Warning: It may require tearing the roof off of closed systems in order to make room for new life. It also comes with the promise of conflict and controversy.

The gospel is good news to those who are in need. This is why the biblical witness continually underscores a preference toward the poor. Those of us who operate with the illusion of self-reliance (that is popular in our culture) have little time or need for God (one hour a week at church seems like a lot). However, for those who struggle daily within systems that enslave them in cycles of poverty, the gift of daily bread is received as a blessing from God. A few years ago I had the opportunity to visit families who live in poverty-stricken neighborhoods in Jarabacoa, Dominican Republic. I met a multigenerational family living in a tiny shack near a polluted stream. The family, with nine growing children, struggled to find enough food to eat. Looking around their house, I commented on the one painted plate that was hanging on the wall of the kitchen. Quickly, the grandmother pulled it off the wall and offered it to me as a gift. In that visit, I learned an important lesson about the willingness of people who have very little to share what they have with strangers. Today's Gospel reading pushes the church outside of our comfort zones to practice radical hospitality as we make room to welcome the poor, the sick, and the neglected. In their midst, the risen Christ offers even us the gift of healing and wholeness.

First Reading
2 Kings 2:1-12 (RCL)

The pairing of the Elijah-Elisha text with the transfiguration narrative provides an interpretive lens on the Gospel reading. The stress here is on the transference of power from one prophetic leader to the next. Elisha inherits the mantle of Elijah as he follows in his path through the water of the Jordan River. The scene parallels both the crossing of the Red Sea as well as the entrance into the promised land by the children of Israel. As Elijah is taken up into heaven, Elisha places upon himself the prophetic mantle of one who will speak God's word to the people.

Isaiah 43:18-19, 21-22, 24b-25 (LFM)

The reading from Second Isaiah points to the promise of God's redemption of Israel. The emphasis here is on the new work that God will do to "make a way in the wilderness and rivers in the desert" (v. 19). This new thing comes despite Israel's unfaithfulness in bringing offerings to God and in spite of the sin that Israel has committed. Yet, God promises to wipe away their sin and remember it no more. The language of redemption provides a description that the Gospel writer will flesh out in his story of the healing and restoration of the paralytic man.

Psalmody
Psalm 50:1-6 (RCL)

This psalm of judgment presents God as one who comes to rule over heaven and earth. Alongside the Elijah-Elisha reading, it reinforces the image of God's sovereignty and transcendence. The psalm shares the image of fire with the story of Elijah's ascension into heaven in the chariot of fire. Here, though, the imagery of fire is used as it descends to bring God's judgment on the earth. In the midst of this judgment, God brings together those who are faithful.

Psalm 41:2-3, 4-5, 13-14 (LFM)

The images of Psalm 41 describe the psalmist's experience of God's redemption. God sustains the sick in their beds and heals their illnesses. Here, the psalm prepares the way for the reading of the Gospel lesson where the healing of the paralytic man provides an embodiment of this poetry. God's restoration and healing prompt the psalmist to sing praise to God.

Second Reading
2 Corinthians 4:3-6 (RCL)

The epistle reading, with its images of veiled sight and Christ as the light in our darkness, serves to prepare the listeners for the transfiguration narrative that stands at the center of this Sunday's festivities for those who follow the RCL. Paul describes the gospel itself as veiled to those who are unable to apprehend the manner in which God's glory shines through it. Thus, the proclamation of the gospel seeks to shine light directly on the face of Jesus Christ who is the one who displays the glory of God.

Preachers may want to hold out the image of catching glimpses of Christ's dazzling presence as that which sustains Christians on our discipleship journey. This movement allows the preacher to address both the gift of faith as the apprehension of God's redemptive work in Jesus Christ as well as point to occasions of doubt and uncertainty in the lives of believers when the light of the gospel seems dim. Through all of this, the church serves as a resource to strengthen the fainthearted and support the weak. In the words of the hymn "We Walk by Faith and Not by Sight":

That, when our life of faith is done,
In realms of clearer light
We may behold You as You are,
With full and endless sight.[4]

2 Corinthians 1:18-22 (LFM)

Paul announces that God's promise comes in the form of *yes*. God's faithfulness to us is seen in Christ and evidenced in the Spirit's anointing in our lives. The reading serves as preparation for the healing of the paralytic man in the Gospel lesson for the day. This man stands as a sign of God's yes to bring redemption to those who suffer. Preachers may choose to develop the image of God's sealing of us and gift of the Spirit as a baptismal image that accompanies us throughout our faith journey. The baptismal rite from one worship book expresses it in the prayer that accompanies the act of anointing the newly baptized with oil:

Child of the covenant,
You have been sealed by the Holy Spirit in baptism,
And marked as Christ's own forever.[5]

This is God's yes to us.

Focal Points for Preaching

End of faith, as its beginning,
Set our hearts at liberty.[6]

The lectionary draws heavily from Mark's Gospel throughout Year B. The book of Mark itself is circular in form as it invites the reader as disciple to follow Jesus from baptism to crucifixion and concludes by sending the reader back to Galilee where the story began. These weeks in the church year when we move from Epiphany to the beginning of the Lenten season follow their own circular movement as we learn to recognize the Spirit's appearance in our lives, respond to the call to follow Jesus, and learn to live into our baptismal identity as beloved children of God. On this journey, we are urged to make room for the surprising and disruptive work of God in our world.

Notes

1. Michael Aune, "Ritual Practice: Into the World, Into Each Human Heart," in *Inside Out: Worship in an Age of Mission*, ed. Thomas Schattauer (Minneapolis: Fortress Press, 1999), 170.

2. See Ched Myers, *Binding the Strong Man: A Political Reading of Mark's Story of Jesus* (Maryknoll, N.Y.: Orbis, 1990), 154ff. In particular, note the argument offered by Ahn Byung-mu that associates the language of the crowd with the "rabbinic expression *'am ha'aretz* ('people of the land')."

3. Ibid., 155.

4. Henry Alford, "We Walk by Faith and Not by Sight," *The Presbyterian Hymnal* (Louisville: Westminster John Knox, 1990), #399, v. 4.

5. "The Sacrament of Baptism," *Book of Common Worship* (Louisville: Westminster John Knox, 1993), 414.

6. Charles Wesley, "Love Divine, All Loves Excelling," *The Presbyterian Hymnal*, #376, v. 2.

Lent
Melinda A. Quivik

The dark purple season, this time of introspection and beefed-up discipline, might be a period preachers anticipate with some anxiety for its increased demands were it not for the gorgeous Easter sermon of John Chrysostom we might be privileged to hear (or deliver!) at the end of Holy Week. In its very heart, the sermon opens for all of us the door to the feast no matter how we spent the forty days:

> Let us all enter into the joy of the Lord!
> First and last alike receive your reward;
> rich and poor, rejoice together!
> Sober and slothful, celebrate the day!
>
> You that have kept the fast, and you that have not,
> rejoice today for the Table is richly laden![1]

Let these words from the fifth century help you surrender to your humanity even as you embrace intentional regimens of daily reflection on the meaning of the Lenten time. Set these words as a watch for yourself against fear that you will fall down under the command for greater almsgiving, fasting, and prayer. Preachers in particular require this grace because just as our worship, teaching, and pastoral care loads increase in these weeks leading to Holy Week, we may also be looked upon by others as examples of dedicated Lenten observance. This adds to the pressure. Let Chrysostom's pronouncement of God's mercy surround you in the Lenten season so that you find it easy and light to take the yoke upon you.

For God has given all of us these days not to pile onto our backs burdens great enough to make us stumble but to give us yet more means by which to love the Lord our God with all our heart, soul, and mind and our neighbors as ourselves. And if we listen to the lectionary texts, we hear in this year a full range of imagistic guidance for feeling fed rather than deprived. We are, in effect, brought into the story of our faith through these readings.

There are many ways to tell our story, of course, but this year gives us special insights into our ancestors and the journey they knew. We hear of Noah, Abraham and Sarah, Peter, James, John, the commandments given to Moses, Jesus angry in the Temple, the Israelites besieged by snakes in the desert, Jeremiah proclaiming the new covenant, and the grain of wheat dying to burst forth. In a nutshell, we hear about death and resurrection as a story that takes many turns, incorporates diverse beginnings and transformative moments, and returns again and again to bedrock foundations. We hear:

- who we are: dust and ashes;
- how we began in baptismal water;
- where we are going with our inheritance;
- how to journey following the wisdom and power of the cross;
- that our ultimate healing is always in the truth;
- that by dying, we live.

This is a journey of repeated repentance, acknowledging our broken lives, returning again and again to the Lord who continues to call us. It is a story we need to hear because all true and good stories give joy, frame meaning, create structure, and, finally, offer hope.

God's story with us is a beautiful story and in some respects we can say that it is a simple story because at its heart is the steadfast love of our Creator, Redeemer, and Sustainer—Father, Son, and Holy Spirit. Yet, we have this Lenten time to ponder and reexamine our lives—who we are as individuals and as communities—because it is not a simple story to live. It requires honesty and courage. It is also crucial for the well-being of Earth and of Earth's creatures, plants, air, water, land, and human beings.

God's purpose for our lives is spelled out during Lent. By giving us the Ash Wednesday commands to fast, pray, and give, God makes it clear that of all the purposes we might find for our lives, the only purposes that give life to all creation bind us to the one who died and rose for us, who shows us the face of God, and who lives in us as Holy Spirit, because through that binding, we are saved to live for the sake of the whole world.

Note

1. John Chrysostom, "Easter Sermon," in *Medieval Sourcebook* at http://www.fordham.edu/halsall/source/chrysostom-easter.html, accessed January 6, 2011.

February 22, 2012
Ash Wednesday

First Reading
Joel 2:1-2, 2-17 or Isaiah 58:1-12 (RCL)
Joel 2:12-18 (LFM)

Understanding the Readings

As Lent begins, the prophet cries out to us, orienting us to pay invigorated attention to our lives of faith. Every Ash Wednesday, in each lectionary year, we are given the opportunity to hear from Joel: "Blow the trumpet . . . the day of the Lord is coming . . . rend your hearts and not your clothing . . . Return to the Lord, your God . . ." We deepen our giving to remind ourselves of how grateful we are for what God has given us. We intensify our prayer to alter the priorities by which we apportion time itself, even in the way we schedule our hours. We fast to engage at the most visceral level with the effects of asserting the will. When something we enjoy or take comfort in is removed for a time, its reintroduction announces its sweetness all the more. When we have seen what we can accomplish toward taking time seriously—giving a particular season its full capacity to work on us—we are changed. In short, this is what the prophet Joel calls for: Turn around. Take a different route. Return to the Lord.

It is not often that the lectionary itself turns to Joel, although we hear this Scripture reading also on Thanksgiving (Year B) and as an alternative (semicontinuous) reading in late October (Year C, Lectionary 30). This rare gift is one we can hungrily await because it is always appropriate on Ash Wednesday to hear Joel's cry of return.

Joel's announcement comes from a time when this prophet of the Temple in Jerusalem knew that the people needed a lamentation deeper than even a funeral rite could engender. "Rend your hearts and not your clothing," he tells them. Some scholars believe Joel was addressing the people's despair over destruction wrought by locusts. But the metaphor Joel uses to describe the dark times that require repentance takes on a much broader scope: "the day of the Lord is coming . . ." What the people are to honor in the marrow of their bones (by prayer, fasting, and almsgiving) is not merely an immediate crisis like a plague of locusts—hard as that destruction can be— but the close of all the ages, the finality of time, the day when the Lord's coming will bring everything to an end.

Describing the day of the Lord, the prophet says it is "like blackness spread upon the mountains . . ." A translation from the Jewish Publication Society renders it: "Spread like soot upon the mountains . . ."[1] Soot is the ash of burned things. And this is the day of ashes. When ashes are placed on the foreheads of the gathered people, the words said are of soot: "Remember you are dust and to dust you shall return." Dust and soot: the ending of every life, every people, and all things. We wear upon our foreheads on this day the finest particulates of endings.

But the imagery of death does not stand alone on this day. As we contemplate the end of all that exists, we also hear words pronouncing the opposite of death: a life-giving God who is "gracious and merciful, slow to anger, and abounding in steadfast love . . ." Whether or not the dangers that threaten the people Joel addresses are real or are truly impending, the prophet knows that the people must assemble in order to return to the Lord. This is a liturgical cry, an invitation to enter into a ritual form that cannot help but cause the appropriate emotional and willful responses to come upon the people.

The RCL reading leaves out the prophet's apocalyptic context (vv. 1-2): the "darkness and gloom," the blackness that will "spread upon the mountains," and the suggestion that the threat is from an enemy army. Without this threat language, the prophet calls for repentance in a less stipulated frame of reference. This may be a blessing for the preacher because it leaves the call open to more numerous interpretations lest the call be too vague to hit home. The LFM, however, extends the reading to verse 18 so that it closes with the Lord having "pity" on the people. Such a vivid anthropomorphism may help to bridge the distance between Creator and creature.

The readings from Joel and Isaiah have much thematic material in common. Isaiah tells us that the Lord hears the cries for justice and sees the people's pride in their cultic practices and is not impressed. The people's religious convictions must be expressed in just action. Isaiah defines fasting in real-world terms: "share your bread . . . bring the homeless poor into your house . . ." An appropriate fast—"remove the yoke . . . offer your food . . ."—will usher in a way of life that nourishes both those who are fed and the one who fasts. It may be tempting to read verses 9-10 as prescribing a conditional relationship between the people and the Lord. Another interpretation, however, sees the if-then language describing what, in fact, the faithful will experience when we actually hear the needs of those around us.

Isaiah is trained on the outward focus of the fast—real, tangible help for the destitute—but does not mention the cultic undergirding for compassionate action. In contrast, Joel names the liturgical foundation for repentant disciplines in terms of both the future and the present. Future orientation sets the context for present-day action in terms of the apocalyptic, the coming day of the Lord; attention to the present concerns the community's need to gather. According to Joel, apocalyptic vision coupled with present need for community create together the context out of which the people are enabled to live in justice. In the Isaiah text, nuance is given to the motivation out of which comes obedience to God. The measure of the obedience, however, is not the apocalyptic threat or the community's internal need but, rather, the actual good that results. This intriguing difference between points of view raises theological questions about the bases for ethical action. Does doing the right thing come from fear of the Lord and the strength gained by living within community (Joel) or from the sheer joy of seeing the fruits of righteous action made manifest in the present (Isaiah)?

Finally, while Isaiah lacks the poignant admonition to "rend your hearts and not your clothing"—which summarizes the heart of both texts—Isaiah carries the resonant line, "you shall be called the repairer of the breach, the restorer of streets to live in," which otherwise is heard only in late August, Year C. Because faith is born and enriched through the imagery of worship, this alternative text should not be ignored every year. Each text, while bearing the stern prophetic word appropriate to this day, nevertheless offers different approaches.

Psalmody
Psalm 51:1-17 (RCL)
Psalm 51:3-4, 5-6ab, 12-13, 14 + 17 (LFM)

Understanding and Using the Psalm

If your congregation does not sing the psalm, considering doing so. The first verse can be sung by one voice to set the tune, and the assembly can then sing the remainder in unison. The psalms are songs. The psalter is our oldest hymnbook. The psalm is placed after the first reading so that the assembly can sing its welcome to the First Testament in a manner analogous to the way we sing our welcome to the Gospel text before it is read. Ignite the emotional power of hearing the Joel or Isaiah reading by bursting into song, "Have mercy on me, O God . . ." (v. 1). By singing, the assembly is united in breath and meter. Together we lament our fault and announce our certainty that God will hear our cry and have compassion.

Psalm 51 contains the beloved language, "Create in me a clean heart, O God . . ." (vv. 10-11) and "O Lord, open my lips, and my mouth will proclaim your praise" (v. 15, *Evangelical Lutheran Worship* [hereafter ELW]), often sung to old and familiar melodies. Despite LFM omission of these and other verses that speak of God's actions in response to our repentance, the psalm in either rendition is a prayer that echoes Joel's admonition to "rend your hearts," because "a troubled and broken heart, O God, you will not despise" (v. 17, ELW).

See also the commentary on Psalm 51 on the Fifth Sunday in Lent, (pp. 146-147).

Second Reading
2 Corinthians 5:20b—6:10 (RCL)
2 Corinthians 5:20—6:2 (LFM)

Understanding the Reading

Lest the readings from the prophets lead us falsely to believe that the life we are called to live as a people turned toward God is an easy one, Paul's description of his trials reminds us that a follower of the risen Christ faces hardships. Paul is writing of his own ministry, to be sure, but his portrait of the life of faith—the place from which he stands and speaks—is shared by all Christians.

Taking into account (1) the physical and psychological deprivations the Christian endures, (2) the orientation toward purity, patience, holiness, and other admirable characteristics required of the witness, and (3) the tools—weapons of righteousness—given for the work encourages us not to be lulled into a complacent assumption about our own choices even from day to day. A witness to Christ lives not only with a left-hand shield for defense but also with a right-hand sword for offense. A witness lives with genuine, not saccharine, love that can involve costly truth telling. A witness lives "as having nothing, and yet possessing everything" (6:10). Notice that this stance, or frame of reference, necessarily incorporates oppositions: defense and offense, love that may hurt, emptiness and fullness. The life of one who follows the risen Christ is layered and rich rather than being flat and simple.

To [re]turn to the Lord is to do so within a relationship as complex as friendship. The phrase "be reconciled to God" (5:20b) does not use a verb that is merely active, something we can assert on our own. Reconciliation requires two parties. In Greek "be reconciled" (aorist passive) calls the hearer to simply receive—as one receives bread in an open palm. In English, "be reconciled" may sound active such that the hearer is called to make the first move toward the other. Theologically, the word is pure invitation to be loved; linguistically, because of translation, the word is an invitation to open one's arms actively. In this way our faith becomes defined in both passive and active expressions.

This is an important note during Lent because it allows us to think of Lent not as an imposition but as a return to what we already know. Our Lenten disciplines come from a way of seeing and living known through oppositions. Because Lenten foci come from *this* place of faith, this way of living, they do not confront us as foreign intruders invading our comfortable routines. Nor do they come to us as burdens added to our already beleaguered lives. Rather, the Lenten foci are welcome and familiar outgrowths of our deepest desires. When we put together all the admonitions of these texts, we see the church comprised of people who possess a gracious openness as their primary mode. The admonitions are not hammers but open hands, beseechings to join together in a common and overt expression of our inner soul searching. In other words, Lent doesn't necessarily introduce into our lives—through these texts and through the practices encouraged in this season—something we aren't already doing. Rather, the church sets aside a period of weeks, a time originally used to teach the catechumens the faith, to reteach all of us—both the baptized and those preparing for baptism—over and over again at a yet deeper level.

The RCL text omits the first half of verse 20, which means the assembly doesn't hear "So we are ambassadors for Christ, since God is making his appeal through us . . ." Paul's primary occupation is summarized in that word *ambassador* and we miss it in this lection. Being an ambassador calls up the role of emissary for a higher power, one who speaks on behalf of the more important person who could not be present.

There are times in the life of the church when a word like "ambassador" is needed in order for the church to consider who and what sends us on our mission. Presently, in many of our churches, the "mission" is defined too much in terms that concentrate on increasing congregational size. The "ambassador" in Paul's letter is he or she who witnesses to the one in whose name all the suffering of discipleship is borne. It is unfortunate that the RCL omits the strong assertion that Christians are "ambassadors *for* Christ," because this gives to witnessing and inviting the requisite richer sense. The LFM text refers to the "ambassador," but leaves out verses 3-10 (the ending of the RCL text), thus ignoring the ambassador's struggles. This allows the LFM reading to celebrate Christ's work of reconciling us to God but does not then move into defining the reconciled as people who live with deep intrinsic contradictions: impostors yet true, known and unknown, dying and alive, and so on. Complexity is thus missing from the portrait of the body of Christ.

Gospel
Matthew 6:1-6, 16-21 (RCL)
Matthew 6:1-6, 16-18 (LFM)

Understanding the Reading

Notice that the Gospel text assumes that the hearers will engage in practices of pious living: (1) almsgiving or, in more contemporary language, challenging ourselves to increase the percentage so as to reach or exceed the tithe; (2) prayer whose purpose is a strengthened relationship with God; and (3) fasting that aims to push our willfulness to the point where it may be difficult to do. The text is written liturgically in that, after assuming we will be "practicing our piety," each practice is addressed in the same pattern of admonitions and encouragements, saying that whenever you practice your piety do not do it to show off but do it secretly for God knows what you do. The liturgical nature of this language is in its rhetorical and repetitive thrust. At the end of the text—in the RCL, at any rate—a summarizing statement regards the good that comes from this secretive way of living out faithfulness as it has to do with the heart. Locate your treasure, and you will find your heart.

The cautions against public displays of piety point to the ancient sin of vainglory.[2] This was one of the serious distractions encountered by desert monastics as they gave their devotion to constant prayer. Unable to maintain focus on prayer, they found their minds wandering in what became predictable patterns. Various thoughts and concerns about the body, the mind, and the soul would turn them from thoughts of God in just this order: food, sex, things, anger, dejection, acedia (a malaise like extreme boredom), vainglory, and pride.

Vainglory is at work if one's tithing, praying, and fasting are done so as to be noticed by others, trapping a person in a false sense of self. Vainglory is distinguished from pride for it misplaces a person's worth as something available through the assessment of others. The wisdom of this Matthean admonition requires us to pay attention to our Lenten practices by reminding us that we do well to look beneath what we are doing to what compels us to those deeds. The motivation can be a clue to how we enter into Lent and how we meditate, at the end, on Jesus' death and resurrection. This text further pushes the thread from Joel through the heart into the heart of God where our treasure truly resides.

Where the text omits the final summary of this admonition (as in LFM), the import of the instruction is left with us as law—a command we are to obey—without telling us of a corresponding consequence. Whether or not verses 19-21 are part of what the preacher explicitly addresses on this day, the preacher will need to emphasize the gospel promise in Matthew that God "will reward you." Here again, this is repeated in a liturgical fashion three times, imbuing the promise with the weight of insistence. What we do in the spirit of offering ourselves to God without an ulterior, vainglorious motive will result in promised gifts.

Preaching the Gospel

A thread runs through all the words from the Scriptures we hear on this beginning day of Lent straight into our hearts. Joel says: "return to the Lord with all your *heart* . . . rend your *hearts* . . ." Psalm 51 tells it again: "The sacrifice acceptable to God is . . . a broken and contrite *heart* . . ." Matthew reminds us: "where your treasure is, there your *heart* will be also . . ." Even Paul lays out what it is to find our hearts, to locate the treasure, because "to be reconciled to God . . . ," to "return to the Lord . . . ," is to have life through using the "weapons of righteousness"—purity, knowledge, patience, kindness, holiness, love, truthful speech, and, not least, God's own power.

The thread leads to the heart and comes out *from* the heart. It is the power of God plunged right into our innermost beings, into the elements out of which we were so wondrously made: the dust of the earth, the soot that is left when the fire has burned, the end of all things.

These texts—whether RCL or LFM—articulate the trouble with the heart, acknowledging the human need for constant return to the Lord because of sin, lack of reconciliation, distraction, greed, and all motivations that come from mislaid and misguided desire. Simultaneously, these texts articulate the blessing God has poured into our hearts, insisting that our striving to fast, pray, and give alms ought to be aimed for the sweetness of what we already have been given: reconciliation with God in Christ Jesus.

In this day's holy communion, the celebration gives praise that the risen Christ is at the heart of our reconciled lives. In other words, as we gather this day around ashes and endings to be admonished about the practices of Lent, we do so only because we have been made able to face our failings by the power of the one whose resurrection makes a mockery of all ashes. This is too much to take in well, and for that reason we creatures of doubt and fear need marks on our foreheads and words from the preacher that say in no uncertain terms, God sees, God knows, God forgives, God makes all things new. Do not dwell overmuch, preacher, on the troubles. Preach the gospel.

Notes

1. *Tanakh: The Holy Scriptures* (Philadelphia: The Jewish Publication Society, 1985), 1007.
2. John Cassian, *The Institutes*, Ancient Christian Writers, trans. Boniface Ramsey, O.P. (Mahwah, N.J.: Newman, 2000); John Cassian, *Conferences*, Classics of Western Spirituality, trans. Colm Luibheid (New York: Paulist, 1985); and Mary Margaret Funk, *Thoughts Matter: The Practice of the Spiritual Life* (New York: Continuum, 1999).

February 26, 2012
First Sunday in Lent

First Reading
Genesis 9:8-17 (RCL)
Genesis 9:8-15 (LFM)

Understanding the Readings

Lent's beginning confronts us with Noah's wild answer—Yes!—to God's command that he build an ark to save all creatures from the destructive powers of God's creation. Noah's legendary acquiescence, risk taking, and ultimate vindication serve as an icon for faith and may be key to answering questions that arise on this day. We may find ourselves asking of this text: Why are you here on this day? What are you directing us to notice? How is that point vital to Lent? We may be haunted by God's pronouncement that "never again shall all flesh be cut off by the waters of a flood."

The questions that arise on this day center on God's identity—the problem of theodicy (God's power and willingness to destroy) and the purpose of the rainbow reminder. I suggest that we can unearth those matters by asking questions about Noah, about God, and about the lectionary choices themselves. First, Noah: Why does he even listen to God? What is the role of empirical evidence when someone is confronted with a conviction that seems to come from the Most High but doesn't "make sense" (i.e., no one else could see a flood impending)? Does Noah have special powers? Is it a mark of righteousness that one spends energy and capital on what appear to be irrational projects? These questions only arise out of the first part of the Noah story, which is prior to the reading for this day, but they must be mentioned because people know this story and find it both attractive (all those animals!) and disquieting (what of the cries of those who drowned?). Children are drawn to this story and are helped to know it through simple, repetitive songs learned in Sunday school and Vacation Bible School. The story—in its first part, at least (the command, the building, gathering the animals, the waters rising, the dove sent out)—makes us wonder whether God cares about those who didn't get in the ark.

We face the flood story as read today with the unavoidable background of dismay over who God is exactly. And these wonderings conjure even more—and deeper— unsettling questions: Why does God say "never again" when we all know that floods wash away whole villages every rainy season somewhere in the world? Dams break. Arroyos fill and trap people in vehicles. If God needs a rainbow to remember, what do ongoing deaths from nature's tirades say about God's omnipotence and omniscience? And, most vitally, the question becomes: *Why* does God establish a covenant? Is God sorry? Is that what the covenant is about? Has God changed in the course of this narrative? Does this narrative signal for us a new understanding of God? Does this story signal a new understanding within God's own self of the power to destroy and to remember? Questions about the actual, plain meaning of this story, familiar and strange as it is, open up avenues for asking about the nature of revelation, of theodicy, and of hermeneutics, all indispensable considerations for preaching.

It is also necessary to back up and look at what immediately precedes the Old Testament text for this day. (The RCL and LFM versions of this text are essentially the same. Although the LFM omits verses 16-17, those verses restate the content of verse 15). Genesis 9:1-7 is about the way human beings must live. God tells Noah and his family what they are to do. They are to enjoy creation and multiply and eat anything they like since all food is intended for them. They are not to kill people. This is the very stern warning that is joined to the Fifth Commandment— "You shall not murder" (Exod. 20:13). The instruction to Noah and his family and, in effect, to all of humanity is to nurture life rather than destroy it.

Genesis 9:8-17 focuses on how God's power works in concert with the human orientation toward what is life giving, telling Noah what God will do: keep covenant and remember. Once the waters have receded, God makes two pronouncements. One of them commands reverence for life on the part of humans; the other informs humanity of God's promise to remember. The question for the preacher, then, has to do with the relationship between God's remembering and the work we have set before us. How does God's covenant make it possible for us to refrain from destroying life? The preacher will want to help the assembly see how God's presence in our midst infuses us with the courage and wisdom we need to honor God's covenant.

Psalmody
Psalm 25:1-10 (RCL)
Psalm 25:4-5, 6-7, 8-9 (LFM)

Understanding and Using the Psalm

As a song following the Genesis reading, with its strong statements from God about the covenant and promises to remember the covenant, Psalm 25 can be heard as a truly appropriate response of the people. Whether the first words are the RCL's "To you, O Lord, I lift up my soul," or the LFM's "Make me to know your ways, O Lord; teach me your paths," the song brings the import of God's rainbow right into the lives of the assembly. It is as if, in response to God's sweeping, outlandish, needed, and eternal claims, we cement those claims, saying, "Okay. We believe you. We want to see what your paths look like. Show us. Teach us." By using the words of the ancient psalter as our response to God, we connect ourselves with our ancestors and give ourselves a chance to "remember" those who first knew the covenant God made.

Indeed, at the heart of the psalm text we hear the word *remember* three times. This emphasis is a stunning link to the rainbow story from Genesis, reminding the assembly of the import of that promise. God will remember. God will remember the destruction of the flood and not let it happen again. God will remember the covenant made at God's own instigation. The RCL selection links even more fully with the covenant pronouncement to Noah because it stretches beyond the LFM portion of the psalm to include verse 10, where we sing the word *covenant*.

Second Reading
1 Peter 3:18-22 (RCL, LFM)

Understanding the Reading

Writing to relatively new Christians in Asia Minor, the author of this letter from ca. 64–90 C.E. encourages the community to understand its life—and especially its suffering—in the context of Jesus' life, death, and resurrection. At the time of this writing, Christians comprised forty thousand people (0.06 percent) in a population of seventy million.[1] This is a tiny band! It is understandable that their strangeness and smallness would invite threats to their well-being. The community to whom this letter is addressed appears to have been strained by persecutions of some sort. Although perhaps not the blatant torture and execution inflicted by later emperors like Nero, Domitian, and Trajan, the community's struggles for the sake of their faith in Christ Jesus leave them vulnerable.

The writer hopes to bolster the tenacity of this new group. By raising the matter of those who did not listen to God's warning about the flood, the letter links the community who will receive it with Noah who did listen and who obeyed and who, therefore, saved his family and all creatures. Then, drawing a parallel between the flood and baptism which "saves you . . . as an appeal to God . . . through the resurrection of Jesus Christ" (v. 21), the letter allows the little community to conceive of itself in truly majestic terms and to be strengthened for the struggles ahead. That both RCL and LFM retain the same verses of this passage signals the import of this text for the day.

The call of this letter to persevere in the face of suffering is emblematic of the role of the epistle in the triad of lections read on a given Sunday even today. The epistle reading helps the church know its task in the context of (1) what is revealed in the Old and New Testaments about the people of God, (2) the ancestors who first framed the metaphors that describe God's power and presence, (3) the life of Jesus on this earth and in his ongoing power because he "sits at the right hand of God," and (4) the witness of the apostles. For us, the epistles are windows into our own beginnings, tributes to the questions that hung over the early Christians and formed them, shaping in turn our own worship practices and therefore our theological understandings. The first letter of Peter, read aloud to its intended assembly as a greeting from an elder to encourage them in their witness, speaks to us in our own time as well.

The task set before them was to think of Noah: what he heard and what he did with it. The strength Noah was given, says the letter, is given to us, too, in baptism. Along with the early church, we are "saved through water" because in baptism God gives us "a good conscience." Another way to say this is that we are washed, cleansed, given new birth, forgiven, and enlightened. This is possible because of the resurrection of Jesus Christ.

Above all, this epistle says that the church is not left on its own to struggle and suffer and lose faith. The existence of the epistles themselves—communications of solidarity between communities—embody the way in which our faith is alive in our shared language. The writer builds faith by creating an edifice of connected imagery from the time of Noah's story to the writer's time to the time now when those same words shape our own belief. It is an astonishing perichoresis in time itself: a dance between the past and the present, both awash in the eternal. This reading leaves us— in our twenty-first-century lives—accompanied by the same angels who ministered to Jesus in the wilderness. They do not pass away.

Gospel
Mark 1:9-15 (RCL)
Mark 1:12-15 (LFM)

Understanding the Reading

Mark's story of Jesus' baptism in the RCL text goes immediately to the wilderness, suggesting that his baptism necessitated moving him right into deep personal struggles. The verbs are strong and mostly wrenching: the heavens tore apart (*schizo*), the Spirit drove him out (*ekballei*), Satan tempted him (*paraxomenos*), and the angels waited on him (*diakonon*). These are all powerful actions, although the

119

power of the last is in the fact of accompaniment, that the angels did not leave him, that the presence of the satanic did not leave him abandoned by heavenly ministers. Something profound lies even here for the sermon: that where violent and dangerous events are taking place, God's servants are at hand.

Paying attention to verbs in a text can offer heft and vitality to the sermon theologically just as it does rhetorically, where focus on verbs in the sermon script encourages vivid language. A strong, active verb holds a punch that wakes us up, helps us feel the immediacy of an act. The preacher might spend some time exploring the actions in the texts and asking: What experience have I had of being torn apart, driven out, tempted, waited on? What do I know of being the one who tears apart, drives out, tempts, waits on . . . ? Such exploration is not an invitation to use the sermon for intimate (and probably inappropriate) self-revelation, but to know the movement in the text well enough to translate it into the sermon.

Mark tells us that the Holy Spirit drove Jesus out into the desert (*ekballei*— see also Mark 1:34, 39, where Jesus casts out demons). Although the word is used elsewhere for the gentler force of being led or sent out (see Matt. 9:38 and Luke 10:2, where workers are sent out into the harvest), in Mark it is violent like an explosion, to throw out. This coercive power comports with the other action in the text with the exception of the dove descending and the angels serving. What does this complex of meanings say about the Spirit, about Jesus, and about the relationship between baptism and temptation? The Spirit not only drives Jesus to a barren and frightful place but also sends the angels. The Spirit's actions, therefore, are neither solely to propel nor to attend gently. We gain more insight into the Spirit's work by embracing them both. The Spirit transforms human lives through complex powers that insist on hardship while enabling its endurance. Sending someone out into danger carries a certain logic, in fact. Wilderness is, after all, where you come to yourself. As a parent shoves a child toward a new experience (going out the door to school, eating a foreign food), the same action can be understood as a gentle coaxing: "It will be good for you!" Where the line is to be drawn—even between the actions of coercion and compelling—may elude us, in the end, for good theological benefit.

In the RCL reading, the experience of the wilderness is closely linked with baptism by virtue of the conjunction of the baptismal scene and the encounters with the devil. One way to read this story is to see that baptism leads to testing one's mettle. Baptism alters the relationship between the person and the world, especially regarding the forces that mean to dismantle the power of the Holy Spirit's presence given in baptism. Although Jesus is called "my Son, the Beloved," he does not get to avoid the desert.

Yet, going to the wilderness is not simply akin to what happens to normal humans launched from baptismal waters into the fracas of the world's inequities and pain. To be sure, Mark unquestionably means to assert Jesus' humanity. Well before his crucifixion Jesus came to know the demonic powers unleashed in the wilderness. We know little of that experience from Mark's Gospel, only forty days, temptation, and wild beasts. For any person, this sounds like a great ordeal. But perhaps he came to know himself as well, or the full extent of his powers through the wilderness testing. There, alone with the forces that sought to undo him—but with the Spirit having played a role in getting him into that situation, and with the angels all around—the story says he held firm. The wilderness depiction, spare as it is here, establishes Jesus' power over the demonic. The devil disappears from this story without a mention. Later, Jesus confronts demonic powers and defeats them.[2]

The Gospel text for LFM is the latter half of the RCL reading, emphasizing Jesus' testing in the wilderness and subsequent preaching. The scene of Jesus' baptism is omitted. This alters the relationship between the day and the Gospel text by shedding the light more on the Spirit's sustaining presence with Jesus than on the Spirit's coming down to him. The LFM texts, then, draw out the connection between God's covenant and the Holy Spirit.

Preaching the Gospel

Boiling down the depiction in each reading of human actions (struggles that result from creation being at odds with itself and missing the point in its responses to God) and of God's actions (the transcendent and immanent power at work in the world for good), we find that these texts describe our own lives. We, too, live in a wilderness of beasts and floods, temptations, imprisonment, and guilt, the bad consciences for which baptism serves "as an appeal to God for a good conscience" (1 Pet. 3:21). The danger with these very familiar stories is that we think we know them and then fail to ask ourselves the questions that can drive our understanding to more penetrating, and truer, levels.

Taken together, these Scripture readings show strong affinities in their imagery for the relationship between human beings and God. God's covenant to remember is drawn out by the images in all the texts, reinforcing the point of the covenant relationship. The watery nature of the flood story is coupled with Jesus in the Jordan River while 1 Peter links Noah with baptism. The rainbow comes to reside in the waters of baptism because we know this water not only to be drowning us but bringing us to new birth, placing the focus this day on how God is present with us now and always in the sacraments.

God's response to our needy situation is to make covenant with all creation, saying "never again," so that now, even in our wildernesses, we are assured that the Spirit is not oblivious to our whereabouts and the angels are still at hand. Even the very brief depiction of Jesus' own wilderness journey in Mark's Gospel shows the fruits of God's covenant: the Holy Spirit drives life experiences even in lonely, dangerous, uncomfortable times and in places where it would be most expedient to give in—which we human beings usually do. Yet, even then we are not left to our own faulty devices; the Spirit remains, and the angels who "waited on him" seem to hover wherever the wild beasts roam. Where do those dangerous creatures live in our lives? They thrive on every street corner and in every home. Wilderness is not just in the mountains or the grasslands but wherever human beings live and move. Destruction is countered in all the places where God's own Spirit attends the living. How do we know this? God's word makes concrete promises. When God sees the bow in the clouds, God says, "I will see it and remember the everlasting covenant between God and every living creature of all flesh that is on the earth."

Lent is focused on the defeat of all that distracts us from what is most essential. These texts show us the Spirit coming and driving human beings to confront and repent our lack of faith in God even while we retain and cling to our faith in the wild beasts.

The one on whom the Spirit descended in the River Jordan is the one whose death and resurrection the church will honor in Holy Week, the ending of Lent. Beginning the movement toward that eventuality by eating and drinking the bread and wine of the risen one on this first Sunday in Lent, remembering his life, death, resurrection, and his coming again—as we do in the eucharistic prayer over the food—assures us that, just as the Spirit came upon Jesus and went with him into the wilderness, Jesus' body and blood becomes our own bodies and we are never left alone. The risen one is inside us.

Notes

1. Fred B. Craddock, *First and Second Peter and Jude*, Interpretation: A Commentary for Teaching and Preaching (Louisville: Westminster John Knox, 1995), 14.
2. David Rhoads and Donald Michie, *Mark as Story* (Philadelphia: Fortress Press, 1982), 65–66, 77–78.

March 4, 2012
Second Sunday in Lent

Revised Common Lectionary (RCL)
Genesis 17:1-7, 15-16
Psalm 22:23-31
Romans 4:13-25
Mark 8:31-38 or Mark 9:2-9

Lectionary for Mass (LFM)
Genesis 22:1-2, 9a, 10-13, 15-18
Psalm 116:10 + 15, 16-17, 18-19
Romans 8:31b-34
Mark 9:2-10

Because the RCL and LFM have entirely different readings this week (with the exception of the RCL's alternative Gospel reading), I will treat each set of lessons separately, beginning with the RCL, followed by commentary on the LFM.

First Reading (RCL)
Genesis 17:1-7, 15-16

Understanding the Reading

Once again Lent sets before us God's covenant promises. Last Sunday God's covenant with Noah following the flood promised that God would remember the past. This Sunday, God promises to Abram and Sarai a future with descendants comprising nations and kings. From the beginning, this text is devoted almost solely to setting out what God will do. The story says "the Lord appeared to Abram," and in response Abram fell on his face. Lying prone with one's face hidden is a posture of utter submission and self-abnegation, and, if not always expressing trust, at least showing honor. This is Abram's one action. The remainder of this story is what God is going to do for Abram and Sarai.

To mark the covenant, God gives to Abram and Sarai their new names, Abraham and Sarah. That these new identities are not their own doing but God's is vital to note because it helps to diminish the idea that Abram's blamelessness or righteousness in any way brings about God's favor. In fact, what may appear to be a contractual relationship proposed by God to Abram is not a contract at all. A contract is an agreement that payment will be made when a task is accomplished. In this story, however, no *thing* will be handed over from God to Abram but, instead, God's own self will continue to be extended in relationship with Abram. There is no end time to this promise, and the covenant is never superceded by subsequent promises. It will last forever. God puts neither a time limit on Abram's walk nor offers an objective reward that Abram will receive.[1]

Concerning the language of the text itself, we notice that God says, "I am God Almighty; walk before me, and be blameless. And I will make my covenant between me and you . . ." God is not using normal contractual language such as "*If* you are blameless, I will make a covenant with you," although it could sound that way. Walter Brueggemann translates God's first words to Abram as "Walk before me, be complete." To be "blameless" is to be whole, to be of one mind, to trust. Furthermore, the unilateral nature of this covenant is evident in God's words, "I, behold, my covenant with you."[2] There are no verbs here. Instead, the closeness between Abraham, Sarah, and God is manifest in that the language connects "I" and "you" by using "covenant" as the link: I-covenant-you.

Finally, two important notes: (1) Sarah is directly addressed, indicating she is not a mere appendage of the patriarch; she receives her own blessing. God has made covenant with her, and God commands that her new name be spoken by Abraham. (2) Because the covenant is also with their descendants, it establishes God's relationship with *a people*, not just with individuals. It is through Abraham and Sarah's descendants that God will make kings and nations.

Psalmody (RCL)
Psalm 22:23-31

Understanding and Using the Psalm

This psalm addresses all people ("you offspring of Jacob . . . you offspring of Israel!") since we are all descendants of Abraham and Sarah. The psalmist calls us to glorify and stand in awe of the Lord who "did not despise" and "did not hide his face from me . . ." The language echoes the meeting of the Lord with Abram when the covenant was set in place and speaks of the coming generations promised to Abraham and Sarah. It calls up the remembrance that God promised to Noah. And finally, it collapses the transcendence and immanence of the Lord who "rules over the nations" and knows "the affliction of the afflicted." This is a cry to a God who is known and honored above all. It is an entirely appropriate response from the assembly to the Genesis 17 story in its encapsulation of the primary imagery.

Second Reading (RCL)
Romans 4:13-25

Understanding the Reading

Writing about this text, Karl Barth makes many remarkable statements, but among them is this: "Grace is the invisible relationship in which all things stand; and the knowledge of it remains always a dialectical knowledge."[3] Without faith, there is no promise. Apart from faith, neither Abraham and Sarah nor we can behold a future that might so miraculously overturn the present. Looking at his and Sarah's aged bodies, Abraham might have lost faith because their weakened conditions could not believably bring forth a future. And yet, apart from—larger than—that factual, law-regulated perception (i.e., bodies deteriorate over time) stands another way of seeing which holds that nothing is impossible with God. The "dialectical knowledge" of oppositions makes it possible to hold onto what was and is not visible because the dialectic insists that the reverse is always present.

Paul spends half of this text making an argument based on the oppositional nature of thinking (law versus grace) and the other half on faith (Abraham did not weaken or waver). A deep temptation when reading this text is to see Abraham's faith as an accomplishment, something held up as an example to the rest of us: See! He could do it! So can you! Keep the faith! And once we've made it through the tough times, God will reckon our faith, too, as righteousness. Barth's assertion about grace holding "all things" opens up the relationship we have with God's promises such that it becomes apparent that God's grandeur (the one "who gives life to the dead and calls into existence the things that do not exist," v. 17) attests to a power beyond what we can reason ourselves into when looking at the things that do exist. To say that all things are held in grace is to point to the source of faith itself. Faith cannot come from what we can observe or else it would not be faith. The promise cannot come from anything generated by creation. The promise must come from the one who brings to life impossible realities.

Gospel (RCL)
Mark 8:31-38

Understanding the Reading

Our minds are set "on human things," and Jesus is set on "the glory of his Father with the holy angels" (8:38). What is human is not what Jesus is heading toward in his own description of it. The path for him will be awful in the true sense of that word (striking awe in those who experience it). From that perspective, Peter's outcry against Jesus' passion is a perfect exemplar of that which differentiates humanity from God. We humans function poorly if called upon to live entirely in the mind-set of God's reign. Jesus' rebuke of Peter consists of hard words spoken in the context of great seriousness about what lies ahead on the cross. God's response to humanity's measly vision is to show us something far greater and lay it out especially in the harshest terms. This gets our attention.

Jesus' words about losing and saving one's life are directed at action or motivation that he seems to be saying is in our control. To follow him, the course of action is to end fixation on self-preservation. The cross we are to embrace is not a predetermined hard row to hoe (as if we are only about God's business when and if we are unhappy). Rather, our cross is the daily journey of focusing on what endures, what matters, what reconciles and seeks the good. It has long been commonplace to speak of the losing and saving of our lives as if we enter into the project with gritted teeth. Rather, consider that what Jesus is calling us to do is receive rest from a burden that is light.

Often the best sermon may come from contemplation of the hardest question that arises from a text. In that regard, the preacher may benefit from paying special attention to the question Jesus asks rhetorically in verse 37: "Indeed, what can they give in return for their life?" Indeed, what does any one of us have that can match the value of a life? Even of our own lives?

For Mark 9:2-9, the alternative RCL Gospel, see below under the LFM Gospel.

Preaching the Gospel

The bedrock commonalities in these texts are rich. Being set on human things, we limp on with limited scope. We see only what is before our eyes unless, by the power that we cannot manufacture on our own, the veil is lifted and we see into the true nature of things. The covenant God promises, the faith God gives us, the vision of what is beyond us are God's gifts. Without them, we are stuck in our desire to preserve what cannot be kept: our lives.

Self-preservation is a mirage. To lose one's life is to lose one's determination to set the agenda and achieve it, to give up on self-justification, to let others remove the pain of distance and the lonely striving after self-constructed greatness, and to look instead for the ways in which God's mercy makes life flourish everywhere. To join that orientation toward others and the earth is to know something of the meaning of Barth's claim: "Grace is the invisible relationship in which all things stand."

First Reading (LFM)
Genesis 22:1-2, 9a, 10-13, 15-18

Understanding the Reading

What story is more wrenching in Scripture than Abraham's willingness to kill his son, Isaac, in response to hearing a voice from heaven? The full story in Genesis 22:1-18 contains a detailed iteration of Abraham's actions. He listened, rose early, saddled his donkey, took Isaac and two others, cut wood, set out . . . and so forth. Although this pericope leaves out all that necessary action in its cryptic recitation of Abraham's arrangements, it does not fail to carry us into the weight of his tasks. In addition, this abbreviated version renders Abraham mute because the conversation (in the full story) between Abraham and Isaac is also left out. Abraham is assumed, in this pericope, to have done what was needed to get the boy to the mountain where he builds the altar, lays the wood, and takes the knife. Then he speaks, but only in answer to God's call. Although the story in this shortened form loses much of its agonizing and beautiful particularity—the time it takes to imagine all these movements readying the task— something of the power is still unavoidably present, because the horror of Abraham's impending obedience stuns the hearer.

This was a test, we are told. As such, God seems to be a harsh examiner. What if Abraham had failed? We do not know. (No matter how many times we hear this story, the question hangs before us: What if we fail? Is there a test being visited upon us even now to which we have not paid due attention?) There is in this story that one gasping moment when Abraham's hand is, we suppose, raised over Isaac, the knife pointing down. Abraham looks as if he is about to fulfill the test exactly. But the story takes a turn. He does not do it. We do not know whether he would have done it. The moment is subverted because the Lord intervenes. The Lord will not let Abraham pass the test as it was first stipulated. Through the test, the Lord learns the heart of Abraham, his willingness to move at least as far toward the command as the story allows us to see.

The story may invite us on the surface to consider what we learn about Abraham, but more important, what does this story show us about the Lord? Is God's omniscience made questionable by God's need to test Abraham's faithfulness? Is Abraham's ability to do such an unthinkable deed an image of the self-denigration required by God? Is the story setting forth an anthropology that shows human capacity to will and act against what we would regularly consider to be in our own best interests?

One way to answer these musings is to assert that the "testing" is already filled with God's knowledge of Abraham, for the story would have been useless if the one to whom God makes this horrifying command could not be counted on to be obedient. One thinks of the story of wise King Solomon solving the question of a baby's true mother by proposing the child be shared by both by being halved. The baby's true mother, of course, offers to give up the child in order to save its life. God could not have spared Isaac and thereby tested Abraham if Abraham had not already been given a vision of God so powerful that the relationship (the covenant relationship laid out a week ago in the lectionary) with God took precedence even over the life of Isaac. The blessing Abraham receives is not only in receiving back the life of Isaac through whom descendants will proliferate but more in being given the possibility of relationship with so merciful a God.

Psalmody (LFM)
Psalm 116:10 + 15, 16-17, 18-19

Understanding and Using the Psalm

In response to the salvation of Abraham, Isaac, and Sarah from the agony of Isaac's expected sacrifice, this psalm sings thanksgiving for the power of the Lord to rescue. The psalmist's great pain—delineated especially in verses 1-9—has been relieved. Verse 10 is translated elsewhere in this way: "I have believed, therefore, I can now speak, 'I was severely bowed down,'"[4] or "I put my faith [in Yahweh] because I said, 'How helpless I am.'"[5] These translations make sense of the despair in verse 11: "I said in my consternation, 'Everyone is a liar,'" which might also be rendered, "I said in my trepidation, 'All humankind is delusive.'" To have felt that everyone has turned against you, that the cosmos has rejected you—such is the sense of Abraham's trial. The psalmist understands that human power to save is a myth. Only the Lord has that power. What, indeed, shall anyone do to give thanks for such a gift? The first two lines of this part of Psalm 116 collapse enormous negative emotion so that the answer to how the singer is to return gratitude ("I will lift up the cup of salvation") becomes all the more pointed. While verse 15 has given scholars much consternation on its own ("Precious in the sight of the LORD is the death of his faithful ones"), it need not be read as some propose: as a question or a mistake in which "death" should be "faith." Rather, the psalmist knows that the pain and death of each of God's faithful people is "precious."

Second Reading (LFM)
Romans 8:31b-34

Understanding the Reading

An obvious parallel exists in the juxtaposition of this Romans text with the story of Abraham's willing obedience to God's command that he sacrifice Isaac. Just as with Abraham, Paul reminds us that God "did not withhold his own Son . . ." But much more is to be found here than a surface connection between stories of sacrifice. No angel stayed God's hand. No ram was sent. "In the words *If God is for us*," writes Karl Barth, "is summed up all that can be said concerning fulfillment, perfection, and redemption, all that can be said of the unobservable central Point."[6] The God who would not let Abraham kill Isaac is the one who becomes the Lamb *for us*.

For God to go that far—to give that much—means, inevitably, that God gives to us everything. To let go of the ultimate thing—one's own heart—means everything else is nothing in comparison. For Abraham to give up Isaac would have meant relinquishing the future.[7] For the Most High God to give up the Son means that giving even everything is far less. Because we cannot fathom this giving, we have no standing to judge or to justify anyone, including ourselves. We are left with only the need for

Christ to intercede for us. In the face of what God has done in Christ Jesus, we have no powers at all. That is the "unobservable central Point"—all power is God's because we owe to God all that we have and are.

If God is for us, no one can oppose us. Why? Because no power strong enough exists in heaven and earth. These texts of Abraham and Romans go hand in glove to help us contemplate the impending crucifixion. In order to approach that insight, the lectionary sets before us the sheer power of Abraham's incredible obedience, the wholly otherness of God "who did not withhold his own Son," and the transfiguration.

Gospel
Mark 9:2-10 (LFM)
Mark 9:2-9 (RCL alt.)

Understanding the Reading

That the transfiguration event is read on this day establishes the context for the death of Jesus. We receive from the Abraham story a terrifying vision of God, and when Jesus is transfigured (or transformed—the same word in Greek) on the mountain, the disciples are terrified. The vision of Jesus in light is classically beautiful and yet it strikes fear. The turn in Abraham's expectation similarly strikes fear because the potential for a less joyous ending hangs in the wings. In each case, however, the terror dissipates in the mercy rendered. On the mountain, the image of great light, the presence of Elijah and Moses with Jesus, the tangibility of it such that Peter wants to fix the moment, and the voice naming the Beloved all vanish and resolve into conversation between friends as they hike back down to the valley. It is a stunning epiphany that is the more awesome for its otherworldly character.

The story tells us that Peter, James, and John were allowed the privilege of this epiphany ahead of the resurrection and before it was revealed to others. But we cannot be sure what the story claims they knew other than that they were given a new puzzle: the meaning of rising from the dead. They couldn't comprehend it, and neither can we who are heirs of the story. By omitting verse 10, the RCL alternative reading leaves the text on a positive rather than a negative note.

Preaching the Gospel

Miracles abound in these texts. The ram appears, giving Isaac his life and Abraham and Sarah their future. Jesus' sudden transfiguration dazzles the disciples and then normalcy returns but with the mysterious requirement that the story not be told to anyone. From where did the ram appear? What shall we see in the fact that all three Synoptic Gospel writers include the transfiguration story, and yet the story says that no one spoke of it? The Second Sunday in Lent shows us (1) an all-powerful God who is utterly demanding and utterly merciful, and (2) an all-powerful God whose brilliance is inexplicable, who transcends the possibilities of normal physical reality, and who walks with us in friendship.

The preacher's task is to help the assembly grasp one more aspect of God's identity, building on the imagery from the First Sunday in Lent of the Holy Spirit's presence and guidance through baptismal promises and covenant to remember. It might be fruitful to consider the sermons in these weeks in the same terms as used in the early church when the catechumens were taught the meaning of the sacraments after baptism had taken place. These sermons might be similarly mystagogical explorations of the stories of Lent and the imagery that moves us always closer toward answering who we worship, finally, as the crucified and risen Lord.

Notes

1. Michael D. Williams, "Adam and Merit," in *Presbyterion* 35, no. 2 (Fall 2009): 88; see also Ralph W. Klein, "Call, Covenant, and Community: The Story of Abraham and Sarah," in *Currents in Theology and Mission* 15, no. 1 (Fall 1988): 120–27.
2. Walter Brueggemann, "Genesis 17:1-22," in *Interpretation* 45, no. 1 (January 1991): 56.
3. Karl Barth, *The Epistle to the Romans* (New York: Oxford University Press, 1933), 135.
4. Hans-Joachim Kraus, *Psalms 60–150: A Commentary*, trans. Hilton C. Oswald (Minneapolis: Augsburg, 1989), 385.
5. Michael L. Barré, "Psalm 116: Its Structure and Its Enigmas," in *Journal of Biblical Literature* 109, no. 1 (1990): 78.
6. Barth, *The Epistle to the Romans*, 326–27.
7. "Abraham and Sarah stand as remarkable existential figures for us in that God asks them to forsake both familiarity and expectation. God previously commanded that Abraham cut himself off from his past. Now God is commanding Abraham to cut himself off from his whole future." Professor Robert Bornemann, lecture in Philadelphia, Nov. 22, 1991.

March 11, 2012
Third Sunday in Lent

Revised Common Lectionary (RCL)
Exodus 20:1-17
Psalm 19
1 Corinthians 1:18-25
John 2:13-22

Lectionary for Mass (LFM)
Exodus 20:1-17 or 20:1-3, 7-8, 12-17
Psalm 19:8, 9, 10, 11
1 Corinthians 1:22-25
John 2:13-25

First Reading
Exodus 20:1-17 (RCL)
Exodus 20:1-17 or 20:1-3, 7-8, 12-17 (LFM)

Understanding the Readings

The lectionaries from both RCL and LFM essentially contain God's directives
for our lives. The RCL text allots more than 75 percent of its attention to the first
three commandments (in the Roman Catholic and Lutheran numbering), which
specifically concern human-divine relations. The last seven commandments, dealing
with relationships between human beings, are simply listed without explanation
or redundant emphases. The relatively greater weight given to the first three
commandments stresses that our primary relationship must be with God because God
(1) has delivered us from bondage, (2) deserves our honor, and (3) has given us all of
creation and the blessing of a day of rest. The LFM text of the commandments leaves
out language that gives detail to the commands about idol worship and Sabbath rest.

The RCL text delineates the shape of the human-divine relationship in several
ways. In the First Commandment, we are told who God is by "name" and by action ("I
am the Lord . . . who brought you out of . . . Egypt"). The commandment tells what
it means to "have no other gods" by naming the forms of idols that we might create,
how we might—but are not to—relate to those idols, what God will do if we disobey,
and what God does to those who do obey, giving steadfast love. This is lost in the
abbreviated LFM version.

The Second Commandment offers no clarification other than that God gives no reprieve to those who wrongfully use God's name. The punishment for failing the commandment is not described.

The Third Commandment, on honoring the Sabbath, requires everyone and every animal in the household to rest. Even the reason for Sabbath rest is provided, a departure from previous commands that gave consequences but not background or underlying rationale. God's pattern of work and rest is to serve as a template for the work and rest of all creation. This insistence emphasizes that time itself—and how we use it—influences our relationship with God and with our neighbors. "People are not to live as if all time were their own, to do with as they please," notes Terence Fretheim.[1] We are to order our hours, days, and weeks in a manner that exemplifies God's own balance of work and Sabbath rest.

This emphasis on giving honor to God because of the blessings we have already received is enlarged and underscored in the Gospel reading from John and in the epistle for this day.

Psalmody
Psalm 19 (RCL)
Psalm 19:8, 9, 10, 11 (LFM)

Understanding and Using the Psalm

Consider what words might be sung in response to the giving of the Ten Commandments. What would be their gist? What would be the goal of the hymn? Surely verses from the center of Psalm 19 would be major contestants for this honor, and most assuredly that is the reason verses 8-11 were chosen for the LFM psalm text on this day: "the precepts of the LORD are right . . . the ordinances of the LORD are true . . . More to be desired are they than gold . . . in keeping them there is great reward." To sing this after hearing the reading from Exodus is to proclaim the goodness of the law, to welcome and give thanks for the precepts that rejoice the heart and enlighten.

Some scholars have argued that Psalm 19 has two parts: verses 1-6 and verses 7-14. Part A (vv. 1-6) is praise for YHWH, the giver of Torah; part B (vv. 7-14), praise for the law. Parts A and B together give praise first for the portions of the creation that speak of God's glory even without words. And then, as if adding to the marvel that is creation, the praise continues for the Lord's own words in the law. The LFM choice to focus the song on this central and ending portion of the psalm can be understood as functioning like the Christian liturgy's "Alleluia" sung as a praise-filled greeting to the Gospel reading ("Lord, to whom shall we go? You have the words of eternal life . . .").

The psalm ends with a petition that the one who sings this praise be kept from violating the honor due the law with the final prayer familiar to many who preach: "Let the words of my mouth and the meditation of my heart be acceptable to you, O LORD, my rock and my redeemer." It is not a prayer in the plural voice but a singular speaker. It is, in other words, a prayer for the preacher alone to send forth rather than a liturgical piece that can be affixed to the beginning of a sermon. The congregation, as one liturgical scholar has put it, does not need to "listen in" on the preacher's plea to God. It would be more appropriate to simply begin with the sermon rather than with the preacher's private prayer said aloud.

Second Reading
I Corinthians 1:18-25 (RCL)
I Corinthians 1:22-25 (LFM)

Understanding the Reading

Paul's words, "the message about the cross is foolishness to those who are perishing, but to us who are being saved it is the power of God," are surely so familiar that the idea of a foolish cross may not startle us. This is an unfortunate outcome of biblical literacy, perhaps, because nothing could be more central to our faith than this Pauline contrast between God's wisdom and our supposed wisdom or the idea of God's foolishness as power. We might make sense of this passage by thinking of the absence of wisdom in the values of our age and our people—Western, developed-world values that measure worth in financial terms and consider power to be held by those who direct more lives more completely than others. In other words, bigger is better and more is nothing but good. Obviously, then, the power of power stands in marked contrast with Jesus' cross.

But this comparison is too facile. It is not just that Jesus' cross flies in the face of the most egregious power and wisdom human beings can muster. Jesus' cross stands as a challenge to all human constructs that believe they bear power and wisdom. Only those who are "perishing," writes Paul, believe in and seek out what is held by human convention to be wisdom and power, paraphrasing Isaiah 29:14: "The wisdom of their wise shall perish, and the discernment of the discerning shall be hidden." Said another way, those who are still in the process of dying don't yet grasp the true nature of wisdom. Those who have already died—that is, the baptized—see more deeply into the meaning of wisdom and power and understand that the world's conventions miss the mark. In Isaiah, the matter is the Lord's disdain for people who talk a lot but do not honor the Lord. Their hearts are not focused in the right place; their worship is hollow. God promises to do "shocking and amazing" things so that the lack of wisdom among those believed to be wise will be unmasked. The people who are thought to have the gift of discernment will be similarly exposed.

So it is with the Corinthians. Paul complains that the "Jews demand signs and Greeks desire wisdom," and both compulsions fail to alight on what is important about Christ Jesus. To receive a sign is to be given a proof that the conclusion you have tended toward is, after all, correct. It is an objective measure. To desire wisdom is to retain distance from what is being sought, to "know" something in a way that makes it a possession, a thing like a prize conferring distinction. The cross is not a thing to possess or a proof to reassure but a relationship that is a vibrant, reassuring, challenging, demanding, merciful, and living home. The cross, as a stumbling block, defies all human reason. Our human leaders do not establish power by giving up, nor do they demonstrate wisdom through silence and enduring pain. This makes no sense to us. But to those who already know the poverty of human values that have not been transformed by the cross, God's power is fully displayed in the crucifixion.

The LFM text cuts to the conclusion of Paul's concern as a pericope comprised of only verses 22-25. By eliminating verses 18-21, the reference to Isaiah is omitted, as well as the familiarity of verse 18, but it could be argued that verses 20-21 carry redundancies and rhetorical excesses. Most importantly, both RCL and LFM retain the central tenet of this text: we look for signs and lean on our own wisdom to guide us, and God answers with the foolishness and weakness of Jesus' cross rather than with what we expect and even want. The church's task is to proclaim God's inversion of our understanding of wisdom and foolishness.

Gospel
John 2:13-22 (RCL)
John 2:13-25 (LFM)

Understanding the Reading

The church hears this story only on this day in the three-year lectionary cycle. Why do we hear of Jesus clearing out the money-changers on the Third Sunday in Lent?

People who have devised rules for use of the Temple and people who acquiesce to those rules have come to the point where Jesus finds they have desecrated the Temple (e.g., the transaction wherein you buy the dove, you get the expected absolution). What exact violation has so enraged Jesus remains unclear. That Jesus drives out the animals has caused some scholars to say he objected to the sheer presence of animals in the Temple. Jesus also disrupts the coin dealers, perhaps due to his objection to the money-changers' excessive profiting from the poor. The exchange of money was to make available coins that were acceptable for temple barter because they did not bear pagan imprints. Whatever the cause, the story points to Jesus' primary anger at the money-changers, for it is their business he overturns. He does not chastise the poor who are doing their Temple obeisance.

Were we to scrutinize verse 16, we might be drawn to critique the churches in our own time that engage in doing business on church property. "Stop making my Father's house a marketplace!" might mean all manner of money-related enterprises. Such self-critique might also cause us to see Jesus commanding us to stop making our churches marketplaces for our own desires, for political agendas, for competitions that stroke the pride of religious leaders, for niche worship (geared toward a segment of the population rather than being intended for all people), and for setting up controversies that create division rather than unity between people. As the subverter of our desires, Jesus sternly—even violently(!)—asserts that the purpose of gathering in God's name is not about us. It is not about the rules we have created; it is about the power of God ("in three days I will raise it up"). Excessive attention to what is not central subverts the primary relationship between God and God's people. Jesus is a stumbling block for the Temple even as he becomes the temple and infuses the Temple with his presence.

Regarding the meaning of Jesus' claim to raise the temple in three days (the only reference in the Gospel of John to the resurrection), interpretation is complicated by the different Hebrew words used in verse 14 (*hieron*—the whole Temple) and in verse 19 (*naos*—the sanctuary of the Temple). Raymond Brown names four possible conclusions, noting that "the temple" could mean the church (Eph. 2:19-21; 1 Pet. 2:5, 4:17), the individual (1 Cor. 3:16, 6:19), heaven (Rev. 11:19; Heb. 9:11-12), or some combination of these.[2] Another interpretation might focus on the Temple as the location of God's presence. In first-century Jerusalem, worshipers found their way to the Temple proper. Scripture tells us that Jesus promised to be present in the waters of baptism, the bread and wine, among the least, and wherever two or three are gathered in his name. Regarding this last, the temple of Jesus' presence resides in the midst of the body of Christ, the *ecclesia*, the church (Eph. 1:23; Col. 1:18). The Gospel of John editorializes that Jesus' talk of raising the "temple" meant, metaphorically, "the temple of his body" (v. 21). We can probe and stretch this text to take in the many ways Jesus' body as temple and as presence is manifest for the baptized today. The temple as Jesus' body, for example, is present even on the altar table and ingested in the meal. Surely such an image is poignant for the assembly as Holy Week comes ever closer.

Preaching the Gospel

One way to find the crux of the readings for any Sunday is to ask in each text what the core human problem is to which God's response serves as the answer.

	HUMAN ACTION/ PROBLEM	GOD'S ACTION/ RESPONSE
Exod. 20:1-7	We need to attend to our relationship with God as primary; the Commandments—impossible to keep—address this need by showing us what we must do	God gives us steadfast love
John 2:13-22	We desecrate the holy temple	Jesus clears away the desecration
1 Cor. 1:18-25	We lean on our own wisdom	Jesus' cross of foolishness and weakness is the true wisdom

You will notice in the chart that the *human problem* states what we humans do and God's *response* states God's actions. This may seem simple, but it can be tricky. If we do not think in terms of who is doing the action (whatever the action is), we can be caught up in determining the value of the action before we determine the actor. For example, having the Commandments to follow is a good thing and it is good when we obey God's commands. So we may think of the gift of the Commandments as God's response to our situation. Examining the texts, however, solely to see who is acting shows us that the Commandments put the onus on us to maintain the relationship God desires to have with us. When we are honest, we readily recognize that the Commandments are impossible to fulfill. (I cannot refrain from making other gods in my life. No matter what I do, it is possible to say that something I have done on the Sabbath fails to honor that day.) What is God's answer? Steadfast love. Undergirding all our failings is the unending power of the Creator, Redeemer, and Sustainer without whom our efforts would end in dejection and pain.

Where do we see this love in the Exodus text? God spoke, therefore we human beings are important in God's eyes. God attends to us! And then God says, "I am the Lord your God, who brought you out of the land of Egypt . . ." God has liberated our ancestors and denied power to slaveholders. This has huge ramifications for God's intention toward all kinds of oppressive structures. God does not allow creation to denigrate creation. "I the Lord your God am a jealous God . . ." So jealous is God that anyone who does not obey (in this case, anyone who has other gods) will be punished for generations. Disobedience is regarded as hatred toward God, and that is not tolerated. (In Exodus 34:14 God's very name is said to be "Jealous," underscoring the serious nature of obedience.) God shows "steadfast love" to the obedient.

One manifestation of that steadfast love is that God gives to all people a seventh day of rest from labor. Much fine thinking has been directed toward the meaning of Sabbath (among others, Abraham Joshua Heschel and Eugene Peterson come to mind)[3] and especially that the day affords reprieve from being identified as mere drones to accomplishment. We are required to set aside time for ourselves. (Notice the metaphor that time is a commodity to be hoarded and brought out for something special!) We are not allowed to forget who and whose we are. We are to use that time (another metaphor: time as a tool!) for just being in the moment, being in the presence of the Holy God who created us, being in the mind-set of "wasting" time and letting ourselves float free from the distractions and preoccupations of the workplace. Sabbath is essential to the whole enterprise of realizing who we are as God's creatures.

God's action is to give us Sabbath and require us to enjoy it. God makes allowance for no work during one-seventh of our lives! One year out of every seven! Most of us cannot manage either to believe in or to structure into our lives that kind of leisure. If we are prudent and serious about our faith, however, we take it, at least, in smaller bits: one day a week. What this means in actual fact is open to discussion, of course, and this third Sunday in Lent is the right time to explore that issue even in the sermon. Do we eschew answering e-mails and texts on the Sabbath? Do we call sporting events leisure instead of work? Do we cook or clean or finish that one last project? How much do we discipline (or relieve!) ourselves of work in order to distance ourselves from the commodifying aspects of our lives?

With regard to the meanings resident in the epistle reading, we recognize the human problem as our desire to believe that we know power and wisdom. God has a reversal in store for us, however, because our notions do not bear fruit. Exercising and wisdom is to be in relationship with the one who died and rose and not in clinging to more shallow understandings. Likewise, in John's Gospel, we see the one who is about to become our wisdom, filled with zeal, speaking in metaphors, misunderstood, and unyielding in his sense of what is and is not honor toward the Father. By asking of this text why we hear of Jesus clearing out the money-changers on the third Sunday in Lent, we then look for and find the core trouble to which God's answer serves to help us endure despite our failings.

In summary, by finding the human problem and God's response, we locate the sermon's thesis, finding that because we want signs and think our own wisdom is capable of knowing God, we desecrate the Lord's dwelling in our midst. God requires that we place God's way first. But this, too, is a problem because we are incapable of keeping the Commandments. God responds on the cross and through the resurrection by revealing all the foolishness that is our so-called wisdom. The sermon could spend some time on the Commandments individually but might to greater benefit unpack the overarching message of the vital human-divine relationship.

Notes

1. Terence E. Fretheim, *Exodus*, Interpretation: A Commentary for Teaching and Preaching (Louisville: John Knox Press, 1991), 229.
2. Raymond E. Brown, *The Gospel According to John I–XII* (New York: Doubleday, 1966), 124.
3. Abraham Joshua Heschel, *Sabbath: Its Meaning for Modern Man* (New York: Farrar, Straus and Giroux, 1951); Eugene H. Peterson, *Under the Unpredictable Plant: An Exploration in Vocational Holiness* (Grand Rapids: Eerdmans, 1994).

March 18, 2012
Fourth Sunday in Lent

First Reading
Numbers 21:4-9 (RCL)

Understanding the Reading

God's actions in this text may be shocking because the story shows both God's mercy and wrath. God has liberated the Israelites from slavery to the Egyptians where they labored, suffered, starved, and watched their people die, and yet the fact that freedom brings new dangers, discomforts, and uncertainties—even death—causes them to forget the pain of their previous life. Throughout the wilderness journey, the people have complained. In Numbers 11:1, 4-6, the complaint engenders God's anger in a form that burns portions of their encampment. The people cry to Moses, he prays, and the fire stops. Later, in Numbers 14:1-4, when the people commence to pick a new leader to lead them back to Egypt, the Lord is ready to cut them down. Through Moses' intervention, the Lord alters the planned decimation and promises that a few righteous persons and the children will enter into the promised land. The people repent, and yet they immediately disobey Moses by traveling into the hill country against his instructions and are killed by the enemies of Israel. In 16:1-33 a power struggle among the priests results in an earthquake that splits the earth open beneath the people. Many are dropped into the earth, it clamps shut on them, and Moses's power is vindicated. Despite witnessing even so great a horror as this, the people do not repent. Instead, they shriek in fear. Once again, in 20:2-8, the people complain about being brought out of Egypt only to die in the wilderness for lack of water. Over and over, the people repeat their cries of frustration. The punishments seem not to have an effect on turning them toward gratitude for their freedom from Egypt. Hearing their cries of thirst, the Lord instructs Moses to strike the rock and water comes forth. It is significant that in all of these instances, the people complain only to their earthly leaders.

Today's reading is the one time the people complain directly to God. Although it is not stated overtly, the order of events in the narrative suggests that God sends the deadly serpents because the people grumble against the Lord. This would be in keeping with past stories in which God sends retribution. Here again, the people complain, and the retribution comes in the form of snakes. That the serpents are poisonous can be taken as an image of God's wrath, for the snakes are seraphim, meaning fiery. God's anger burns as fire against the people. For the second time in their trek, the people realize their fault and repent of it. The healing can begin.

God's final act in this pericope is forgiveness in the form of a healing totem. The cause of death is lifted up on a pole—an analog to Jesus being lifted up on the pole of the cross. The pole erected by Moses at God's request is not, allegorically, the cross of Jesus' crucifixion, but the story suggests typological resonance and serves to set up the image of the ultimate goal of Lent: to prepare us for the deep healing that comes through the death of God's Beloved. Those who look to the cross are healed just as those who suffered the serpents' fire in the wilderness were healed by looking at what would otherwise have killed them.

In summary, God (1) liberates the people, (2) causes them to suffer, (3) forgives them, and (4) heals them. This is the pattern of the action of the word of God in our time: (1) God's mercy and grace (2) cause us to realize our need, which (3) helps us to know our utter dependence on God through whom, then, (4) we are healed. Most intriguing is the conjunction of the source of death with the source of healing, inviting the preacher to ponder how Jesus' cross is, likewise, the source of our death and our healing. Since baptism is our death and rebirth, we can see in the cross the face of both our suffering (guilt) and salvation (resurrection).

2 Chronicles 36:14-16, 19-23 (LFM)

Understanding the Reading

This last chapter of 2 Chronicles describes the fall of Jerusalem based on, and abridged from, what is recorded in 2 Kings 23–25. The destruction of Jerusalem is pivotal and horrible for the Israelites, and it inaugurates the seventy years of exile in Babylon. The story tells that the Lord had made repeated overtures to the people to enlist their allegiance (v. 15), but the messengers were met only with mockery (v. 16). The destruction, then, resulted from the people's disobedience.

Without the inclusion of verses 17-18, however, the assembly will not know that the Lord turned to the enemies of Israel, the Chaldeans, to punish the people's disobedience. The missing verses tell that the Chaldeans slaughtered young and old and confiscated the temple treasury, carrying it off to Babylon (an event that occurred 597–581 B.C.E.). Knowing the identity of the enemy invader is necessary to make sense of verse 19, which tells only that "they burned the house of God . . ." Absent verses 17-18, the assembly will not know who "they" are or in verse 20 who "he" is (King Nebuchadnezzar II, ruler of Babylon 605–562 B.C.E.).

Woe to those who "scoff at [the Lord's] prophets," for verse 21 says that the enormous devastation was to fulfill what the prophet Jeremiah had been told, and that the people had not given heed. The word of the Lord to Jeremiah suggests the people will remain in exile (the land will lie in waste) a long time—seventy years. This is a length of time that matches and mirrors the time during which the people had disregarded the Sabbath, turned away from the Lord. Thus, one way for the people to imagine the long suffering they have to endure is to see it as punishment meted out in like measure to their failings.

The final two verses promise deliverance and here is where we find the last of God's action in this text. The first actions were to send messengers (out of love) and then to send the Chaldeans (out of anger). At last, the Lord inspires Cyrus, king of Persia, to let the Israelites return to Jerusalem where the king has been charged by God to rebuild the Temple. Who is King Cyrus? His capital was in today's southern Iran and, at the height of his power, he may have ruled as far as Syria, Lebanon, and Israel. He reigned in Babylon from 539–530 B.C.E. Both biblical and extrabiblical records account him a tolerant and peaceable ruler. He gave hope to the exiled, but we must note that the Lord is responsible for the great heart of Cyrus's benevolence.

Psalmody
Psalm 107:1-3, 17-22 (RCL)

Understanding and Using the Psalm

As a response to the first reading, this psalm appropriately tells the story of rebellion, punishment, repentance, and healing. "Then in their trouble they cried to the Lord and you delivered them from their distress" (v. 19, ELW) appears four times in the psalm. This verse is, in fact, the antiphon for Psalm 107, emphasizing the stress on turning to God and the liberation that follows. Whether or not meter plays a role in determining antiphon, it may be significant that the meter of verse 19 differs from the primary meter of the psalm as a whole. If content is a determinative factor, the concern of verse 19 succinctly tells the people's story of failure and redemption. Also occurring four times in the 43 verses is the language of verse 21. In the psalm verses given in NAB for this day, verse 21 is sung once, but it also perfectly expresses a conclusion to the Numbers 21 story: "Let them give thanks to you, Lord, for your steadfast love and your wonderful works for all people."

On the whole, this psalm is a liturgy of thanksgiving for deliverance from an enemy. The psalm could be singing of liberation from Egypt or from serpents in the wilderness. It is expansive in its imagery for why God is due the peoples' gratitude.

Psalm 137:1-2, 3, 4-5, 6 (LFM)

Understanding and Using the Psalm

Psalm 137 is the cry of a people exiled to a strange land, sitting by the riverbanks, remembering home and weeping. There can be no singing with such mourning. The musical instruments are silenced. The psalmist promises to honor Jerusalem above all things that give joy. The intensity of this feeling, a ferocious longing, is enhanced by the final thought in verse 9—omitted here and as a matter of course when this psalm is used liturgically—because it speaks of the happiness of dashing the enemy's little ones against the rocks. Assemblies are given reprieve from having to voice such horrifying thoughts, but the psalmist is not afraid of them. It is good to know what is in this psalm as a whole in order to share in the psalmist's convictions about home. This is, after all, a psalmist who prays: "If I forget you, O Jerusalem, let my right hand wither" (v. 5). Given the graphic nature of the vengeful desire voiced in this psalm, the curse on the psalmist's own hand is no idle wish.

The psalm may be sung by the assembly in alternating verses, in unison, antiphonally, or it could be sung by the choir. It may be sung as it appears in the psalter or in one of the many versions that have been written over the years. Two of them are set to the haunting Latvian folk tune, "Kaz dziedaja."[1]

Second Reading
Ephesians 2:1-10 (RCL)
Ephesians 2:4-10 (LFM)

Understanding the Reading

Ephesians is not necessarily a letter sent to the church in Ephesus.[2] The letter does not address particular struggles as in letters known to have been addressed to specific communities. The audience for this epistle is wide and ranges over the centuries. The author's purpose is to describe the church and its relationship with Christ, and as such, its concerns are as relevant to the issues facing the church today as when the letter was written.

The pericope for this Sunday attends to the themes of the Gospel and Old Testament readings by focusing on the result of the Son of Man having been lifted up as a mode of healing for the people. In short, we were dead and have been brought to life by the grace of God. Our nature is to follow "the ruler of the power of the air." (What an intriguing image! Is the power of air vapid?! Is it destructive because it is pervasive or because it has no real heft?) We are given over to the power that is antithetical to God's purposes and for that reason, we are "children of wrath." The serpents of disobedience have sent into us fiery desires, and we end up at war with each other and with ourselves, entangled in anger, competition, scraping. It defeats us, kills us, locks our sights on paltry goals set in the short term.

From this dead life, "God, who is rich in mercy . . . , made us alive together with Christ . . ." This defines the church: God has acted toward us as God has acted in Christ by raising us up with Christ to be seated beside him in heaven. The church, then, is not simply a body of persons who do good in the world. We are "created in Christ Jesus for good works . . . ," but the first actor is God, who, through grace, has made a way for us not to be ruled by the "power of the air." Instead, the church is a heavenly institution. It is not a club organized to maintain itself. It exists so that through the church God's enormous kindness might be visible. This is esoteric, to be sure, but it is not vague.

As a whole (vv. 1-10 in RCL), this pericope includes both the human situation of sin and captivity and God's gracious response. The LFM text (vv. 4-10) offers only God's graciousness for the assembly to ponder, leaving off the full context for God's actions.

Gospel
John 3:14-21 (RCL, LFM)

Understanding the Reading

The Gospel reading immediately connects with the Old Testament text, likening the serpent lifted up on the pole to the "Son of Man" lifted up. The words are Jesus' speaking to Nicodemus, the religious leader who had come to him in the darkness of night. Nicodemus seeks Jesus out to say he sees what Jesus is doing. I want to say Nicodemus approaches Jesus to ask him something, but the question doesn't come to Nicodemus until Jesus tells him about being "born from above," making this an achingly real encounter. Have you and I not met someone from whom we simply wanted *more* and didn't quite know how to get it or request it? You hang around, if you can. You hope something *more* will happen. That greater knowledge comes to Nicodemus as soon as Jesus begins to speak of the mystery of second birth. It is the invitation for Nicodemus to reveal his desire to understand, and it gives Jesus the opportunity (or so the Gospel writer has set it up) to hold forth on the conjunction of the serpent and the Son of Man, the vast difference between them.

Jesus' words remind us that the serpents came to kill the people, whereas the Son came to save, not to condemn. But the difference not only does not obliterate the link, it suggests a deeper connection than is ever stated outright. The cross of Jesus' crucifixion is the source of our salvation but, even more than that, it is so because it is the very image of the truth about ourselves. When we meditate on the cross, gaze upon it, sit at its feet, ponder its reality, we are looking at the result of human contempt for God's gifts. "For God so loved the world that he gave his only Son . . ." and we did not understand—*do* not understand—but instead despise him. "Crucify him!" the people shouted. Jesus' face resides in the faces of "the least of these" in all parts of the earth today, and we do not understand their difficulties, do not care for them, instead despise them by failing to structure our lives and the gifts of the earth in a way that eases their struggles and gives life instead of death. This is the same as shouting, "Crucify him!"

When we look at the face of Jesus in the least among us, we are looking at the cross, seeing the truth of our actions, acknowledging the reality of our sin, and beginning the path toward amending our ways. We are, in effect, looking at what heals. The healing is not our doing; the healing comes because Jesus' face on the cross has been imparted to all who are in need. We are healed by God's gift, placing into our path daily, hourly, the opportunity to face the truth. "The light has come into the world . . ." But we love darkness. Mostly, we look away. The light of truth that hangs on Jesus' cross exposes our situation. The people in the wilderness, however, did not look away. Their healing radiated from the serpent on the pole. This Sunday's text means to turn our sight to the cross in such a way that we can see our own healing lifted up on it.

Preaching the Gospel

Common themes run through all of the preaching texts for this day. Numbers and 2 Chronicles both describe the result of people having turned away from God, the suffering that ensues, and the respite granted them through God's compassion. The Gospel reading encapsulates the opposition between death and life as it is depicted in Jesus' crucifixion where healing comes from what reveals the deepest pain. The epistle turns attention to the church where the healing Christ is resident *in* the body of Christ, the church, as it gathers in the name of the crucified and risen Son.

This day's preaching texts all point to the death that comes from looking at the truth (the fire of God's wrath) and seeing there—in the cause of God's anger—what cries out for our repentance. The darkness of continued attachment to what does not give life is familiar and comfortable. Liberation brings danger and reveals the truth about ourselves. Healing comes through exposure to the truth about what can only imprison and kill us. Out of mercy, God sends the light that heals, that makes darkness vanish, that illumines what must be seen.

Again, the images today are rich with palpable impressions, one of which is surely the image in the Old Testament readings (both RCL and LFM) that God designs retribution and sends pain and suffering upon the people. A helpful essay by Walter Brueggemann on God's relationship with King Nebuchadnezzar II (the destroyer of Jerusalem) sheds light on how believers understand God's actions.[3] It is disquieting for us to contemplate God's alliance with superpowers unless the alliance is with our own country. Brueggemann notes that the biblical record shows us God's "provisional" alliances. Turning this idea to the 2 Chronicles text, we see that in the story of God's use of the Chaldeans to destroy Jerusalem, God's next alliance is with good King Cyrus, the Persian. God does not carve out an indelible bond with any of the warring powers; only with the little band of Israelites does God continuously extend unending care and steadfastness. For them, the alliance with God is not provisional. For them, God's steadfastness does not waver. Even when the relationship requires severe recrimination on God's part, the goal is always liberation and justice for the people. For that reason, the preacher need not dwell on theodicy issues that may come to reign in people's minds hearing today's texts. Instead, the attention should hold to God's acts of endless compassion.

Notes

1. Ewald Bash, "By the Babylonian Rivers," in *With One Voice* (Minneapolis: Augsburg Fortress, 1995), #656; Susan Briehl, "Once We Sang and Danced," in *Evangelical Lutheran Worship* (Minneapolis: Augsburg Fortress, 2006), #701. A Jamaican tune, arranged by Bread for the Journey, "By the Waters of Babylon," is found in *This Far by Faith* (Minneapolis: Augsburg Fortress, 1999), #67.
2. Ralph P. Martin, *Ephesians, Colossians, and Philemon*, Interpretation: A Commentary for Teaching and Preaching (Atlanta: John Knox, 1991), 3.
3. Walter Brueggemann, "The Non-Negotiable Price of Sanity," in *Journal for Preachers* 28, no. 1 (Advent 2004): 28–36.

March 25, 2012
Fifth Sunday in Lent

First Reading
Jeremiah 31:31-34 (RCL, LFM)

Understanding the Readings

The prophet Jeremiah lived at a time of intense warring and devastating power struggles in the lands of the Middle East during the seventh century B.C.E. He grew up in the home of the priest, Hilkiah, who lived two miles outside Jerusalem. To be outside Jerusalem was, in fact, to be an outsider, and so we can think of Jeremiah's early, formative perspective as that of someone looking in from elsewhere.

The word of the Lord came to him in his adulthood, and he preached or prophesied what he heard. The word of the Lord was directed at Jerusalem and Judah and foreign nations with both love for the people and anger at their disobedience. God appointed Jeremiah "over nations and over kingdoms, to pluck up and to pull down, to destroy and to overthrow, to build and to plant" (Jer. 1:10). The oppositions in his call are of supreme importance because they describe Jeremiah's task as, first, to condemn and, then, to create anew. Of Jeremiah's fulsome awareness of political reality in his time, R. E. Clements writes that the prophet did not speak words of vapid comfort to the people but knew that "hope took full and serious account of the measure of Israel's sins."[1] Crucial to Jeremiah's prophecy was the double edge of judgment, on the one hand, for wickedness, and, on the other hand, forgiveness like that of a lover to the beloved, a husband, in fact, to his wife. Chapters 30–33 are separated from the rest of Jeremiah as a compendium of hope-filled visions of Israel's restoration.

So it is that what we hear on this fifth Sunday of Lent is a concluding statement of what God has come to know about the people with whom God has made a new covenant. It is as if God sees the futility of teaching them and begging them. It hasn't worked for the people to hear the prophet say, "Know the Lord," for they don't do it. They don't live in a way that demonstrates that knowledge. Instead, God sees that the law must be an implant: "I will put my law within them, and I will write it on their hearts . . ." (v. 33). What is written on the heart lies so intimately close to the source of life that it cannot be ignored. It is not an objective word that comes from outside and maintains a distance by requiring a conscious, rote memory. Instead, the word is subject to the living body in whom it dwells. The word of God's law is as central as a beating heart. It is the very stuff of daily life. The old covenant required a new covenant, a new way of being in relationship, another gift from God to a people who have been so incapable.

That this covenant with Israel is a wholly new beginning is evident in the last line: "I will forgive . . . and remember their sin no more" (v. 34). The slate is wiped clean. The people have not earned this allegiance from God, but they receive it anyway. The image of intense connection between God's desire for the people and who they actually are is unmistakable. "I will be their God, and they shall be my people" (v. 33). The text has already imaged the relationship of marriage, and here it is cemented.

Psalmody
Psalm 51:1-12 (RCL)
Psalm 51:3-4, 12-13, 14-15 (LFM)

Understanding and Using the Psalm

The pith of Psalm 51 is in the verses contained in both the RCL and LFM pericopes, the famous prayer: "Create in me a clean heart, O God . . ." It is, essentially, a confession of sin, and a plea for forgiveness and help. By adding verse 15 in the NAB (v. 13 in the NRSV and ELW versions), the LFM includes a promise that, upon restoration, the psalmist will teach other sinners the ways of the Lord.

Some scholars have noted that the psalmist's plea, "Renew a right spirit within me," (NRSV/ELW vv. 10-12; NAB vv. 12-14) resonates with the Lord saying in Jeremiah 31:33, "I will put my law within them, and I will write it on their hearts." Certainly, a consonance exists between these texts. After all, that is the reason these psalms are set as responses to the first reading. The assembly is invited to sing with the psalmist a prayer that, in this case, echoes the situation of the people in answer to which the prophet's proclamation of the Lord's new covenant has ushered in a new hope. The prophet announces that the Lord will forgive and remember the people's sin no more, and the people's response is to sing of the Lord's mercy.

The RCL verses not included in the LFM lection detail more clearly and in different perspectives the depth of the psalmist's awareness of guilt and need for renewal. In RCL verses 4-5, the psalmist stands in the presence of the Lord in utter depravity of sin—"Against you only have I sinned . . ." (ELW)—signaling such a thoroughly repugnant turning away from God that condemnation would be the only appropriate response. This pervasive notion of sin, however, must not be read in the Augustinian sense that links sin with sexuality or the origins of human life. Rather, the Hebrew understanding here points to the cause of sin lying so deep that its beginning cannot be found. It is primordial.[2] Yet, it is that completely faulty self who also, then, in verse 6 can sing of God's great compassion and mercy: "you delight in truth deep within me . . ." (ELW). That the Creator would want what gives light and honesty from deep within the human creature is a stunning understanding.

Psalm 119:9-16 (RCL alt.)

Understanding and Using the Psalm

This great love song to the law responds with joy and commitment to the promise of the law being written on the heart in the new covenant. Psalm 119 is the longest of the psalms and structured so that every section is named for a letter of the Hebrew alphabet. This is the bet section, the second. Each section has a clear pattern of eight lines. The entire psalm has been described as a necklace of wisdom sayings, a poem or a didactic poem, and an anthology. Overall, it is a special song to Torah.

In these verses, the psalmist speaks of God's law in such a way that it could as well be any of us in our time. "By keeping to your word" (ELW) is the psalmist's prescription for staying out of trouble, staying "clean." It is a prayer that the psalmist be restrained from departing the commandments. It acknowledges the need for instruction in God's law, the benefit of learning the commands by heart. The comparison of the Lord's decrees with other kinds of riches is typical of wisdom sayings, and it is just such lines that cause scholars to see this great poem as an anthology.[3] The image of the new covenant in Jeremiah 31 being written on the hearts of the people finds an echo here in the psalm. How fitting, then, for the assembly that just after the people hear the Jeremiah 31 passage, they respond with the words of Psalm 119:15-16: "I will meditate on your commandments . . . I will not forget your word" (ELW).

Second Reading
Hebrews 5:5-10 (RCL)
Hebrews 5:7-9 (LFM)

Understanding the Reading

The writer of Hebrews addresses the identity of Christ Jesus. The preceding verses (esp. 4:14—5:4) had set up the attributes of earthly priests who share with the great High Priest the call from God to serve. Human priests do not set themselves up in exalted offices, in order to bring gifts and sacrifices to God. The pericope itself begins with a favorable comparison between Jesus and human priests: "So also Christ did not glorify himself . . . but was appointed . . ." (v. 5). In contrast, however, with the great High Priest who is perfect, human priests are able to sympathize with sin because they are themselves beset with weakness. Christ Jesus does not share with human priests that source of sympathy. Instead, he suffered innocently.

The text has been referred to as a "hinge" in the epistle as it summarizes the proclamations that (1) Christ received divine authority from God, the Father; (2) Christ's compassionate authority derives from his own suffering; and (3) Christ's salvific authority comes from his perfection. The surrounding parts of the letter articulate these assertions. Having dealt (chaps. 1–5) with Christ's superiority to prophets, angels, and Moses prior to the hinge, following it, the letter lays out the purpose for its being written (chap. 6), compares Christ's priesthood to that of the Levites and Melchizedek (chaps. 7–10), and finally recounts the faith of the ancestors in order to inspire in the recipients of the letter renewed faith in the face of their oppression (chaps. 11–13). This sets the pericope in context.

Reading more closely, what we learn of Christ Jesus' identity in verses 5-10 is this: he did not glorify himself, he prayed and pleaded, he shouted and wept, he was reverent and submissive, he "learned obedience through what he suffered" (v. 8), and because of all this, "he became the source of eternal salvation for all who obey him . . ." (v. 9). The text describes God's actions in the voice that identifies the Beloved and then in the prayers and obedience of Jesus. There is no overt reference to the actions of humans in this text except in verse 9, in which those "who obey him" receive Christ's salvation. Thus, the human problem this pericope offers, although not overtly stated, is that human beings need to be saved. The letter's overarching concern is to make the case that the one who alone can extend salvation is Christ Jesus, the High Priest.

Over against the human deficiency in humanity's need for eternal salvation stands the enormous figure of Jesus who obeys God even as he struggles with his path and pleads to be spared death. The image is that of an emerging power that is fully revealed at the end of a long trial. It would be good for us to remember that this text is about Jesus, not about us, in spite of how often we hear admonitions (from the larger culture in various ways, to be sure, but also from the pulpit and fellow disciples) to shun self-glorification, to be submissive, and to let suffering teach us character and strength. It is good to remember that we are not Jesus, that his abilities and intentions cannot be ours, and that there is a kind of excessive self-regard that can creep into our self-assessment if we compare ourselves to God's own Son.

As we come closer to Holy Week, we rightfully bring to the forefront of worship our admiration for Jesus and what he has done for us. This is natural and it especially invites readings from an epistle like Hebrews, written to bolster a people who were teetering in faith. Mention of the voice from heaven at Jesus' baptism, "You are my Son, today I have begotten you . . . ," helps us to remember the Epiphany and to connect death with baptism. The grain of wheat falls and takes on new life, just as in baptism we are drowned and reborn.

The LFM text hones in on the humanity of Jesus in his suffering, leaving out the contextual references to "the order of Melchizedek" and, as a consequence, also omitting the relationship between the Father's voice at his baptism and his identity as the "eternal salvation for all who obey him . . ." The unmistakable suggestion in the text as it appears as verses 7-9 shows us a Jesus who is supremely human and obedient without the tension between his attributes as fully human and fully divine.

Gospel
John 12:20-33 (RCL, LFM)

Understanding the Reading

In Raymond Brown's translation, the central statement in this text, verse 25, would read roughly like this: the one who loves (*philein*) this life destroys (*apollynai*) it; the one who hates (*misein*) life in this world preserves (*philaxein*) it to live eternally. Brown calls attention to the fact that this statement has variations in the Synoptics, all of which are as different from each other as John's is from them.[4] We are accustomed to these oppositions in John's Gospel and, indeed, the statement follows right after Jesus' assertion that the wheat must die in order to bear fruit. Hating and loving life play some role in dying in order to rise.

There are problems, however, for us in this language of loving and hating. A strong point needs to be made, certainly, about the kind of hating and dying that occurs in baptism: the death of the old person and the birth of the new, the drowning and rising, a shift in the scope of a life and in its purposes for being. Once I was a child and life was all about what I needed; now I am an adult and I have the maturity to care about other's needs, as well as my own.

But the admonition to hate life and lose it can easily become prescriptively destructive because the mouths of too many preachers may paint this hating and loving with too broad a brush. Do we all love our lives too much to give them up for others? No. Some among us actually already hate our lives and ourselves because of the agony life has tossed our way. Some have already given up everything; there is nothing more to abdicate. Such persons have, as Lisa Dahill describes it, no self left to hate or love, no life to offer.[5] In such situations, to whom is Jesus speaking? Or might we need to affirm that when you have no life to lose, it is time to turn in that life and find another? Perhaps we need to say that whatever life one is living, if it is not *life giving*, it is not worth keeping.

Jesus says to us, "Unless a grain of wheat falls into the earth and dies . . ." He is describing a death that does, in fact, bring forth life. For such an outcome, however, the grain cannot fall and die just anywhere. It falls into a place where sprouting can take place, where nurture can be found, a little water, some minerals. The grain does not bear fruit without a fertile bed.

What does this mean in your context? How can you bring the dying and rising to life for the assembly on this last Sunday before the church heads into Palm Sunday (life and death together) and then Holy Week and then the Resurrection? This is a pivotal day, this fifth Sunday in Lent, and it must offer a widely available understanding of hating and losing, dying and gaining, for the images are critically important. The cross is the dying we are caused to look at because Jesus finds us in our waywardness and shows us the failings of humanity in his agony, the dying of the one who loves us more than any other.

Preaching the Gospel

The questions in the section just above are not idle. They are real questions for the preacher: What does dying-in-order-to-live look like in your congregation, in your community, in your state or geographical region, in your nation and in relationships between nations at this time in the year 2012? Who or what is already dying in your context? Where is life to be found? Where is God at work transforming deadliness into rebirth? Who are the people in your neighborhood or in the extended lives of the assembly through whom we might be able to recognize the hand of a God who has truly written the law on their hearts, fixed a promise of forgiveness, served as witness to the rising out of darkness and into the light?

Asking these questions risks inciting the preacher to come up with an inspiring list of persons and endeavors in which the work of God's mercy and renewal shines through but which end up demoralizing the hearers. The inspiration can come across as yet another law: "See how good these other people are! See how much their faithfulness and energy has accomplished!" The meaning behind such examples can sound like: "See how much you all are failing because you are not like these other people! Get with it!" In contrast with the noble work of those listed, I cannot measure up. I can only see my inabilities. And to have yet another law laid on me leaves me feeling only my iniquity and not the Lord's forgiveness.

The problem with such lists—depending on how they are fashioned—is that they hold up as exemplars people who are seen to be so heroic, so unblemished (one readily thinks of Mother Teresa) that they cannot inspire me to join their goodness. In comparison with them, I only feel my inadequacy. I can see that what they do is magnificent, but I can't envision the energy or discipline or know-how to do it myself. This is why the Bible's narratives and characters are so obviously life giving. The characters are not heroic. The narratives are about flawed people like you and me. Abraham once gave Sarah away to a warlord; Sarah laughed at the Lord's messengers; Hagar despaired; David killed a man to gain a lover; Paul killed Christians; Mary had a questionable past; Peter denied Jesus. Need we continue?

The sermon must offer up a vision, and on this day that vision needs to lift up the reality—the really alive, tangible, palpable existence—of the law "written on their hearts" so that moving on into Palm Sunday and Holy Week will be for the assembly an invitation to embrace the root love God has for God's people. This is not a time to churn on people's failings to observe Lent or to make the command to follow Jesus into an impossible chore. Rather, focus on the ways in which all these texts show us how God is at work, giving mercy, instilling knowledge of what is good and just, lifting us up, being the source of our salvation. Focus on what God is doing in the texts and then, analogously, what God is already doing in lives of the gathered people. Bring out what the people of this assembly already have done to express the law that is written in them. See the faces of the people light up with conviction and hope.

Notes

1. R. E. Clements, *Jeremiah*, Interpretation: A Commentary for Teaching and Preaching (Atlanta: John Knox, 1988), 177.
2. Hans-Joachim Kraus, *Psalms 1–59: A Commentary*, trans. Hilton C. Oswald (Minneapolis: Augsburg, 1988), 503.
3. Hans-Joachim Kraus, *Psalms 60–150: A Commentary*, trans. Hilton C. Oswald (Minneapolis: Augsburg, 1989), 415.
4. Raymond E. Brown, *The Gospel According to John I–XII* (New York: Doubleday, 1966), 473–74. I have rendered Brown's version to make it inclusive.
5. Lisa Dahill, *Reading from the Underside of Selfhood: Bonhoeffer and Spiritual Formation* (Eugene, Ore.: Wipf and Stock, 2009).

Holy Week
Gordon W. Lathrop

Holy Week lives at the center of the liturgical year. It not only functions as the calendrical goal toward which Lent has been bringing us. It also celebrates the story toward which all of the Gospel readings, throughout the whole year, have been leaning. If, as Martin Kähler already argued,[1] the Gospels themselves are something like "passion stories with extended introductions," then in Holy Week we get to the main story itself. Or if, as Austin Farrer proposed,[2] every finger of the Gospel stories points toward the resurrection, then in Holy Week we come to that to which they have been pointing. Many cultures, including that reflected in the book of Exodus, began the year in the spring: "This month shall mark for you the beginning of months; it shall be the first month of the year for you" (Exod. 12:2). Christians elaborated on that tradition, using the solemn commemoration of the death and resurrection of Jesus at one Passover time in the early first century not so much to mark the new year for us now as to mark the heart of the year, the festival around and toward which our years constantly turn and from which, according to Christian faith, our years take new life.

Of course, the Passion and the resurrection story are told every Sunday, not simply once a year. Indeed, Sunday itself—more than Easter and more than Christmas—constitutes the primary festival of Christians. The regular recurrence of the Christian meeting on the first day of every week always intends to celebrate the resurrection and bring us to encounter the Risen One. This Risen One is known in the very presence of the gathered assembly itself, the body of Christ. He is known also in the prayers of this assembly, as Matthew bears witness ("For where two or three are gathered in my name, I am there among them," Matt. 18:20). We give evidence of our trust in this presence of the Risen One as, in churches making use of the classic Western liturgy, we call out "Glory to you, O Lord" and "Praise to you, O Christ," before and after the reading of the Gospel. And yet, in the midst of this encounter with the resurrection, we also encounter at least a part of the Passion story in the regular, weekly celebration of the holy meal: "Take; this is my body . . . This is my blood of the covenant . . . poured out for many" (Mark 14:22-24). The Risen One is the Crucified One, according to Christian faith. Here in the weekly meeting, like Thomas in the Fourth Gospel (John 20:26-27), we are invited to see his wounds with the eyes of faith.

Preachers, who know this deep and ancient meaning of Sunday, work—Sunday in and Sunday out—to use the texts of the day to illuminate the meaning of the death and resurrection of Jesus for the current assembly and its current times. Indeed, without this regular unfolding of the riches of that meaning, thinking about preaching in Holy Week would be daunting, too huge a task, too much to interpret, too much to say. But, with such regular preaching, we come to Holy Week and Easter as to a beloved center, a fresh source, a renewal of the story that has called us to faith throughout the year.

Then Easter is a kind of great Sunday for the year. That assertion rings at least as true as the more common "Every Sunday is a little Easter." Indeed, regarding the year as if it were a great "week," then the fifty days of Easter are a "Sunday" to that "week." Those fifty days were spoken of by second- and third-century Christians as if that period from Easter to Pentecost were a single great day of rejoicing. In those days, at the heart of the year, at the renewed beginning of the year, the whole story of the death and resurrection of Jesus and of the outpouring of God's Spirit on us from that death and resurrection is rehearsed again in fullness.

But if the Great Fifty Days constitute Easter, then all Holy Week makes up a kind of beginning of that days-long festival. It is like the evening before the feast. Just as ancient Jewish festivals actually began with sunset on the preceding evening, so the content of the annual Christian festival of the death and resurrection of Jesus Christ begins to unfold already in Holy Week. In a sense, the whole thing—Holy Week and Easter Sunday and the Fifty Days and Pentecost—is Easter.

At the fulcrum between the "Easter eve" that is Holy Week and the "Sunday" that is the Fifty Days, stand the Three Days. Together the celebrations of these three—the evening of Maundy Thursday through Good Friday, the evening of that Friday through Saturday, and the evening or Vigil of Saturday night through Easter Sunday—constitute a single liturgy. It is this single liturgy that is especially the heart of the Christian year.

We rightly note this accent on the whole festival and its whole content. We are not gradually killing Jesus again in our observances. Jesus Christ, the Crucified, is risen. Now. He is just as risen on Palm/Passion Sunday, on Good Friday, and at the Easter Vigil, as he will be on Easter Sunday morning. What we are doing with these liturgies is parsing out the story of the crucified Risen One, telling it from different moments and in differing voices, so that its full meaning may once again encounter our year and call us to faith.

The double character of cross and resurrection fills the whole week. Passion Sunday, devoted to proclaiming the agonizing Passion according to the Synoptic Gospel of the year, is nonetheless a Sunday, the day of resurrection. On Maundy Thursday, it is the Risen One who even now washes our feet, turns us toward each other in love, and is present as "given and shed for you." On Good Friday, the one who says "I am" so that the whole cohort of soldiers and police fall down (John 18:6) and the one who grounds our confident "bidding prayers" for all the conditions of the world shows us that Jesus Christ is the *risen* Crucified One. And, at the same time, the Risen One celebrated in the words of all of the Vigil stories of salvation, is also the one who shares the suffering of the escaping slaves and the slain Egyptians, is also the ram caught in the thicket, is also the one with the three young men in the midst of the fire. Jesus Christ is the *crucified* Risen One.

This time of the year, with these remarkable, multisided texts and their remarkable, participatory liturgies, is an astonishing time. It contains the resources to speak more profoundly than we usually speak, to remind us of real evil—also within ourselves—to hold real sorrow, to remember the wretched and poor ones, to begin to wipe away tears, to image hope, to enliven joy, to turn us toward mutual love, and to bring us to trust in God again.

My deepest recommendation to you, dear pastor and preacher, as you consider planning this coming Holy Week and as you think about how the lectionary texts may once again be celebrated in your place, is that you do all you can in your congregation to recover these Three Days and their ancient, single liturgy. If you are new to these services, begin with observing them somewhere else, in a congregation known for its vigorous and healthy celebrations. But then, let the mutual, communal foot washing return to Thursday. Let the Johannine Passion, with its magisterial Christ, sound on Friday. And especially, most urgently, hold the playful, profound, astonishing Vigil. Hold it in the early evening, so the children may come and participate. Hold it in the middle of the night, if your congregation includes mostly adults. Hold it toward dawn as a deepening transformation of the sunrise service. But hold it. Or, if you already do all of these things, then work again on refreshing them. These lectionary texts that we now turn to consider will then come home. Your year will indeed have a center.

In what follows, you will note that, with exception of the special case of the Easter Vigil, the Gospel text of any set of readings comes first. This does not reflect the actual liturgical order, of course. Rather, it means to reflect how, in Christian liturgical use, also all of the other readings are heard as pointing toward the one who lives at the heart of the Gospel text. Such is "liturgical hermeneutics" or the interpretive practice of Sunday and of Easter as the "Sunday to the year." Such is the way that Christians read these ancient texts when they read them in the assembly called together in the Spirit around the risen Christ. This approach does not exhaust all that there is to say about these texts, of course, but it is the surest way toward faithful preaching. You may also note that many of the texts we now turn to consider recur every year in Holy Week, not only in Year B. Thus, in the Revised Common Lectionary, almost all of our texts are marked for Years A, B, and C. They will be familiar to you from last year. The exceptions, unique only to Year B, are these: the Processional Gospel, drawn from either John or Mark, and the Markan Passion for Passion/Palm Sunday; the Gospel from Mark 16 at the Easter Vigil; and the alternative first and second readings and alternative Gospel for Easter Day. Also in the regularity of these texts we are coming back to center.

Especially in this year, however, you will note two strong voices that speak to us: the writer of the Gospel according to Mark and the writer of the Gospel according to John, the Lion and the Eagle, to use the old images drawn from Revelation 4 and 5.

These voices are in dialogue here. Mark sounds on Passion Sunday, speaking of the suffering of the Messiah, utterly unlike what had been expected. John speaks throughout the week—and most strongly on Maundy Thursday and Good Friday—calling us to see the glorification of the "lifted-up" Son of Man. Then the voices alternate at the Vigil and on Easter Sunday morning: the hidden promise of the resurrection in Mark 16 and the encounter with Mary Magdalene in John 20. These two voices, throughout the week, are further surrounded by other texts, most especially all four of the servant songs of Isaiah, singing out from Passion Sunday through the following Wednesday.

These texts are rich indeed.

I wish you well, dear preacher—no, I wish you the very Spirit of God—as you bring us home again, to the center and source of our faith.

Notes

1. Martin Kähler, *The So-Called Historical Jesus and the Historic, Biblical Christ* (Philadelphia: Fortress Press, 1964), 80.
2. Austin Farrer, *The Glass of Vision* (Westminster, UK: Dacre, 1948), 145.

April 1, 2012
Sunday of the Passion / Palm Sunday

Revised Common Lectionary (RCL)

Liturgy of the Palms
Psalm 118:1-2, 19-29
Mark 11:1-11 or John 12:12-16
Liturgy of the Passion
Isaiah 50:4-9a
Psalm 31:9-16
Philippians 2:5-11
Mark 14:1—15:47 or 15:1-39 (40-47)

Lectionary for Mass (LFM)

Processional Gospel
Mark 1:1-11 or John 12:12-16
At the Mass
Isaiah 50:4-7
Psalm 22:8-9, 17-18, 19-20, 23-24
Philippians 2:6-11
Mark 14:1—15:47 or 15:1-39

The Sunday of the Passion, more commonly called "Palm Sunday," functions as an entryway into Holy Week. It is, of course, the last Sunday in Lent, a final Sunday marking our Lenten way toward Easter. It is also the first day of the great and holy week, the week of these remarkable liturgies and texts. And, through it all, it is a *Sunday*, a celebration of the resurrection of Jesus Christ who gathers with his community. All of these things come to expression in the lectionary texts. In Year B, the procession of palms is interpreted by the reading of either the Markan or the Johannine account of Jesus' entry into Jerusalem. In the process of this reading and this procession, the community of the local congregation enters into Holy Week and into its recounting of the story of the death and resurrection of Jesus. The reading of the Passion according to Mark is the first great moment of this recounting. But, on this Sunday, we are also again meeting the Risen One: he is present in the community, in the readings, in the preaching, in the holy supper. The procession itself is a little image of his resurrection, even though its story remembers him on the way to the cross. The whole double-sided celebration—Sunday and yet Passion, joyful procession and yet cross—proclaims this center of our faith: the Crucified One is the Risen One; the Risen One is the Crucified One.

In spite of the length of this service, I would urge your congregation to consider seriously engaging as many of its participants as can walk or be carried or pushed to be part of the procession. I would urge your lectors to read (or, better, sing! See the various musical resources provided for this day) the fullest form of the Passion according to Mark. And I would urge you not to neglect to preach. The sermon may be brief, but the texts themselves, including especially the Markan Passion, and the very fact that this service is the entryway into the whole following festival, give the preacher remarkable material. The congregation needs to hear, once again, an announcement of the gospel as the reason why we keep this week.

Liturgy of the Palms

Processional Gospel
Mark 11:1-11 or John 12:12-16 (RCL)
Mark 11:1-10 or John 12:12-16 (LFM)

Two different versions of the story of Jesus' entry into Jerusalem immediately prior to his execution provide the options for the Gospel reading as the procession begins. The oldest of these is the one from Mark. Written down in about 70 C.E., it may have been built upon the memory of an actual crowd demonstration that occurred in Jerusalem sometime during the lifetime of Jesus, perhaps, indeed, not long before he was killed at Passover time or perhaps at another time, at the Feast of Tabernacles in the fall, a dating which would account for the tabernacles (or Sukkoth) imagery: the green branches and the quoting of Psalm 118. If there was such a historical entry or demonstration, it would then have been seen as radically different from the processions that took place in Jerusalem when Roman officials entered there. For example, Pilate would have come up from the seacoast to claim his seat in the praetorium, riding on horseback or on a horse-drawn vehicle, accompanied by armed cohorts of Roman soldiers, many also on horseback, by imperial Roman standards, by the blowing of trumpets or the sounding of other instruments, by the pushing of people out of the way, and probably not by the welcoming of the residents. Here was power, come to control. If Jesus' historical entry was at all like the stories we have, it was not powerful. The colt, the green branches, and the cries of the people make a strong contrast to warhorses and military display. And the "hosanna" of the people is a beseeching prayer. It means, "Save, now, please, O God!" It is a prayer in the mouths of those who are oppressed and in deep need.

In any case, in its Markan context, the story is used to reveal once again— according to the deep intention of this Gospel—the paradoxical identity of Jesus. The seemingly providential provision of the colt for "the Lord" would have suggested that God is involved in this story. The tabernacles imagery of leafy branches, of a procession to the Temple, and of prayers for salvation (see Lev. 23:40; Neh. 8:15; Ps. 118:25-27) would have recalled the idea of the fruitful land as the place where the people were to live before God, under God's blessing, one theme of the ancient feast. The designation of Jesus as the "one who comes in the name of the Lord" would have been heard as expressing messianic expectation: as Peter confesses in Mark 8:29, Jesus is the Christ. But Jesus' answer to that confession (8:30-38) is also present in the story. He is coming here to his death. He is riding a colt, thus associating his entry with littleness. The people who are celebrating are a needy and oppressed people, suffering under Rome and crying out for help. The foretelling of the presence of the colt is like the foretelling of Jesus' suffering and death (cf. 8:31; 9:31; 10:33-34). God is indeed involved, but in an unexpected way: this Jesus is God "the Lord" coming in weakness to suffer with us and so be the end of the way of imperial power, to so be the salvation of us all and of all the earth with its leafy branches.

A further note: although the casting of cloaks (*himatia*) on the back of the colt and on the road may be taken simply as a narrative sign of respect, it could be that the author of Mark wants us to remember that Bartimaeus just threw off his cloak (*himation*) in the story immediately preceding (10:50), when he came to Jesus to have his sight restored and so to follow him "on the way" (10:52). Then we might notice how clothing functions in the rest of the story. We might pay attention to these details and, contrary to our usual way of reading in the present, very literal time, we might think about their symbolic force. A young man is stripped naked as Jesus is being arrested and brought to execution (14:51-52), just as Jesus himself will be stripped (15:17, 20, 24). And then a young man is clothed and seated to tell the women that Jesus is risen (16:5), just as the former demoniac was clothed and seated with Jesus, healed and in his right mind (5:15). Clothing, of course, is symbolic of the self. Perhaps, with Bartimaeus and the crowd of the procession and the fleeing young man and all who have ever taken off clothing in order to be immersed in the baptismal font, we are to put ourselves into the way and the story of the cross. In Christ, we will be finally clothed in the resurrection and brought to our right minds.

The story as it is in the Fourth Gospel, the latest of the canonical versions, written down thirty to forty years after Mark's account, is clearly an abbreviation and reworking of Mark. Nonetheless, narrative details are added that have come to matter to the Christian imagination. Here are the *palm* branches (cf. Neh. 8:15), otherwise unmentioned in the Gospel tradition, and here is the *donkey*, together with the mixed quotation from Isaiah and from Zechariah, found first in Matthew. A reference to that quotation from Zechariah 9:9, however, about the peaceful, nonwarlike entry of a mysterious king, was probably intended in the earliest levels of the tradition of this story. For early Christians, this king was Jesus. In John, the whole narrative seems to support the comment of the Pharisees in 12:19, a comment that the author of the Gospel believes to be paradoxically true of the crucified Glorified One: "Look, the world has gone after him!"

Processional Psalm
Psalm 118:1-2, 19-29 (RCL)

This psalm of thanksgiving came, over time, to be associated with the Feast of the Tabernacles in the Jewish tradition, with the carrying of leafy branches and the building of huts on the land out of them, with processions to the Temple, and with the pouring out of water and praying for rain. In imagery and in explicit words—the tree branches, the procession to the Temple, "hosanna," and the "one who comes in the name of the Lord"—the psalm came to influence the telling of the story of Jesus' entry into Jerusalem. It also came to influence the Christian theological and liturgical tradition much more widely. For Christians, Jesus is the "stone that the builders rejected." For Christians, the resurrection is the "day that the Lord has made." And at almost every Eucharist the community sings of Jesus as of "the one who comes in the name of the Lord." The RCL proposes that the psalm might have a role in the entrance liturgy. Perhaps the choir could sing it as the assembly gathers, especially if the procession itself makes wise use of the communal singing of the traditional hymn of Theodulph of Orleans, "All Glory, Laud, and Honor."

Liturgy of the Passion

Gospel
Mark 14:1—15:47 or 15:1-39 (40-47) (RCL)
Mark 14:1—15:47 or 15:1-39 (LFM)

We do not know to what extent the Passion story—the story of Jesus' suffering and death—circulated as a whole composition prior to the writing of the Gospels and to what extent it was written first by the author of the Gospel of Mark. In any case, the oldest form of this story that we possess is the one we find in Mark. There we find the story thoroughly combined with Mark's own theological purposes. Older, of course, are the references in Paul, such as the traditional formulation in 1 Corinthians 15:3-4: "I handed on to you as of first importance what I in turn had received: that Christ died for our sins in accordance with the scriptures, and that he was buried, and that he was raised on the third day in accordance with the scriptures . . ." Mark provides us a layered narrative reassertion of these classic statements of faith.

The very changes that Matthew, Luke, and John made in the story, as they received it from the Gospel according to Mark, help us to see some of the unique traits of this version. Mark alone has the fleeing young man (14:51-52). Mark alone has Jesus answer the question of the high priest with the astonishing "I am" (14:62), words that those hearing the story in the church will know as the very name of God (cf. Exod. 3:14). And only Mark has such a clear, confirmed report that Jesus was indeed dead (15:44-45). Those three traits by themselves might give preachers a word to say: God, the very God of the exodus, has in Jesus shared our lot of suffering and death, indeed, shared the lot of unjust and cruel death that our kind has repeatedly inflicted on one another. "I AM" goes to death, is dead. We are invited to bring our sorrows and the sorrows we know of the world here. Like the young man and like everyone who is immersed in baptism, we may be immersed naked into this story. We will discover, on this Sunday, that we are raised up together with Jesus. The meal we come to eat and drink, the meal of his death made into a gift of life, testifies to that resurrection and invites us to the way of trusting God and loving our neighbor.

There is, of course, much more to the story. Mark, in a trait followed by Matthew but not in quite the same way by Luke or John, begins the Passion account with two meals. The first is the meal at the house of a leper, a classic outsider. The second is the Last Supper. In Mark, both interpret the meaning of Jesus' death. In the first, in a gracious counterimage to the horrible account of the meal at which John the Baptist was killed (Mark 6:14-29), a woman anoints the head of Jesus, enacting herself a prophetic sign of his messiahship that is to be forever part of the gospel. She does not bring in his head on a platter. Nonetheless, Jesus interprets her act as a sign of his death. He makes of her a preacher of the gospel. He says that he is indeed the Christ, in his death. Then, when we no longer have his body to anoint, we will indeed have the poor. Listening to this woman preaching-in-sign, we will be invited to turn to them in love. In the second meal, Jesus interprets his death with the words at the gift of the bread and the cup, noting that his blood is poured out "for many." Those words (*hyper polloon*), which are rightly translated in modern versions of the "words of institution" as "for all," actually point to the crowd, the unwashed multitude, the others and the outsiders, the *hoi polloi*. The covenant made by Jesus' blood is for them—thus, it may also include us. Indeed, these are the very "many" who also show up in the fourth servant song on Good Friday, in Isaiah 53:12.

The Markan Jesus also interprets his own death with his vow not to drink wine again until he drinks "it new in the kingdom of God" (14:25). It is important to remember that ancient meals had a structure in which first the food was eaten and then, especially at a festival or a banquet, a cup or cups of wine were liberally shared at what was called, in Greek, a *symposion*. In the Markan Last Supper, the *symposion* takes place first in Gethsemane. There Jesus prays to be delivered from the symbolic cup (14:36) that he will drink in his death. Then, as if to act out this image, Jesus first refuses the pain-deadening myrrhed wine the soldiers offer him before they kill him (15:23), while as he dies, when his death is accomplished and as he cries out the first line of Psalm 22, he drinks the sour wine given him (15:36). For Mark, this very sour wine is the new wine of the kingdom. The Markan symbolism is strong and intended to be understood in the Christian community. The kingdom of God comes hidden in Jesus' death, as it is to be proclaimed openly in his resurrection. Not only is the sky—that seeming barrier to God and the mysteries beyond—split open when Jesus stands in the water at the outset of the Gospel, under the dove and the voice of God (Mark 1:10), but the temple curtain—another seeming cosmic barrier—is also torn at this death. We who hear the story know of these rendings and are invited to live as if they were so, in the company of God's life-giving, death-defeating, fear-ending mercy come among us. And, like the disciples, we, too, are invited to drink this cup, the cup of his death become the cup of the arriving kingdom (10:39; 14:23).

There are yet more paradoxical reversals in this Passion story. It is not only that the anointing of Jesus as Messiah is an anointing ahead of time for his burial or that the cup of the kingdom is the sour wine given as they are killing him. It is also that the "twelve" are an image of God's new Israel, the twelve tribes of the exodus reconstituted as witnesses on earth to the true God. Yet, here, one of them betrays Jesus, one denies him, and they all desert him. More: Jesus does in a sense "call for Elijah" (15:35), for the precursor of the coming of God's kingdom, and that kingdom does come, and yet that call is his misunderstood cry to God as he is dying. Jesus is indeed the rabbi (14:45), the builder of the new temple (14:58; 15:29), the Son of the Blessed One (14:61; 15:39), the King of the Jews (15:9, 12, 18, 26, 32), the one who saved others (15:31), but these things are all said as they are arresting, accusing, beating, mocking, and killing him, when "he cannot save himself" (15:31). To the hearers in the Christian assembly, all of these things are true, but they are true of the weak one come among us, of the crucified. Such is Mark's purpose.

In all of these reversals, there is room for the hearers in your congregation as the Passion is read or chanted and as you preach. This story comes as a thing to eat and drink, as water to pour out over the heads of people for whom death, and mutual betrayal, and loss, and failure, and sin, and sorrow have become too much. Henceforth, there is no place of sorrow or death where God in Jesus has not first come. Indeed, in Jesus God has come to where God cannot be, to the places where our experience says God is not. At the deepest place of abandonment, the Spirit of God has set a fountain of life-giving water. This Passion Sunday not only bears witness to that fountain. It offers us to drink.

First Reading
Isaiah 50:4-9a (RCL)
Isaiah 50:4-7 (LFM)

This passage from Second Isaiah is the third of those four pieces of prophetic poetry that have been called the servant songs. Current exegesis is clear that the "servant," of whom the prophet speaks, is Israel as a whole, in a corporate identity. Here, that nation, called to be the witness for God in the world, has indeed been accused and abused, but the people who once listened to God and were given the charge to teach the world are here invited to trust that the Lord God is the final judge. Christians have seen this servant as Jesus. He is the obedient one, the teacher, the one who willingly went into false accusation and insult and false trial. Even more, on this Passion Sunday, his story—the very Passion according to Mark—comes as a word that can sustain the weary.

Psalmody
Psalm 31:9-16 (RCL)
Psalm 22:8-9, 17-18, 19-20, 23-24 (LFM)

The psalm in the three-year lectionaries is intended to function as a response to the first reading, as a way that the assembly sings as it receives the word of the first reading. Here, both the RCL and the LFM use a classic psalm of lament, in each case one that has been associated in Christianity with the interpretation of the death of Jesus. Psalm 31 provided one of the words from the cross (v. 5) as these occur in Luke's Passion story. In fact, some liturgical materials appoint this verse as an antiphon or response to be sung when Psalm 31:9-16 is used. Psalm 22 is the classic "psalm of the Passion," its first line being quoted in the Markan Passion and much of its imagery (for example, "for my clothing they cast lots," 22:18) having influenced the telling of the story of Jesus' death. Thus, here, the words of the servant in Isaiah are answered as if the servant himself were singing one or the other of these psalms. That both psalms are psalms of lament, however, is wonderfully helpful. The lament psalms were intended to be songs available to anyone in trouble, so that their words could be used to bring widespread human sorrow to expression and, at the same time, to bring the lamenter through to a song of thanksgiving. For Christians, this use of the lament psalms becomes an image of the announcement of the gospel: in Jesus' cross is room for all our sorrows, all our griefs. In his resurrection, drawing us up as well, is the song of thanksgiving.

Second Reading
Philippians 2:5-11 (RCL)
Philippians 2:6-11 (LFM)

This passage from Paul's letter to the church at Philippi is made up of one of the great hymns of the New Testament. Perhaps Paul wrote this hymn himself. Perhaps he is quoting a hymn already known in the community to which he is writing. In any case, he is inviting the members of the community to be formed by the same humility and self-emptying of which they sing in Christ. The passage is thus one of the oldest accounts of Jesus' death and resurrection, older than the Markan Passion, that yet presents to us in poetic form some of the meaning of the Passion story we are celebrating today. As this poem was sung, so the Passion story today may be sung. As the song exults in the risen one, so the Passion story leads us to kneel before God's self-emptying mercy in Christ and acknowledge that this powerless one is the only Lord who matters. It is Sunday, and on Sunday, in resurrection confidence, the assembly confesses "that Jesus Christ is Lord, to the glory of God, the Father."

April 2, 2012
Monday in Holy Week

Revised Common Lectionary (RCL)
Isaiah 42:1-9
Psalm 36:5-11
Hebrews 9:11-15
John 12:1-11

Lectionary for Mass (LFM)
Isaiah 42:1-7
Psalm 27:1, 2, 3, 13-14

John 12:1-11

Both the LFM and the RCL provide readings for a Eucharist to be celebrated on each day in Holy Week. The LFM follows the expected order for a daily mass, providing only a first reading, a responsorial psalm, and a Gospel. The RCL provides a full set of readings, imagining that there may be some communities that would need readings for a full daily Eucharist or for some other daily word service. In many places, Holy Week calls for an intense practice, not otherwise followed in the rest of the year. In order to assist communities who have such a daily gathering, we here will look briefly at all of these readings, before we turn to the great liturgies of the Three Days.

Gospel
John 12:1-11 (RCL, LFM)

The Gospel on this Monday is the Johannine version of the story with which the Markan Passion began yesterday. Here, however, the story has been assimilated to the account of the raising of Lazarus, an event that in the Fourth Gospel is seen as the immediate motivation for the killing of Jesus. Thus, the meal is still at Bethany, but in Mary and Martha's house, with Lazarus at the table, not in the house of Simon the leper. The unnamed anointing woman of Mark has become Mary herself. She anoints his feet, not his head, as if in a kind of foreshadowing of the foot washing that Jesus himself will enact at the meal of John 13. And the nard has been bought not to anoint his body "beforehand for its burial" (Mark 14:8), but to "keep it for the day of my burial" (John 12:7). Mary's anointing of his feet and wiping with her hair seems to reflect the Lukan version of the story (Luke 7:36-38), in which an unnamed woman ("who was a sinner") attends to his feet. That John conflates these versions of the story and names the woman as Mary of Bethany has doubtless brought on the quite unbiblical tradition that this woman was Mary of Magdala, "Mary Magdalene." In any case, it seems likely that the author of the Gospel according to John knew both Mark and Luke and used their stories for his own evangelical purposes.

Far from being, as in the Lukan narrative, more of a sinner than anyone else, both women in John's story are exemplary. Mary acts in gratitude and kindness, anticipating Jesus' death. And Martha "serves" (*diekonei*), that is, she takes the role, so important to the ancient Christian community, of setting out food for the community to eat (cf. Luke 22:27; Acts 6:2-3). She is the "minister" or presider of this gathering.

While the Johannine version of the story does not explicitly begin the Passion narrative here, it is a bridge to that narrative. According to John 11:45-53, the raising of Lazarus became the occasion for the intense plotting on Jesus' life by the religious authorities. This meal causes an extension of that plotting (12:9-11). John seems to be saying that by raising another from the dead, Jesus himself becomes vulnerable to death. Furthermore, those who have life from him are also under threat. These assertions are profound expressions of Christian faith, the trust that life comes from Jesus' death and the knowledge that those who are raised up by him are also frequently threats to the status quo of a world organized toward death.

The Johannine story, thus, like the Markan version, gives a down payment on the Passion story to come. The anointing nard is to be preserved for Jesus' burial. The care for his feet points toward the foot washing of the final supper, the foot washing that is itself a Johannine symbol of the life-giving service Jesus does for us all in his dying like a slave. Judas objects, and his forthcoming betrayal is mentioned. And the presence of Lazarus, reminding all of the story of his raising by Jesus, leads to further plotting.

The little community at this table may be taken as an image for the Christian community. Gathered around a meal, the community has signs of Jesus' life-giving death at the heart of their gathering and hears a reminder that care for the poor will now continue to be the way the community encounters him and cares for his body. Among them are people of diverse motives, people made alive, people in deep gratitude, people inclined to betrayal. Most of us evidence a mixture of these motives. But, in the most striking symbol of this Johannine version, the house is "filled with the fragrance of the perfume."

Near the beginning of Holy Week, this Gospel presents us with a remarkable image. Our own local community is this gathering at the table. And, throughout this week, the fragrance of the life-giving, death-defeating story of Jesus' death and resurrection, of his feet and head anointed and our feet washed, of our lives saved by him and turned toward the poor, will continually fill the house of our gathering.

First Reading
Isaiah 42:1-9 (RCL)
Isaiah 42:1-7 (LFM)

The use of the Isaian servant songs to mark this week continues here. This passage is usually considered the first of those four songs, so powerfully important in Second Isaiah. Israel's vocation—what it means to be "the chosen people"—is recounted here. The people themselves, as a single identity and in quiet and humble ways, are to bring forth justice in the world. They are to be like a light for the nations. They are to be God's covenant with the earth, bringing the hope for Torah to all foreign places, all the "coastlands."

Christians, of course, aware of the failure of all of us throughout history to be such signs of God, have sung this song about Jesus. He is the one who does not make a spectacle in the streets, does not crush people who are already only dimly burning with life or with faith. He is the light. In his death, he is the new covenant for all. And he is the source of real justice.

Still, like Lazarus who is threatened because he shares the new life that Christ gives and, like Mary, who is disparaged for her caring for feet ahead of time, we, too, are called to share with Jesus and with ancient Israel the life of the servant of God. For us, Jesus is the servant. We are servants in the servant.

Psalmody
Psalm 36:5-11 (RCL)
Psalm 27:1, 2, 3, 13-14 (LFM)

The RCL appoints part of Psalm 36 to respond to the first reading, the great servant song. That psalm, like the passage from Isaiah, celebrates that God's life-giving mercy and God's light are for all peoples (v. 7), indeed, all animals and all the earth (v. 6). As if in a transition toward the image of the Gospel, all these peoples are welcome to the feast in God's house. Of course, the psalm originally intended the Temple as that house. But Christians may hear a reminder here of the house at Bethany and the house of our own congregation, this week filled with the fragrance of the story of the servant.

The responsorial psalm of the LFM sings as if it were in the mouth of the servant. With Jesus the servant, we are given words of confidence in God even in the face of extreme adversity. With Jesus the servant, we wait in this week for the word of the resurrection, "the goodness of the Lord in the land of the living" (27:13).

Second Reading
Hebrews 9:11-15 (RCL)

Three of the RCL selections for the second reading in Holy Week come from the letter to the Hebrews. That letter, written anonymously, probably in about the year 75 or 80 c.e., makes an extended use of metaphors drawn from the Temple and temple sacrifice in order to proclaim one way to understand the death of Jesus. Those metaphors have a powerful use in this week of the narratives of that death. Metaphors, of course, involve calling something by the wrong name. They thereby say something that could not otherwise be said. Jesus was not a priest, in the literal sense. And his death was certainly not a temple sacrifice. But his death was greater than all sacrifices, indeed the end of sacrifice—the end of all such "dead works" (9:14). What he "offered" (another metaphor!) was himself. In a note that recalls the Isaian servant's work, Hebrews makes clear that this offering has now established a new covenant for all people. In that covenant, we receive God's astonishing love in Jesus Christ, and, redeemed by his act in the Spirit, we turn away from "dead" religious works toward the needs and the bodies of the poor, so clearly recalled at Bethany's table.

April 3, 2012
Tuesday in Holy Week

Revised Common Lectionary (RCL)
Isaiah 49:1-7
Psalm 71:1-14
1 Corinthians 1:18-31
John 12:20-36

Lectionary for Mass (LFM)
Isaiah 49:1-6
Psalm 71:1-2, 3-4a, 5-6ab, 15 + 17

John 13:21-33, 36-38

The lectionaries continue to read from John and from the Isaian servant songs as Holy Week moves on. But RCL and LFM, otherwise so close together in their choice of readings this week, diverge on the question of which exact passage from the Fourth Gospel to use as the Gospel for this Tuesday. RCL sets out the classic text about Jesus being "lifted up" and thus drawing all to himself. LFM anticipates the story of the betrayal of Jesus that will be told by both lectionaries tomorrow, giving the Johannine version of Judas's "going out" at night to do the betraying, but also adding a few verses about the forthcoming denial of Peter. Both lectionaries thus continue to provide us with images meant to interpret the meaning of the death of Jesus.

Gospel
John 12:20-36 (RCL)

This passage in the Gospel according to John follows immediately after the Johannine version of the entry into Jerusalem. Thus, that certain Greeks are presented as wishing to see Jesus (v. 21) becomes one illustration of the speech of the Pharisees: "Look, the world has gone after him" (v. 19). The Greeks come as part of that world, part of that "all" that will be drawn to Jesus (v. 32). The author of this Gospel clearly wishes to express that followers of Jesus—most certainly the people who carry on the work of the Twelve—have a responsibility to help others, including especially the Gentiles, to "see Jesus," even though we will come to know that the deepest seeing of the risen crucified one is the "seeing" that occurs in faith (cf. 20:29) and that is associated with hearing this book of the Gospel itself (20:30-31). The Greeks disappear in the further narrative here, or, rather, they dissolve into *us* as *we* are hearing the account of this book. We are the Greeks. Listening, we may come to know and believe and, in that sense, "see."

What we hear immediately is the Johannine version of the central paradox of Christian faith. The Gospel according to John calls the execution of Jesus his "glorification" and his "lifting up." That the cross is "glory" depends on the ancient idea of the *kabod YHWH*, the mysterious and weighty Glory of God which is light and burning fire but which is also God's passionate love, God's "burden" for the people and for the earth. For John, this Glory is encounterable in the crucifixion of Jesus and in the still-wounded hands of the Risen One. That the cross is "lifting up" is an expression that combines the horrible image of raising up impaled and crucified victims onto the killing stakes of their execution with the idea that "up" is closer to God and closer to Glory. The play with these images is already present in chapter 3 of the Gospel, where birth "again" and birth "from above" are intermingled (3:3-7), side by side with the intermingling of "ascension" to know the things of God (3:13) and lifting up to save the people of God and all the world (3:13, 16). Indeed, as Moses's serpent was "lifted up," so that the people might see and be healed, so Jesus is "lifted up" so that we and the Greeks might "look" and live. These layered images are meant to invite us to see how the death of Jesus is overwhelmingly, divinely life giving. For John, the death of Jesus, his resurrection, his ascension (another way to speak of his "lifting up"), and his gift of the Spirit to enliven and to forgive are all a single great event. The resurrection and ascension are already present in the cross. The cross is always present in the resurrection, ascension, and gift of the Spirit. Such is the lifting up of Jesus in this Gospel.

But, according to this text, even more occurs in the crucifixion than the provision of a place for us to look and be healed. Jesus' death provides a drawing, centripetal, coherent center for the whole world. According to most Greek manuscripts of the Gospel, all *people* will be drawn to him. According to one very important ancient papyrus (p66) and to the uncorrected original version of the foundational *Codex Sinaiticus*, all *things* will be drawn. It does not greatly matter which we read. Either brings us to see that this text is the Johannine community's version of the idea that is sung in the hymn quoted in the letter to the Colossians, a book that may be from a time not long before the writing of the Fourth Gospel: "in him all things hold together . . . through him God was pleased to reconcile to himself all things . . . making peace through the blood of his cross" (Col. 1:17, 20).

This is the very idea that will be enacted in the Good Friday liturgy when the assembly prays for everyone and everything in the great Bidding Prayer, empowered by the sense that the death of Jesus is the beginning of the healing of all harms, the salvation of all things. How is this so? A preacher will be pressed by this text to articulate something of her or his atonement theology. It seems like John's Gospel is saying that by God in Jesus sharing our awful death, death itself is destroyed. By

God in Jesus sharing our disorder and many failed centers, a center for all things is reestablished. All things are brought into loving order. All people are drawn. Thus, the death of Jesus is the "hour" that has been awaited, the very hour of the judgment of the opponents of God who have dominated and terrorized the world. The death of Jesus shines as a light in the darkness.

These all are magisterial images of salvation. For John, Jesus' death, while looking like defeat and suffering, is the great victory of God.

More paradoxes surround and illumine this central one. The Fourth Gospel uses this as the place to quote the passage about keeping life by losing it (12:25), an idea that in Mark occurs as part of the first Passion prediction (Mark 8:35). Furthermore, the idea of following Jesus by "taking up the cross" (Mark 8:34) is even intensified here: for John the followers of Jesus will be "where I am." The astonishing thing is, of course, that "where Jesus is" is the cross. Also for followers, the way of life is paradoxical. This is no promise of "heaven." Or, rather, this promise of the cross is also a promise of the life that is in the "lifted up" one.

John's Gospel also makes this the place where the seed imagery, found elsewhere in the earlier Christian tradition (cf. 1 Cor. 15:36-44; Mark 4:3-9, 13-20) as an image for the resurrection and for the arrival of the kingdom of God, is intensified as an image for the death and resurrection of Jesus. For John, Jesus himself is the sown, dying seed who becomes the source of the hundredfold harvest.

We Greeks may see the single seed, fallen into the earth. But we are invited to hear of the great harvest and to eat of the life-giving Bread made from the resulting, risen, hundredfold grain.

John 13:21-33, 36-38 (LFM)

For commentary on this text, please see the Gospel (RCL) for Wednesday of Holy Week, below. Note, however, that the LFM Gospel for this day also includes not only the beginning of the betrayal of Judas, but also the Johannine foretelling of the denial of Peter. In John, this text is made to illustrate what has been earlier said (in 12:26) about following Jesus and being where he is. In the early second century, when John was likely written, Christians knew that Peter had indeed finally "followed" Jesus by sharing a tortured execution with him. That idea is again referred to in the appendix to John (21:18-19), probably added after the original Gospel was completed. Peter will deny Jesus. He will then also be forgiven and invited to follow, even to death.

First Reading
Isaiah 49:1-7 (RCL)
Isaiah 49:1-6 (LFM)

The second of the great Isaian servant songs is heard on this day. While these songs probably intended to speak of the vocation of all Israel, a vocation being restored during the exile of the people and witnessed to by the prophet, this text especially seems available to be interpreted as of a single person, perhaps the prophet himself, whose calling is to "bring Jacob back to [God]" (v. 5). Still, all the *exiled and suffering* people could be envisioned, whose undertaking is to bring the whole history of all of the descendants of Jacob to reconciliation with the God whom they are seen as having deserted. The present suffering people are to bring back the whole people of Israel, those from an earlier time and those to come. One way or the other, the remarkable thing is that this is too little a vocation, "too light a thing" (v. 6). The reconciliation with God is to be for all people. A despised and abhorred people—"the servant"— has the role of showing God's restoration to the nations (v. 7). Christians find this despised and abhorred one in the crucified Jesus. For us, he is "light to the nations" (v. 6). The role of the servant, gathering all the peoples, echoes what we hear in the Gospel: "and I, when I am lifted up from the earth, will draw all people to myself" (John 12:32). "Look," as the Pharisees say, "the world has gone after him" (John 12:19).

Psalmody
Psalm 71:1-14 (RCL)
Psalm 71:1-2, 3-4a, 5-6ab, 15 + 17 (LFM)

The psalm appointed by both lectionaries means to give us words to sing as if in the voice of the servant, whose "song" we have just read from Isaiah. Here the suffering one (vv. 4, 10-11, 13) has also been chosen by God since birth (v. 6; cf. Isa. 49:5). In the context of the servant song, the psalmist's praise of God's glory (vv. 8, 14-15, 17) becomes a witness to all nations of the saving mercy of God. Christians use the language of the psalm as one way to understand the death of Jesus, the servant, the "portent" (v. 7), whose death is the very Glory of God, according to John.

Second Reading
1 Corinthians 1:18-31 (RCL)

This passage from Paul provides us with the most basic text for the Christian "theology of the cross." It is important that this text be read at some time during the great and holy week. Here we find the Pauline version of the same root paradox that fills the RCL Gospel. For all that Jesus Christ looks like nothing to the world, faith trusts that this Crucified One is the wisdom of God, the true sign of God, and the source of our life from God, our righteousness, sanctification, and redemption. One mercy of this paradox is that all the odd and lowly people who make up the church— people like us—are drawn—with all things!—into the movement of God's saving mercy for the world. God works with things and people that are almost nothing to bring down the pretended and supposed mighty and continually to make the world anew. The cross of Jesus really is new life for the world.

April 4, 2012
Wednesday in Holy Week

Revised Common Lectionary (RCL)
Isaiah 50:4-9a
Psalm 70
Hebrews 12:1-3
John 13:21-32

Lectionary for Mass (LFM)
Isaiah 50:4-9a
Psalm 69:8-10, 21-22, 31 + 33-34

Matthew 26:14-25

The servant songs of Isaiah continue to be read to us throughout Holy Week, finally leading us to the great fourth song as the first reading of Good Friday. Here, on the way to Good Friday, we again read the third of these songs, the first reading we also heard last Sunday. Wednesday in Holy Week also presents us with the day that some in the Western church have called "Spy Wednesday." The betrayal of Judas is recalled in the Gospel, either in its Johannine (RCL) or its Matthean (LFM) form.

Gospel
John 13:21-32 (RCL)
Matthew 26:14-25 (LFM)

The account of the betrayal of Judas occupies the Gospel today. In the RCL that account is taken from John, in the LFM from Matthew. Attending to both can help the preacher think about the ways in which the story's narrative details evolved in the early Christian movement. And knowledge of such development can beckon us to avoid either simplistic literalism or psychologizing. The point of preaching, for example, is not to ask, "What must Judas have been feeling?" The purpose of the story was never to answer such a question. Storytelling details certainly did seek to respond to popular curiosity about the events around Jesus, but as these details are preserved in the Gospels—and as they are recounted with significant differences—they almost always correspond to theological points the authors are wishing to make and symbolic images of the meaning of Jesus to current faith that the authors wish to set out. These books are not "you are there" reports. They are words about Jesus and faith in the current assembly.

Then, what about Judas? Recent public discussion of the second- or third-century Gnostic text called the *Gospel of Judas* has brought on the suggestion that Judas has gotten a bum rap. The Gnostic book proposes that he did indeed betray Jesus and so bring about Jesus' death, but that this was the wonderfully creative and obedient thing to do, the thing Jesus himself wanted, the thing that would horrify the gathered disciples, since it led to the release of Jesus from fleshly existence to go back beyond the skies to the realm of Light. This proposal, of course, is not only far from what the New Testament Gospels say, it also represents several characteristic Gnostic points of view. For Gnosticism, release from the body and from the earth is a good thing. Not for orthodox Christianity. For Gnosticism, individuals acting are far more important than communities gathering. Not for orthodox Christianity. And for Gnosticism, contrariness, the making of bad things to be understood as good, is a whole way of thought. The *Gospel of Judas* gives us one rather pure, world-denying, and world-escaping spirituality. It does not give us any insight into the "historical Judas."

Is there any insight into the historical Judas in the canonical Gospels? Probably not much. They, too, are dealing in images and storytelling for their own purposes, but those purposes are deeply in accord with classic Christian faith, the faith your Holy Week services are seeking to serve. Jesus did not "want to die." Yet his awful death, including the idea that someone close to him sought to hurt him, has been made by God the source and center of life. That action by God, affirmed by Christian faith, has been projected by the Gospels back into the life of Jesus as Jesus' own foreknowledge of the betrayal. Given the widespread witness to this theme of betrayal, however, it is probably true that one of the inner circle of Jesus' first followers, a man whose name was probably Judas, a significant participant in the earliest Jesus movement, did indeed participate in some way in arranging for Jesus to be executed by the Romans. We do not know why. The shocking and yet necessary point that lived on in the stories of the communities and that echoed some themes found in the lament psalms (e.g., Ps. 41:9; 55:12-14) was that betrayal was possible from the most central leaders of the church.

Of course, it still is. We, too, have the potential to be as Judas. That remains one of the points of the stories in the Gospels.

But the most amazing and profoundly deeper point of the Gospels is that Jesus eats with Judas, knowing his perfidy. The outreaching of love, the possibility of forgiveness, the all-encompassing passion of God *includes Judas*. This is an image, a proclamation of gospel mercy, available also to us now. The continued availability of that meaning now is more important than whether or not the story is a historical report.

In Matthew's Gospel, after the prophetic imagery of the thirty pieces of silver is mentioned, imagery that Matthew has drawn from Zechariah 11:13, Judas is seen dipping in the same bowl with Jesus. This latter detail Matthew has taken from Mark, though Matthew has added the dialogue in which Judas is explicitly identified (26:25). In any case, Judas is most likely being pictured as dipping unleavened bread in the ritual *haroset* of the Passover seder. To Matthew, such a gesture of shared dipping was a gesture of affection and love as surely as was the kiss in the garden (Matt. 26:48-49). The image is thus the more horrible of the betrayer, but the more deeply gracious of Jesus. Matthew seems to be saying that this Jesus is also there for us, in our betrayals. We may be warned by the awful words, "It would have been better for that one not to have been born" (26:24), but we may be invited to repentance as well by the gracious sign. As the pastoral epistles will later put the matter: "If we deny him, he will also deny us; if we are faithless, he remains faithful" (2 Tim. 2:12-13). And Matthew, like the Markan Gospel on which he largely depends, goes even further. In the passage immediately following the LFM Gospel, Judas is clearly among those to whom Jesus gives the Eucharist, including "my blood . . . for many for the forgiveness of sins" (26:28).

The Fourth Gospel has developed this narrative yet further. Here Jesus hands Judas the bread he has dipped (John 13:27). Since, in John, the meal account itself has been replaced by the foot washing (see below, the Gospel for Maundy Thursday), this bread is the only food actually mentioned in the entire Johannine version of the Last Supper, and this bread is given to Judas. That very bread-gift then becomes the occasion to quote a lament psalm (Ps. 41:9; see John 13:18). At the same time, this gift from Jesus becomes the moment when Judas, according to John, is possessed by the adversary of God and of God's people, by Satan. Such possession was not present in the earlier accounts of Mark and Matthew, but it does appear in Luke (22:3), though not at this meal moment. For Luke, demon possession provides a reason for the betrayal. For John, Judas is thereby aligned with the "ruler of this world" (12:31) who is judged and driven out by Jesus' own death. Powerful words in this passage express that judgment. When Judas goes out, after receiving the bread—a sign of Jesus' love but also a sign of his acceptance of death, thus judging and driving out Satan—the words follow: "And it was night" (13:30). Reading this book, one recalls that for John Jesus is himself the light of life. Judas goes away from the light, to betray the light, and that light nonetheless shall not be overcome (John 1:5).

At the church's meals, the holy bread is also held out to us. May we cling to it as to food that judges what is world-hurting and potentially perfidious in us, as well as food that gives us life. The bread that is Jesus himself judges and heals. Even when we are faithless, may we stay near to the one who is faithful. May we continue to find in him and in his gift the light that leads to life and love.

First Reading
Isaiah 50:4-9a (RCL, LFM)

The third servant song again images the whole people of Israel as a servant with the task of quietly and reliably teaching the world what God says. That word of God, given day by day into the ear of the servant, a word from which the servant does not turn even when receiving it includes being disgraced and insulted, finally comes to those who listen as a word that sustains the weary (v. 4). For Christians, this servant is Jesus Christ, and the word that sustains the weary is finally a word that includes the account of his suffering. Indeed, more than sustaining the weary, this word raises the dead. And this word from the suffering servant helps us, even when we are guilty of betrayal. In Jesus Christ, the one who holds out the bread of himself to us, is vindication. Because of him, who will declare me guilty? Formed by forgiveness, I, too, may learn, as a servant in the servant, to listen to the word of God and to speak a word that will sustain the many weary ones around me.

Psalmody
Psalm 70 (RCL)
Psalm 69:8-10, 21-22, 31 + 33-34 (LFM)

Once again, the psalm here has us respond to the first reading as if we were singing in the voice of the servant. Psalm 70 expresses the faith of the servant in a prayer that turns to God as the only sure refuge and reliable judge. Psalm 69 actually uses the imagery of sour wine or vinegar (v. 21) given mockingly to the suffering one, imagery that was picked up by Christians, most significantly in the Markan and Johannine Passions, the accounts read in this Holy Week of Year B.

Second Reading
Hebrews 12:1-3 (RCL)

Here is one of those words intended to sustain the weary. For the letter to the Hebrews, the primary example of faith, the center of the cloud of witnesses, is Jesus Christ in his suffering—even, we will say on this Wednesday, in his being betrayed by a close follower—trusting that God is the sure refuge. For us, even for us as partly having something of Judas about us or at least as not having so sure a faith, the astonishing gift that comes as we gather with the others, sing the songs of faith, hold out hands—the hands of faith—for the bread-gift, hear the word for the weary, is that we are gathered into the faith of Jesus. It is not so much that we try to be like him. It is, rather, that the community, in the Spirit, is gathered into him and finds itself trusting God as he did.

April 5, 2012
Maundy Thursday / Holy Thursday

Revised Common Lectionary (RCL)
Exodus 12:1-4 (5-10) 11-14
Psalm 116:1-2, 12-19
1 Corinthians 11:23-26
John 13:1-17, 31b-35

Lectionary for Mass (LFM)
Exodus 12:1-8, 11-14
Psalm 116:12-13, 15-16bc, 17-18
1 Corinthians 11:23-26
John 13:1-15

With Thursday evening, the Three Days, the very central days of Holy Week, begin. The idea of the Three Days is an intentional evocation of the word of Hosea ("on the third day he will raise us up," Hos. 6:2), a remembrance of Jonah being three days in the belly of the great fish, and a celebration of the gospel-book promise that Jesus would be raised on the third day. That promise, of course, was itself an evocation of Hosea and Jonah: in the resurrection of Jesus we have the action of God which Hosea proclaims, the salvation which Jonah signs. For us, the Three Days are a single proclamation of and encounter with the death and resurrection of Jesus. The two days that tell the story of his dying—the evening of Maundy Thursday through Good Friday and into the afternoon of Holy Saturday—also contain images of his resurrection. The third day that proclaims his resurrection—the evening of the Vigil through the celebrations of Easter Day—also contains images of his dying. The Three Day feast is a *unitary* feast, a single new proclamation of our salvation in Jesus Christ.

The feast begins tonight, with all of the gifts of that salvation running out to greet us like the father of the prodigal son running out to clothe that wanderer in a new robe and ring. Here, in this liturgy, at the end of Lent, we are clothed in forgiveness and in a new community, and we are led in to a feast. Our feet are washed. Our ears hear a story that stands at the "beginning of months" (Exod. 12:2), as if the very hearing were giving us a fresh beginning of time, a really new year. Then, at the end of this evening's liturgical events, many congregations strip their altar table and all of their meeting space of fabric and color, of lights and decoration, of the food of the meal itself, while someone sings either Psalm 88 or Psalm 22, psalms that can be taken to represent the suffering and death of Jesus. While this ceremony probably originated in the simple need to wash the altar and its space in preparation for the rest of the celebrations of these days, it has come to stand starkly for the death of Jesus. From that death, all the gifts of forgiveness, new community, festival meal, and a new beginning of time flow out to us like the resurrection. The risen Crucified One greets us in this service. At the hands of my sister or brother kneeling before me, he washes my feet. In my hands, he washes the feet of my neighbor.

Thus, the texts we hear tonight are read within the context of several intense actions. They come to expression in juxtaposition to those actions. Many churches have begun to keep the classic liturgy of this night: public reconciliation and communal absolution at the conclusion of the Lenten way and in preparation for the Easter feast; the foot washing actually enacted, preferably by anyone in the congregation who wishes, not simply by a select few or by only the clergy; the Eucharist, remembering this as the night of its institution according to the Gospels and the Pauline narrative; and the stripping of the church in preparation for Good Friday and Easter.

It would probably be important for the preacher on this evening to consider some brief ways that she or he may orient the assembly again to what they are doing in these Three Days, to the great outline of the events to follow and to the reasons for our keeping them. We are not trying to travel back in time and imagine the events of Jesus' death and resurrection. We are not trying to emulate ritually his patience and love while suffering. We are not trying to kill him again in cultic imitation and then trying to raise him up. And we are not simply keeping a springtime feast with nice images of new life. No. In the face of real evil and suffering and death in our world, such "trying" on our part would be painfully ludicrous. Rather, in these services we are gathering where the word of God can be heard and tasted and seen now, today, a word that shows how God in Christ goes to the place where we thought God cannot go—into suffering and death with us—and thus how God makes a fountain of life to spring up there, where we thought there was only death. And we see again how that fountain is intended for the life of all the world.

We start to drink again from that fountain tonight.

Gospel
John 13:1-17, 31b-35 (RCL)
John 13:1-15 (LFM)

In the classic Western lectionary, carried on by both RCL and LFM, the Gospel for tonight is not the account of the Last Supper as it is found in the Synoptics, but the Johannine account of the foot washing. It is fascinating to trace the development of this idea in the Gospel tradition. Mark has Jesus speak of his coming to serve after the third Passion prediction, as part of his call to the disciples that they should serve: "the Son of Man came not to be served but to serve, and to give his life a ransom for many" (Mark 10:45). Matthew replicates this location for the saying (Matt. 20:28). Luke, however, moves both the call to service and the verbal presentation of Jesus as a servant to the account of the Last Supper, after the gift of bread and cup. Jesus then says, "For who is greater, the one who is at the table or the one who serves? Is it not the one at the table? But I am among you as one who serves" (Luke 22:27). But the author of John seems to have read all the accounts, and to have chosen to represent Jesus as actually serving at this final meal. And the service that is represented is slave service, the service of washing the feet of the guests. Indeed, it begins to be clear that the Fourth Gospel means us to understand that this service stands for Jesus' death, for his giving himself to the uttermost in service to the lost and needy world. Such is the Johannine version of the Markan phrase, "to give his life a ransom for many."

The fascinating thing is that in the Fourth Gospel the foot washing virtually takes the place of the meal. We have already seen that no food is mentioned here, apart from the bread that is given to Judas (see above, on the Gospel for Wednesday in Holy Week). Furthermore, in John this meal is not the Passover, since in this book Jesus is "the Lamb of God" (John 1:29) and by the Johannine chronology he is actually to be killed at the same time that the Passover lambs are being slaughtered, the "day of Preparation" (19:31) before the Passover begins. More, the foot washing does not take place before the meal as the guests arrive, as one might expect, but, rather, "during supper" (13:2b). Here the very content of the meal is Jesus' humble service.

It seems as if the author of the Fourth Gospel, not unlike Paul in the much earlier letter to the Corinthians, means to call the meal practice of the churches to a deepening reform. The church's meal is not to be just any meal. In this meal Jesus serves the participants with his serving love, with his very death. The Fourth Gospel is probably not so much recommending an ongoing foot-washing rite as urging that people see and hear the slave service of Jesus when they eat his meal in church. And the Gospel is urging that those who eat and drink then be formed to turn in slave service toward the others of the assembly and of the world. John wants us to see that this supper matters.

Nonetheless, it is helpful that the present Maundy Thursday rites of the churches have sought to proclaim Jesus' gift at the meal, both by keeping the meal itself and by keeping, at least here, a practice of foot washing. Amish and Mennonite communities, as well as other "third-wave reformation" churches, have long kept the steady connection between foot washing and the practice of the Lord's Supper. Now mainline churches are discovering again that such a practice also belongs to their own deep tradition. Roman Catholic communities have known the action of the priest or the bishop washing a few representative feet on this evening, as if in dramatic imitation of Jesus. But the call of the text to wash each other's feet now—not the single leader acting out of the role of Jesus—is the more fascinating challenge given to all of our congregations today.

I hope that your preaching on this evening will be made more concrete by the actual practice around you of many members of your congregation, in turn, washing each other's feet. That, too, will be a preaching of the Maundy Thursday word, visibly and tangibly, like water from that fountain God places amid our death, like the prodigal welcomed home again.

The new community we are given in Christ, the ones who are served by Jesus and invited to serve each other, arises from his death, comes to us like a sign of his resurrection from the dead. That is why his "departure from this world"—his death and resurrection in Johannine terminology—includes loving "his own . . . to the end" (13:1). And that is why the slave service at this meal is prefaced by the astonishing words about all things being placed in his hands by God (13:3), words that Christian faith would use to describe the glorified, Risen One. Those words are not followed by some gesture of universal authority, however, as might be expected from the magnificence of the statement, but by Jesus' stripping off of his outer garment, foreshadowing the stripping of crucifixion (19:23-24), and by his taking up of towel and basin and water and feet. The Risen One is the Crucified One.

We gather in assemblies today, after the death of Jesus and after we have been baptized into that death with him—indeed, after we have come to be counted among those who have thus *bathed* (13:10). Baptism is doubtless what "bathing" means here. But we gather still in need of our feet being washed: in need, literally, but also in need metaphorically. We are always in need of the service of Jesus and in need of being formed by him into serving ones ourselves, turned toward our neighbor. We are in need of having leaders and being leaders who, like our Lord and Teacher, model love and service. We are in need of assemblies continually reformed by the serving Jesus in their midst.

In this evening's assembly we gather to hear the gospel of Jesus' death and resurrection—in our ears, but also on our feet. That gospel always brings us, once again, to understand: "You do not know now what I am doing, but later you will understand" (13:7). This evening, this renewed encounter with the risen crucified one, is meant to be that *later*.

First Reading
Exodus 12:1-4 (5-10) 11-14 (RCL)
Exodus 12:1-8, 11-14 (LFM)

The Three Days for Christians function as our Passover feast. The several rites spread out over these days are as our *seder* and our *haggadah*, our ordered meal and our saving narrative. This is quite literally true. Jesus was killed at Passover time, and when Christians started in the second century to keep an *annual* (and not only a *weekly*) feast in commemoration of his death and resurrection, his exodus (see Luke 9:31!), they chose to keep a renewed version of Passover. Their feast was originally a night of "vigil kept for the Lord" (Exod. 12:42), just as the book of Exodus required.

That vigil became our Easter Vigil. At first, it was held on the same day of the full moon that was the day used by the Jewish community for *pesach*. Then, because of the importance of Sunday, it came to be pulled to the night of Saturday to Sunday immediately after that full moon. The two days of preparation for this vigil ultimately became our Maundy Thursday and our Good Friday. The whole thing was the "Christian Passover." That history is why this reading is set here, at the beginning of the Three Days.

That history also is yet another reason why it is not wise for Christian congregations to hold their own "demonstration *seder*." When they are invited, Christians visiting a synagogue or the home of Jewish friends to learn directly how Jews are today keeping Passover can be a profound and wonderful thing. A Christian congregation holding a Jewish Passover meal is not. Such a practice may rightly be seen as a kind of religious imperialism. Furthermore, the form of Passover among Christians is the liturgy of the Three Days, especially the Easter Vigil. That form is as old as—in some ways, older than—the medieval patterns that came to shape what Jewish families do today. Both the Jewish *seder* and the Christian Vigil were legitimate further developments in the history of the festival after the destruction of the Temple in 70 c.e.

In any case, for the Christians, Jesus is the new Lamb. His is the blood on our bodies and lives, the blood that saves us. His resurrection is the crossing of the sea from slavery to freedom and to the new beginning of time. And the watching kept to the Lord, for us, is also the watching for his return and the watching for his presence in all the needs of our neighbor.

The Passover feast itself was probably, at its ancient beginning, a similar overlaying of new meaning on an old festival. The sacrifice of lambs by herdsmen in the spring most likely intended, originally, to try to guarantee the renewed fertility of the flock. Israel then used such a springtime occasion to tell the story of the exodus, of the escape of slaves and the salvation worked by God, and thus to point to a deeper new life and new year before God, more life giving than any fertile flocks. Then Christians overlaid a new story—a Passover story about Jesus' execution—on this old feast, finding in the death and resurrection of Jesus the new grounds for freedom and life. The chain of these reinterpretations comes down to us, to each one of our Three Days celebrations in each place. We, too, are charged to renew our feast in the springtime by seeing to it that the word of the serving Jesus and the responding service of the new community are what we actually celebrate.

Psalmody
Psalm 116:1-2, 12-19 (RCL)
Psalm 116:12-13, 15-16bc, 17-18 (LFM)

The psalm responds to the foundational text about the Passover by pointing especially to the cup of the Eucharist, the new Passover meal for Christians this evening. For the

Christian community, this psalm of trust speaks about Jesus Christ. He is the one who is fulfilling his vows of self-giving and sacrifice. He is the faithful one whose death is precious in the sight of the Lord. And the thanksgiving that rises in this house is grounded in his resurrection.

Second Reading
I Corinthians 11:23-26 (RCL, LFM)

The Pauline account of the Last Supper provides the second reading. For many Christians who expect that this evening should especially commemorate the founding of this meal such a reading is to be expected. But the pressure of the Johannine account to make sure that our gathering for a meal is deeply reformed to accord with the gospel, that it does indeed proclaim the serving death of Jesus and form us all in his service toward each other, is nonetheless a salutary pressure. For churches that frequently hear one or the other version of these "words of the institution," the text may otherwise be too familiar, missing us in its meaning. In fact, the Pauline account is the oldest such account, likely written about 25 years after the death of Jesus. And the apostle is also writing the account with the intention of reforming the worship practice of the Corinthians. Paul wants to make sure that the saving death of Jesus is proclaimed clearly in the meal the Corinthians keep. Jesus' "body for you" and his "new covenant in my blood" need to come to expression. But, as the context makes clear, this proclaiming "the Lord's death until he comes" (11:26), for Paul, must imply a new welcome to the poor and excluded ones, not a humiliation of "those who have nothing" (11:22). In many ways, the reform that Paul seeks in Corinthian practice is very like the foot-washing reform that the Fourth Gospel proposes in its own time, about 50 years after Paul's writing.

Both words of reform come to us, along with the many layers of the Passover tradition. In these texts, in the slave service of Jesus, in the words at the Eucharist, this Holy Thursday proclaims the death of the Lord. And, with words of forgiveness, with the washing of feet, with the bread and cup of the holy supper, it wraps us in his resurrection. As both Paul and John urge, may it also form us again in love.

April 6, 2012
Good Friday

Revised Common Lectionary (RCL)
Isaiah 52:13—53:12
Psalm 22
Hebrews 10:16-25 or 4:14-16; 5:7-9
John 18:1—19:42

Lectionary for Mass (LFM)
Isaiah 52:13—53:12
Psalm 31:2 + 6, 12-13, 15-16, 17 + 25
Hebrews 4:14-16; 5:7-9
John 18:1—19:42

The renewed Good Friday liturgy contains a simple sequence of at least these things: an opening prayer for the new community redeemed in Christ; these readings followed by preaching; a "bidding prayer" or "solemn intercessions," in which all humanity and all the earth are named before God in supplication; the carrying forward of a cross, meant to stand for the actual cross of Jesus' death; and some form of prayer and song around that cross, perhaps using a recast form of the old "reproaches," perhaps ending with a victorious hymn. At the heart of this observance, in these readings, stands the fourth servant song and the Passion according to John. The mood of this liturgy is serious, but it is not lugubrious. What is happening here is not a movie full of torture scenes to frighten and, alas, to entertain us. Rather, just like John's account, the cross is being proclaimed here as God's astonishing victory, God's far-reaching salvation for all things.

Gospel
John 18:1—19:42 (RCL, LFM)

On first glance, the image that seems to be invoked by the Johannine Passion account, the Gospel for this day, is like that of a beautiful *Christus Rex* carving: an image of the crucified Christ on the cross, but utterly without blood and suffering; rather, a figure clothed in rich royal and priestly garments and *reigning*. At every turn in the story, this reigning one comes to the fore. According to the Johannine narrative an entire detachment—about six hundred soldiers!—together with some police are dispatched to arrest Jesus, as if an emperor were being arraigned. When Jesus agrees that he is the one that they are seeking, what he says is the divine name: "I AM" (John 18:5-6). Hearing that powerful word, all of this army coming to arrest him falls to the ground. And we have only begun. Throughout what follows, it is as if Jesus himself is in charge. He speaks magisterially to the high priest (18:20-21) and to Pilate (18:34, 36-37; 19:11), discussing "my kingdom" (18:36). He makes Pilate afraid (19:8). He is seen as a threat to the emperor (19:12). And, when at last he is dead, he is buried in a garden, a kind of evocation of paradise (19:41), and is embalmed with one hundred pounds of mixed myrrh and aloes (19:39), an embalming worthy of the greatest monarch and worth more than a king's ransom.

But, on second glance, the signs woven throughout the story are still the signs of the suffering one. John's Gospel is *not* "docetic," not the story of one who only *seems* to suffer and die. After all, the soldiers recover and Jesus really is arrested. More than arrested, he is bound (18:12). Magisterial as his bearing may be, he is struck in the face (18:22), ritually defiled (18:28), brutally flogged and painfully mocked (19:1-2), stripped of clothing (19:23), and crucified (19:18). He is thirsty (19:28). And he is really dead (19:30, 33). They thrust a lance in his side to make sure (19:34). None of these sufferings are told in excruciating detail, but they are told.

The point of this narrative interweaving, of course, is that the Crucified One is the Risen One. His death is his glorification, his lifting up, and it is the salvation of the whole world, of the "all" that is drawn to him. One ought to remember here the same interweaving that marked the Johannine narrative of the supper: knowing that all things are given into his hands, Jesus gets up and uses those hands to wash feet (13:3-5); the all-holding one does slave service. So also here. The king, the Son of God, the very presence of the I AM, dies, and "it is finished" (19:28, 30).

Once again, this Passion account will call upon the preacher to preach the atonement. Whatever your "atonement theory" is, in whatever way you answer the question, "Why did Jesus die?" or, to use Anselm's phrasing, "Why did God become a human being?" the Gospel of John will push you further. John seems to say that by sharing our death, by actually dying among the wretched ones killed in our political and self-serving machinations, absolutely everything has been changed. God has gone where God cannot go, and death and fear and loss and hopelessness are themselves forever transformed into their opposites.

So, Jesus is king, but his throne is the cross, and his royal array is that given to him by a mocking army eager to kill him (19:2). Even so, in such condemnation, he is indeed "the man," the *anthropos*, par excellence (19:5). More, Jesus is killed, and yet he is the Lamb of God (19:33; cf. Exod. 12:9) for a new Passover out of death itself. Jesus is made utterly alone, and yet he gives us to each other as a new family (19:26-27). Jesus is thirsty, and yet from him pours life-giving water (19:28, 34; cf. 7:37-38). Jesus is made to stop breathing, and yet he breathes the Spirit of God, of life and forgiveness, from the cross into our assemblies (19:30; cf. 7:39; 20:22-23). All of these paradoxical images are intentionally and uniquely present in this version of the Passion story, and they are there to invite us to trust once again that God brings life from the cross.

The image of blood and water flowing from Christ's side may have yet a further intention. Very likely it was already true for the evangelist that the "blood and water" indicated baptism and the cup of the holy supper. In any case, only slightly later in the life of the church it became common to say that the sacraments flow out to us from the side of the crucified Christ, just as the Holy Spirit that enlivens our communities also has its source in his final breath. Both assertions are ways to say that the Jesus Christ crucified is, in a needy and captive world, source of life.

The preacher today needs to follow the lead of this narrative. The point is not to make people feel bad about Jesus dying nor to describe that death in alienating and grisly detail. It is, rather, to hold out the images of suffering so as to make room for your hearers to bring their own histories and the histories they observe all around them in the world into this story. And it is then to show the image of Jesus as reigning, as source of life, in order to invite your hearers to trust that God is raising them and all the world up together with Christ.

The liturgy will go on to make the same point in another way. After this text is sung or read and after the sermon, the assembly will pray for everything and everyone, in a kind of confident celebration that by the cross of Jesus all things are indeed being held in his hands and so held into hope.

First Reading
Isaiah 52:13—53:12 (RCL, LFM)

With Good Friday, we come to the fourth and last servant song. Once again, it is most likely that the song was originally intended to describe the vocation of the whole people of God, considered as a single identity and considered as suffering for the sake of leading many in the world to God, for the sake of making many righteous (53:11). Still, this fourth song, even more than the others, can easily be read as of one mysterious figure. Down through the ages, Jewish inheritors of these Scriptures have wondered who this servant might be. The apocryphal—or "deutero-canonical"—book of Wisdom, for example, took images from this song to apply to the fate of the righteous wise man (cf. Wis. 5:4). But for Christians, the subject of the song is Jesus Christ the Servant. He is the "root out of dry ground" (53:2), the "man of suffering" (53:3) who is held of no account. Yet that plant has become the very tree of life, and that ignominious suffering has been made the source of our forgiveness.

There are several stark passages in the fourth servant song that cause it to correspond rather directly with the Johannine Passion. "Kings shall shut their mouths because of him" (52:15), and Pilate is afraid (John 19:8). The servant is "like a lamb that is led to the slaughter" (53:7), and Jesus is the Lamb of God (John 19:31-33), who is silent before the slaughterer (19:9). His tomb is with the rich (53:9; cf. John 19:39-42). God has willed his suffering (53:10; cf. John 13:1, 3), and yet God has "prospered" him (53:10), in what Christians believe is the light and community and forgiveness and justification of the many that flow from the resurrection.

Since ancient Christian times, this text has been read to make sense of the death of Jesus. It is read again for this purpose today.

Psalmody
Psalm 22 (RCL)
Psalm 31:2 + 6, 12-13, 15-16, 17 + 24 (LFM)

If the fourth servant song has given images to the Christian community for understanding the death of Jesus, then these psalms have provided actual words for the telling of the story of that death. Especially is that true of the RCL selection, Psalm 22, sometimes called the "psalm of the Passion." Both psalms are psalms of lament, used here as response to the reading of the fourth servant song and as if in the mouth of the servant, with whom we are singing along. But Psalm 22 gives us the word that Mark says Jesus cried out as he died (22:1), the image of the pierced hands and feet (22:16), and the detail of the divided clothing (22:18). Still, both psalms move on, as lament psalms so often do, to the confident trust in the deliverance of God. For Christians singing these psalms, the "great congregation" (22:25) is the gathering of the assembly of the church where the news of the resurrection is proclaimed, and the meal of the poor (22:26) is both the Eucharist of the Risen One and the care for the needy that flows from those who follow the Risen One. Indeed, the heart of that assembly may take courage (31:24) as it waits for the Lord today and in the great Vigil of Easter. These psalms of the Passion are also words of the resurrection.

Second Reading
Hebrews 4:14-16; 5:7-9 (RCL alt.)
Hebrews 10:16-25 (RCL)

The temple-cult imagery remains strong in these two possible passages from the letter to the Hebrews proposed for the second reading. The passage from chapter 10 uses the metaphor of Christ's flesh itself as the new way into the Holy of Holies and his blood as the very means thus to come into the presence of God. From this metaphor, the writer urges us to take new courage for drawing near to God (who is, after all, "a consuming fire" [Heb. 12:29]) and renewed commitment to meeting in the Christian assembly (10:25), the place where the "pure water" of baptism flows (10:22) and where the "confession of our hope" (10:23) is renewed. Also in Hebrews, as in the Christian reading of Psalm 22, the assembly arises out of the death and resurrection of Jesus. Also in Hebrews, as in John, the water bath can be seen to flow from Christ's flesh. Confidence to approach God is also urged in the alternate passage from chapter 4, though here there is not quite so much temple-metaphorical language—simply that Jesus is our "high priest"—as there is a call for us to see that Jesus Christ, in his sufferings, shared our lot and our needs. In him is merciful understanding for us.

With a surfeit of images, more than any preacher can develop on any one Good Friday, we are surrounded in these readings with words for the meaning of Jesus' death. Yet the words do not exhaust that meaning. The purpose of the readings is to point toward the crucified Risen One, present now, in the power of the Spirit drawing us and all the world into the life-giving mercy of God. The preacher will pull a few of those pointers forward, glad that the room will still be filled with the resonances of passages that remain uninterpreted, inviting the hearers to continue to explore the meaning of Jesus' death with the rest of their lives.

April 7, 2012
Holy Saturday

Revised Common Lectionary (RCL)

Job 14:1-14 or Lamentations 3:1-9, 19-24
Psalm 31:1-4, 15-16
1 Peter 4:1-8
Matthew 27:57-66 or John 19:38-42

The Revised Common Lectionary, with these texts, provides readings for a service that might be held on the Saturday in Holy Week when that service is *not* the great Vigil of Easter. Let me urge you not to have such a service and not to use these texts. The next service in the liturgy of the Three Days is rightly, wonderfully, the Easter Vigil. *The* service for Holy Saturday is the Vigil. The gathering place of the assembly on this day is rightly silent, in glad and quiet preparation, until the Vigil. Many worship books that otherwise make thoroughgoing use of the RCL, as for example the *Book of Common Worship* (1993) and *Evangelical Lutheran Worship* (2006, hereafter ELW), in fact omit this set of readings. And the Lectionary for Mass has no comparable set, since, in Roman Catholic congregations, no mass will be held on this day until the first mass of Easter, which is the Easter Vigil. Instead of holding some other kind of Holy Saturday service, let me urge you again to recover the practice of the Vigil in your assembly.

But the problem is not simply the integrity and flow of the single liturgy that is celebrated over these Three Days. It is also that the texts themselves, the texts in this set, are much less clearly marked by both the cross and the resurrection, both death and life, than have been all the texts of Passion Sunday and the Three Days thus far. It would be easy to use these texts in a manner as if we were thinking that Jesus is now dead and we are going to raise him up with our celebration tomorrow. That is simply not true. It makes of liturgy a play acting, rather than a proclamation of God's truth. It might be possible, if one were very careful, to push these texts to do the double evangelical work so important to the message of this Holy Week. The comments below will try to offer help in doing that. But the best advice is to avoid using these texts at all. Of course, some intentional communities, communities that meet every day for daily prayer, will indeed be meeting, say, in the morning of Holy Saturday. It might be possible to adapt this set of readings for use in morning or noon prayer. Even then, however, they will need to be used with care. Jesus did indeed die, sharing the dereliction of the wretched of the world and sharing our death. And it is certainly true that for many people life itself is an agonized waiting in near-death, a waiting for a resurrection that never comes. Christian faith trusts that Jesus Christ has shared that awful waiting, the awful question of Job, but that he has placed the very life of God also there. God is there where we thought God could not be. Jesus Christ died, but—in a way we cannot quite bring to accurate words, a way best represented in symbols and images—we have been brought to trust that he is not dead now. That trust is the reason why we have Christian meetings for worship at all, also in Holy Week.

Gospel
Matthew 27:57-66 or John 19:38-42

The Gospel in this set of readings is simply the account of the burial of Jesus as it is present in either Matthew or John. For the burial in John—for its astonishing report of a huge amount of burial spices and for its use of the garden image—see above in the Gospel for Good Friday. A preacher might use these images to proclaim that the Crucified One is the reigning one, greater than any dead emperor, and that his death is the source of new access to paradise as a place to walk together in harmony before God. The garden here will in the next passage of John show up as the place where Mary Magdalene meets Jesus, thinking—not entirely inaccurately—that he is the gardener. "Gardener" is not quite the right name, but the one who was crucified does by the cross create and tend the new garden.

The Matthean version of the burial has no garden and no spices. It does have the rock-cut tomb, the great stone, and, especially, the story of a setting of the guard. Here the resurrection is implied simply by the guarding against it, or against a *pretense* of resurrection. The story quite obviously simply waits for its continuation, for the stone to be rolled away, the guards to be dumbstruck, and the real thing to happen. The story here is both a defense against the rumor that Jesus' resurrection was an elaborate hoax and, at the same time, a preparation for a much more literal understanding of the event of the empty tomb than is found in John. As such, it is harder to use this Matthean burial text, by itself, than it would be to use the Johannine one in signifying how the Crucified One is the Risen One now, in availability to all those who wait in agony. The symbolic materials are simply much stronger in John. To the Johannine text, we might say "the gospel of the Lord!" and "Praise to you, O Christ." That would be harder with the Matthean text.

In any case, if one of these texts is used it must be in order to preach the gospel, not in order to pretend that Jesus is now dead and buried.

First Reading
Job 14:1-14 or Lamentations 3:1-9, 19-24

The reading from Job presents the agonizing question of human mortality. Job's speech, in answering again to his so-called comforters, here has become direct address to God. He begs God to note that human beings have limited lives and that God ought to leave them alone and not be constantly judging them, a judgment they can never endure. Trees, cut down, can sometimes sprout again. Not humans. He further begs God to hide him in Sheol, thus in death itself, rather than bring him to endure God's wrath. Indeed, his final question in this passage expects a negative answer: no. If humans die, they will not live again. If they could, things might be different. But they do not. Such is the nature of this astonishing biblical text, this contradiction to the easy current American idea that human beings have immortal souls that live on beyond death, whether or not there is a God.

Were this text to be used on Holy Saturday, it must not be made a foil for Christian denials. Christians must not set themselves up as Job's comforters, lying about both the human condition and God. No, what Job says is true. Rather, Christians believe that Jesus Christ has shared Job's predicament and Job's anguished outcry. And so, God has shared that predicament and outcry. God is not a judge above mortal humans, but—amazingly—one of them, planting life in the midst of death. Only in the crucified Risen One, and not simply in the nature of things, is death so transfigured.

The Lamentations text also expresses the agony of suffering and death. Here, the suffering itself is from God, from God's powerful wrath. But, in spite of the text's sense of "no escape" (3:7-9), there is here more hope than in Job: the "mercies" of the Lord "never come to an end" (3:22). Read on Holy Saturday, the text functions like an anticipation of Easter. Still, what is "new every morning"—also on the morning of Holy Saturday—is that the Crucified One is risen. It is not our hope that will raise him up. Our hope, rather, is given birth by that news.

Psalmody
Psalm 31:1-4, 15-16

For commentary on this text, see the Psalmody for Good Friday (LFM), above.

Second Reading
1 Peter 4:1-8

After the Job text, if that reading is dealt with carefully, respectfully, this is probably the most interesting text appointed for this set. The suffering and death of Jesus are here made into the grounds for an appeal to Christians that they live differently from the surrounding culture and that, above all, they live in love. But at the heart of the text is the notion that the gospel has been proclaimed even to the dead (4:6). This idea, also mentioned in 1 Peter 3:19-20, ultimately developed into the idea of the "harrowing of hell." That is, the crucified Christ, in his death, has indeed gone to Sheol where he has taken hold of Adam and Eve—taken hold of humanity, thus— and pulled them up to life with God. In the Eastern churches, an image of this event became the primary icon of the resurrection. In a literal timetable of events, Holy Saturday became the day when this occurred. But one need not be literalist about the idea. And one can use something more like the Johannine chronology: everything— death, harrowing of hell, resurrection, ascension, gift of the Spirit, founding of the sacraments, gathering of the church, everything—took place when Jesus died. When God came into death, God took hold of humanity and pulled it up to life, to "live in the spirit as God does" (4:6). That "in the spirit" does not mean apart from the body, but in the Spirit breathed out by the crucified. Contrary to this Spirit, all of us are, like Job, judged in the flesh, in our mortal, turned-in-upon-itself flesh, and that judgment is death. In the Spirit is life. Not only Adam and Eve but all of us are pulled up out of judgment in the resurrection.

April 7/8, 2012
Resurrection of Our Lord / The Great Vigil of Easter

Revised Common Lectionary (RCL)

Genesis 1:1—2:4a*
Psalm 136:1-9, 23-36
Genesis 7:1-5, 11-18; 8:6-18; 9:8-13
Psalm 46
Genesis 22:1-18
Psalm 16
Exod. 14:10-31; 15:20-21*
Exodus 15:1b-13, 17-18
Isaiah 55:1-11*
Isaiah 12:2-6
Proverbs 8:1-8, 19-21; 9:4b-6 or
    Baruch 3:9-15, 32—4:4
Psalm 19
Ezekiel 36:24-28
Psalm 42 and Psalm 43
Ezekiel 37:1-14
Psalm 143
Zephaniah 3:14-20
Psalm 98

*The following three texts and responses
are in ELW only:*
Jonah 1:1—2:1
Jonah 2:2-3 (4-6) 7-9
Isaiah 61:1-4, 9-11
Deuteronomy 32:1-4, 7, 36a, 43a
Daniel 3:1-29*
Song of the Three 35–65

Romans 6:3-11
Psalm 114 (not appointed in ELW)
Mark 16:1-8 (RCL), John 20:1-18 (ELW)

Lectionary for Mass (LFM)

Genesis 1:1—2:2 or 1:1, 26-31a
*Psalm 104:1-2, 5-6, 10 + 12, 13-14, 24
    + 35 or Psalm 33:4-5, 6-7, 12-13, 20-22*

Genesis 22:1-18 or 22:1-2, 9a, 10-13, 15-18
Psalm 16:5 + 8, 9-10, 11
Exodus 14:15—15:1
Exodus 15:1-2, 3-4, 5-6, 17-18
Isaiah 54:5-14
Psalm 30:2 + 4, 5-6, 11-12a + 13b
Isaiah 55:1-11
Isaiah 12:2-3, 4bcd, 5-6
Baruch 3:9-15; 32—4:4
Psalm 19:8, 9, 10, 11
Ezekiel 36:16-17a, 18-28
*Psalm 42:3, 5; 43:3, 4 or Psalm 51:12-13,
    14-15, 18-19*

Romans 6:3-11
Psalm 118:1-2, 16-17, 22-23
Mark 16:1-7

* When a selection from the twelve Old Testament readings given here is what is used in a particular
Vigil, the *Evangelical Lutheran Worship* (ELW) indicates that these four are always among those
chosen. The passage from Romans and the Gospel are also always used.

W̲e have come to the principal event of Holy Week and Easter, the Great Vigil. In many ways, of course, the word *vigil* is misleading. We might, from this title, think that the service is one of *waiting* for Easter. It is not. The service is Easter itself, the heart of the celebration already, from its very beginning. As the assembly is welcomed and greeted, as the fire is ignited, as the paschal candle is lighted, Christ is proclaimed as risen. We ought not try to figure when in the service we can begin to celebrate the resurrection of Jesus. The whole service is such a celebration. Christ is risen before we began. No, the word *vigil* comes to us from the ancient practice of Passover as "a night of vigil" (Exod. 12:42) as well as from the more general Christian custom of beginning the celebration of Sunday itself with a night service, a "vigil." If our Easter Vigil waits for something, then it waits for the word of the resurrection, celebrated in this night, to be made known in all the earth and for God finally to raise up all things as Jesus Christ has been raised up. It waits for the *eschaton*, for the manifestation of God's great day.

In this night and in this assembly gathered in the night, the resurrection of Christ will be proclaimed repeatedly. It is proclaimed by the night itself, since, according to the stories, it was at night, in a way beyond our knowing or controlling, that Jesus was raised: we gather in that mystery. It is also proclaimed by the springtime equinox and the full moon, seen as signs of the renewal of the very earth being worked by God in the resurrection. But, then, the resurrection is proclaimed by the metaphor of fire and the spreading of candlelight and by song about that fire and light as signs of the risen Christ. It is especially proclaimed by an astonishing range of biblical stories of deliverance, all read as words for the resurrection. And, in the ongoing service, it is proclaimed by the presence of the risen body of Christ in brothers and sisters singing together in the light and around these readings; by the welcoming of new members of this body through holy baptism and by the watery remembrance of the baptism of us all into the death and resurrection of Christ; by confident prayer in the Spirit of the risen Christ; by the sharing of the peace of the Risen One; by the holy supper of his presence; and by the sending of the assembly to bear witness to these things. All of this is Easter.

Our concern here is primarily with those readings. Many of the passages listed above have been used by various groups of Christians in the celebration of this night for a very long time. Already in the second century, the "paschal homily" of Melito of Sardis, the text of which we still have, begins by referring to the narrative of the exodus as having just been read aloud and goes on to make reference to many other biblical stories that we still use. Melito was probably building on an old Jewish practice, a practice evidenced in the Aramaic translations of the Torah called *targumin*, of reading or telling the stories of the "four nights" during the nighttime observance of the Passover: the night of creation, the night of the deliverance of Isaac, the night of the exodus, and the night yet to come, the night of Messiah's appearance. Our paschal Vigil tells all of these stories, especially if one regards—as Christians do—the story of the resurrection of Jesus as the very "night of Messiah." When we actually begin to find Christian lectionary lists, in fourth- and fifth-century Jerusalem for example, something very close to the list of twelve Old Testament readings found in the ELW has already been assembled as the list of readings for this night. Modern lectionaries have worked with this old information, some making all the possible readings available, others editing that list. I would urge you to use as many as you can in your community, finding alternative ways for them to be read or proclaimed.

One evidence of the antiquity of this service is the centrality given to the readings from the Old Testament. Unlike the chapters here for other days, I will begin with those central "prophecies," those hugely important Old Testament narratives that make up the main body of our night of vigil to the Lord. Stories from Israel's history, stories of deliverance mostly, are seen as witnesses to the way God works, a witness culminating in Jesus' resurrection. Furthermore, these same stories of the deliverance of the people and of the forming of the people to trust in God are also taken as stories appropriate to baptism, as a description of what happens to the baptized and as words for the faith in which the baptized are formed. The passage from Paul's letter to the Romans then caps this series of baptismal images and the Gospel of the resurrection sums up all the images of deliverance. In what follows here, I will be reflecting on the texts in this way, on the texts as images both for the resurrection of Jesus Christ and for our baptism into that resurrection.

It is important to do this. The word *resurrection* is not quite the right word. What happened to Jesus Christ did not simply involve a dead man coming out of his grave. That is not nearly enough to say. It may even be quite wrong. What we call "the resurrection" involves the crucified Jesus Christ becoming accessible, his living body encounterable by the assembly that meets him in faith through Word and Sacrament and in the presence of the community. It involves all the forms of the presence of Christ in the assembly, most especially the presence of his body and blood in the Eucharist. More, it involves this same Jesus Christ being present throughout the cosmos, especially identified with the wretched poor. It involves, indeed, the beginning of the raising up of all things. More, it involves the creation of a new community under the Spirit of his resurrection, baptized persons walking together as witnesses in the world, as his body. By using such an abundance of images for the resurrection—and thus also for baptism into the resurrection—we are able to proclaim a little more faithfully the overwhelming mercy and renewal that Christian faith has meant by "resurrection."

Preaching in this service does not need to be long. But it does have the possibility of calling attention to at least some of these images and how they work to bring us again to faith in the God who raises Jesus and pours out the Spirit of that resurrection. Indeed, it does have the possibility of making a little clearer again what we mean by "resurrection." It does have the possibility of being, next to the readings, another verbal way of our encountering Jesus Christ, now through a living and contemporary voice.

The lectionaries provide a set of responses from the Psalms and from some other Old Testament sources for each of the Old Testament readings. Using a few of these can be quite good, perhaps especially the "Song of Miriam and Moses" from Exodus 15 and one or two psalms. These biblical sources also provide remarkable images for us. But I would suggest that some readings might be read without response and that others might have as response the use of a great range of hymns and songs.[1]

It is important to note also that this great liturgy of the resurrection speaks both sides of the story, both death and life. Also here the Risen One is the Crucified One. That will be clear, of course, in the holy supper, where "my body for you" and "my blood for you" bear witness to the cross, turning it into source of life. Furthermore, it will be clear in the action or remembrance of baptism, since baptism involves a burial into death for the sake of a rising to new life. But it will also be clear in the readings. The new creation itself, like the image we read in Genesis, arises out of chaos and destruction, now the chaos of Jesus' death. Further, because of Jesus standing with them, we can mourn the dead of the great flood or the Egyptian dead on the seashore, as well as whatever slaves did not escape. More: all those bones that God will raise up to be a great host are indeed dry and dead. Jonah is thrown overboard and the three children are thrown into the fiery furnace: their lot is to be death. But God does raise up that great host. Jonah is spit out onto land. Another one stands with the children in the furnace, and they are not burned. And Jesus Christ is risen—the risen Crucified One.

Such is the celebration of this remarkable night.

The Vigil Readings
Creation
Genesis 1:1—2:4a (RCL, ELW)*
Genesis 1:1—2:2 or 1:1, 26-31a (LFM)

This poem of the creation of all things was probably written during the time of the exile. It provides an image of how the many things that were regarded by other peoples as gods were created by the one God; it makes the observance of the week into a regular witness to God's creation; it gives a reason for the keeping of the Sabbath; and it calls all things good before God. For Christians, the God who makes an ordered world out of chaos also is the God who gives life to the dead and justifies the ungodly (cf. Rom. 4:17; 5:6). In Jesus Christ's resurrection a new creation has begun. He is the Word God speaks to all things. Baptism brings us to begin to walk in that new way, in God's good earth, as the Spirit hovers over the water of the font where we were baptized. We might say that Jesus Christ and baptism into him bring us into an eighth day, a day acknowledging the great goodness of the seven, a day celebrated in the midst of the seven, but a day giving us what an ordinary week could never deliver. Or, we might say that on this great Sunday of the resurrection, God says again, "Let there be light."

Flood
Genesis 7:1-5, 11-18; 8:6-18; 9:8-13 (RCL, ELW)

The old myth of the flood is like yet another creation story. God begins again, and wicked humanity is drowned in the new version of the chaos out of which comes the recreated world. Christians have long seen the Spirit that descends in the Gospel's story of Jesus' baptism as imaged by the dove that announces the end of the flood. And Christians have long seen the eight survivors of the flood as a type of the baptized (see 1 Pet. 3:20-21), living now with all the animals, under God's rainbow, on God's beloved earth. But an even more profound reflection will see that the crucified Christ identifies with all those, humans and animals, swept away in all events of devastating death, and yet God also makes the risen Jesus Christ and the community around him to be the ark itself, wherever there is a flood of loss.

The Testing of Abraham
Genesis 22:1-18 (RCL, ELW, LFM)
Genesis 22:1-2, 9a, 10-13, 15-18 (LFM alt.)

To our sensibilities, this is a horrible story. What would have happened to Isaac's trust in his father? Does God really mean it? How does Abraham know it is God? But our sensibilities were not present in the creation of the story. It is nonetheless a story that retains even for us its primal power. It is not a story marked by our psychological interests. It may have originally been a story meant to require Israel to turn away from the widespread ancient practice of child sacrifice. Using a ram was a better idea. In any case, Christians have seen Jesus Christ in the ram, God's provision so that we would never again ritually slay our children and each other, God's provision for new life. And Christians have seen the baptized in Isaac, spared from death by the angel and the ram to live anew, and also in Abraham, formed deeply to trust that God is life-giving, new-family-making, not death-dealing. Perhaps, even more profoundly, our Lord Jesus is Isaac. Only, he is not spared. Rather, he is raised up. The story, finally, is a story of deliverance, but the deliverance is from religious malformation. The resurrection brings us to a different kind of religion.

Exodus
Exodus 14:10-31; 15:20-21* (RCL, ELW)
Exodus 14:15—15:1 (LFM)

For Christians, the two great stories of the Old Testament are the narratives of the creation and of the exodus. At the Vigil, the two greatest images of the resurrection are these same stories. In the resurrection of Jesus Christ, there is a new creation. In the resurrection of Jesus Christ, there is a new exodus: the world itself is brought out of slavery into freedom. As the stories say that God acted to deliver a small, enslaved people to be God's own people of priests and witnesses for the world, so Christian faith says that Jesus has come across the sea of death and brought to God a new people of witnesses and priests for the sake of the life of the world. In baptism, we are joined to that crossing of the sea, to that promise of dancing on the safe side. Just as the flood narrative, this narrative as well is a new creation story. God hovers over the sea, not defeating enemies in nature, however, but defeating people who want to enslave others. Still, we may also weep for Pharaoh's conscripted soldiers. They, too, image a kind of slave in need of freedom.

God's Marriage to the People
Isaiah 54:5-14 (LFM)

The RCL does not use this passage, it would seem, largely because of its possibility of sexist misuse. God here is "husband," and the neglected city or the cast-off people is "wife," saved (or not saved!) only by the action of the husband. This is not a helpful image in the present time, when many peoples around the world still act as if this unjust way of relating men and women is the divine order of things. One might hope that a future revision of the Roman lectionary would follow the lead of the RCL. In the present LFM, however, this passage from Isaiah retains the only reference there is to the flood story. The Noah story is here reused to talk about God's commitment to the people, just as the Vigil (in the ancient lectionary as in the RCL and ELW lists) reuses the Noah story to image God's action in the resurrection of Jesus. The Bible itself, like the Vigil, is marked by a continual rebirth of images. Carefully interpreted, not making too much of the supposed gender of the partners in the image, one can indeed say that in the resurrection, God has "married" the earth and its inhabitants. Easter is the celebration of the nuptials. So the "Easter Proclamation" of the ELW sings out, more carefully than this passage, "This is the night in which heaven and earth are joined—things human and things divine."

Come to the Waters
Isaiah 55:1-11* (RCL, ELW, LFM)

The image of water, wine, and milk being offered freely to the thirsty and food being given away without cost to the hungry, of this food replacing "that which is not bread," is a wonderful one. This image is then intensified in this passage about grace from Second Isaiah: the people may freely return to God, who is full of forgiveness; and the word of God, which makes and revives the world, will do its work more surely than rain will bring about harvest. Indeed, the harvest from the word falling like rain will be bread that is really bread. For Christians, all of this—forgiveness, the life-giving word, true bread, wine, and milk given away to all who come—are found in the resurrection of Jesus Christ. And those waters are the very waters that come from the side of the crucified, slake every thirst, and flow in the font of baptism.

The Wisdom of God
Proverbs 8:1-8, 19-21; 9:4b-6 (RCL, ELW)
Baruch 3:9-15, 32—4:4 (RCL alt., ELW alt., LFM)

In both of the optional passages, wisdom is personified as Woman Wisdom, a figure whom God has found and has used to create all the good earth. According to Baruch, God has then given this Wisdom to Israel. She has appeared on earth as the book of the law, as the Torah. If Israel would cleave to her, the nation will live, coming out of the defiling death of exile. According to Proverbs, Wisdom herself has set out a feast, bread and a prepared cup of wine, so that simple and foolish people may eat, be wise, and live. For Christians, Wisdom has appeared upon earth not only in the Torah, but in Jesus Christ and in the Spirit that is poured out from his death and resurrection. She cries out in him, "Come to me, all you that are weary and are carrying heavy burdens, and I will give you rest" (Matt. 11:28). He is the way from death to life, the way we learn in baptism. And the feast of Wisdom is found in the food he sets out, in the power of the Spirit: his own body and blood, crucified and risen.

A New Heart and a New Spirit
Ezekiel 36:24-28 (RCL, ELW, LFM)

The powerful image at the heart of this Ezekiel passage is the replacing of a stony heart with a real heart of flesh and the replacing of a rebellious and violent spirit with the very gift of the Spirit of God. It was one way to express the hope of the prophet for an exiled people. But the image is so strong, it can easily come to stand for hopes for all of humanity, torn apart as we are by violence, by a defiling of the land with blood, and by yet more stony hearts. For Christians, the Spirit that fills the Vigil, the Spirit poured out from the death and resurrection of Jesus, the Spirit of service and mutual love, is the very gift we hope for all people. And the "clean water" (36:25) is the water of baptism into the death and life of Jesus, the water of birth in this same Spirit. Living the baptismal life in the risen Christ, gathered into him at any place on the good earth, is being brought "into your own land" (36:24).

Dry Bones Live
Ezekiel 37:1-14 (RCL, ELW)

Yet another image from Ezekiel for the hope of the return of an exiled people is this image of the valley full of dry bones. The narrative presents itself as a prophetic vision set off by the complaint of the people that they are "dried up," their "hope is lost" (37:11). The image, of course, was not at its origin a proposal of a literal resurrection, but a metaphor for the recovery of hope and thus of life. Read at the Vigil, however, it both evokes the story of the resurrection of Jesus and calls that story out to us for our life and hope. It metaphorically breathes on us the Spirit of the Risen One so that we may live, revived in our actual present bodies. The word in the Vigil and the word alive in the catechesis around baptism, then, are like the prophesying of the prophet, speaking to our bones.

Gathering of God's People
Zephaniah 3:14-20 (RCL, ELW)

The readings appointed for the Vigil include not only central passages from the Torah, the "five books of Moses," and from the major prophets, but also texts from the minor prophets. Here is Zephaniah, a prophet probably active in Judah during the reign of Josiah. Whether or not this final passage of his book is from this prophet or from a later exilic or postexilic redactor, it is a magnificent hymn about the deliverance of the city Jerusalem. Once again, the image is of God "marrying" the people, though nothing much is made here of God's or the people's gender. Rather, the image is of God being in the people's midst, rejoicing in them, and gathering in the outcast, the sick, and the shamed. For Christians, the "day of festival," even the day of the marriage, is the resurrection of Jesus Christ. In him, God is in our midst. Through him, the Spirit gathers all the people into a strong new city of refuge, the assembly of the church. Baptism is such a gathering.

Jonah Saved
Jonah 1:1—2:1 (ELW)

Two of the remaining readings, those from Jonah and from Daniel, function like ancient Jewish comic books or graphic novels: the stories are largely fictional; the images are arresting; the message is profoundly serious; but the reading itself is meant to be rather fun, even funny. Both texts are rather late, probably intended at their origin to urge fidelity to God and awareness of God's care for other nations in the midst of the oppressive empire and pagan religion of the Hellenistic Greeks. The astonishing thing about Jonah is that this narrative figure is called to preach to Nineveh, the terrible and oppressive city of Israel's past, the great image of the enemy. No wonder he goes in exactly the opposite direction, toward the West, toward Spain (Tarshish), not toward the East, toward Nineveh. After all, what was God doing, caring about Nineveh? The story of the storm, and of Jonah thrown overboard, and of the great fish, and of the salvation of Jonah follows. Since the Gospels themselves, the Jonah story and its three days have been considered an image of the resurrection of Jesus (cf. Matt. 12:39-41). Indeed, Jesus dies with the rebellious, and his resurrection is the new possibility of their faithful turning, in witness and love, toward those they consider enemies. Once again, resurrection is a coming through the sea of death toward a new, more open, and more faithful life, an image that all the baptized may treasure.

Clothed in Garments of Salvation
Isaiah 61:1-4, 9-11 (ELW)

The last reading from Isaiah is drawn from the very last chapters, from what is possibly Third Isaiah, the continuation of the prophecy of the school of Isaiah into a time after the return from exile. It is a beautiful passage in which the prophet—or, perhaps, as with the "servant" of Second Isaiah, the nation itself—is anointed with the Spirit to announce good news: recovery, return, comfort, liberation, healing. Three major images are used: God clothes the naked with festal clothing and with garlands. God makes the people to be as strong trees. God causes the people to build up old ruins. Since at least the Gospel of Luke (Luke 4:17-21), Isaiah 61 has been taken to speak of Jesus and his ministry. He is the one anointed by the Spirit to announce the good news. Indeed, he is the good news himself. For Christians, the word of his resurrection, his restoration, is at the heart of that good news. The anointing oil and the garment of baptism are signs of the garments of salvation. And the vocation of the assembly around the Risen One includes a continued turning toward the oppressed and mourning world, a continued building up of the ruins.

Deliverance from the Fiery Furnace
Daniel 3:1-29* (ELW)

The last reading is this wonderful old story. One may hope that your congregation will enjoy hearing it again, with its narrative repetitions, so characteristic of Aramaic storytelling, and with its horrible emperor and toadying officials resisted by the faithful Jews. The joy of the story may rightly merge into the joy of Easter. Even when Nebuchadnezzar continues to get it wrong at the end, thinking that the faith of Israel can be propagated by violence (Dan. 3:29), the hearers will know that that conclusion is utterly misguided. Perhaps you can lead your congregation in hissing this villain! Such a response might fit the character of the story. Christians have seen the story of surviving the fire as another image of the resurrection. They have seen the baptized as called to stand alongside Shadrach, Meshach, and Abednego in resistance and witness, unafraid of death. But mostly, they have seen the "fourth" man in the fire, the one with "the appearance of a god" (3:25), as the very presence of the crucified and risen Christ. Jesus Christ stands with all the persecuted ones of the world. His cross shares the fire with them. And, in the midst of every fire, he is their—and *our*—life.

New Testament Reading
Romans 6:3-11 (RCL, ELW, LFM)

This passage from Paul can be seen as summing up all of the images for baptism that we have been considering. What will follow in the liturgy shortly will either be actual baptisms or, at least, a remembrance of baptism by the whole assembly. While we celebrate the resurrection of the Crucified One this night, for Christians this resurrection pulls us along. A major means of the pulling is baptism. Easter is not only about a past event. It is about our being gathered into that event and henceforth living our lives from it.

Gospel
Mark 16:1-8 (RCL)
Mark 16:1-7 (LFM)

If the Romans text can be seen to receive and sum up the images of baptism we have been encountering in all the readings, then it is fascinating to see the account in the Gospel of Mark as receiving all of the images we have been exercising for the resurrection of Jesus. In Mark's Gospel, Jesus is not there in the tomb but he will be seen, as he promised, "in Galilee" (16:6-7). The appearance does not take place in the narrative itself. Indeed, the women do not even pass on the promise but, rather, flee away, afraid. This puzzling ending has brought readers of Mark to realize that they are thereby being sent back into the Gospel book itself where, with Jesus' coming into Galilee (1:14) they learn to see the risen Crucified One *in the very stories of the book*, in the assemblies of those who gather in Jesus' name around this book, and in the little and marginalized ones who are received by those assemblies (see 9:37). What readers of Mark have learned can be extended to all the stories we have read tonight: the resurrection appearance of Jesus has come to us in these stories. These stories are part of what Paul means by testifying that Jesus died, was buried and was raised "in accordance with the scriptures" (1 Cor. 15:3-4). In these stories, we begin to see him, so that we can learn to see him as well in the little ones of the world. The promise given to the women at the tomb comes to our assembly tonight. Here you will see him.

John 20:1-18 (ELW)

For commentary on this text, see the Gospel for Easter Day, below.

Note

1. For assistance in planning, for ideas about diverse ways of reading, and for suggestions for hymns and songs, you might look carefully at three other Augsburg Fortress publications: *Worship Guidebook for Lent and the Three Days* (2009), *Music Sourcebook for Lent and the Three Days* (2009), and *Indexes to Evangelical Lutheran Worship* (2007).

April 8, 2012
Resurrection of Our Lord / Easter Day

Revised Common Lectionary (RCL)
Acts 10:34-43 or Isa. 25:6-9
Psalm 118:1-2, 14-24
1 Corinthians 15:1-11 or Acts 10:34-43

John 20:1-18 or Mark 16:1-8

Lectionary for Mass (LFM)
Acts 10:34a, 37-43
Psalm 118:1-2, 16-17, 22-23
Colossians 3:1-4 or
   1 Corinthians 5:6b-8
John 20:1-9

Holy Week and the Three Days have led us to Easter Sunday morning, to the first day of Easter, the first of the "fifty days of rejoicing" to follow. If you are a preacher in contemporary North America, this is probably the one celebration during all of these days where you will see and be speaking to the most people. Indeed, the Sunday morning liturgy of this day may be one of the most attended services of the year. Before you, around you, will be the Easter Christians. But also a great array of regular participants will be there. In addition, there may be the curious, people who decide to use the crowded attendance as a way to hide a little as they try on what Christianity may be meaning these days. In any case, it is important that all be welcomed. We do not "earn" the gospel of Jesus Christ by having faithfully worked through Lent and Holy Week. As in the parable of the equal wages, all of us are freely and graciously given the *denarius*, whether we have worked or not. So, taught by the reading at last night's Vigil, let everyone come to the waters; let those who have no money come, buy and eat.

It is, however, important that the gospel be preached at this liturgy in clarity, that the water and the food of God actually be set out. It is important that this service not be devoted to "gospel lite," as if the gathering were only about springtime or new beginnings or new clothes, or only about a kind of pretending that things are happy, or, for that matter, only about the new life and not the death of Jesus Christ. No. The heart of this day, like the whole of the week behind us, is both the passion and the resurrection of Jesus. Both. This day, too, is a day for the preaching of the cross as the source of new life. The Risen One is the Crucified One. Here, by the power of the Spirit, in the presence of each other, in the preaching you do, and in the holy supper, Jesus holds out to us his *wounded* and life-giving hands and so gathers us into the life of God.

Our celebrations may then surround that center. Let there be springtime flowers and, especially, let there be music. The gospel of cross and resurrection as the grounds of our hope is rightly surrounded and expressed by a great array of wonderful music. And, even, let those who will, put on beautiful clothes and hats. For Christians, the clothes of Easter morning may be a sign of our sense that God has raised us up, in our bodies, together with Jesus Christ. Still, the use of such a sign must not shame or exclude the poor or the sick, though it is not uncommonly people in hard straits who especially wish to put on such signs of life. In any case, the word of the cross welcomes us all and helps us avoid pretense.

Preaching on this day is a remarkable opportunity to speak the grace of God and to ground one of our most popular celebrations in its own deepest meaning: the crucified Risen One.

Gospel
John 20:1-18 (RCL)
John 20:1-9 (LFM)

In the Fourth Gospel, there are not several women who go to the tomb, as in the Synoptics, but Mary Magdalene alone. As the story proceeds, she becomes the one to summon Peter and the "beloved disciple" and then she is the first to see the risen Lord. Indeed, sent to tell the others of the resurrection, she becomes what the later church calls "the apostle to the apostles." She is an image of what ministry and preaching are about in the earliest churches, before a later time when women were largely silenced. And, according to this narrative, the people of the most ancient community were receiving the gift of the resurrection gospel all together, as a community. Mary is not left alone with her encounter. She has already summoned the others. Now she is sent back to the others. (For the supposition that Jesus is the gardener, see the Gospel commentary for Good Friday, above.)

The dialogue of recognition between Jesus and Mary enacts what has been said earlier in the Gospel: "the shepherd . . . calls his own sheep by name . . . and the sheep follow him because they know his voice" (John 10:2-4). Mary is called by name and she knows the voice.

The "do not hold on to me" passage (20:17) must not be interpreted as Jesus' refusal to be touched by a woman. On the contrary, Mary is here commissioned as a preacher. The passage means to make clear to the hearers that the one whom she and the other Christian preachers announce—the one whom this Gospel book announces—is the ascended one. For the Fourth Gospel, the death of Jesus, his resurrection, and his ascension are all finally one thing: his "glorification" or his "lifting up." For the Fourth Gospel, the Jesus who was killed has paradoxically ascended to fill all things, every place where God is, which is every place there is. Thus, he cannot be held by only one or only a few. But Jesus has also ascended to fill the preaching of Mary and, as we will see in John 20:19-31, to be present in the meetings of the church. Two things follow: The Jesus who is met here is the Jesus who has been killed; the crucified is the risen and ascended one. And, for all of its interest in the faith of an individual, the Fourth Gospel always also envisions that individual in community.

Peter and the beloved disciple see the empty tomb. Of the two, according to the text, it is the beloved disciple who believes. This beloved disciple, of course, is frequently identified with John, after whom the Gospel is named, though there is no such identifying in the book itself. Rather, in the book the beloved disciple seems to be the mysterious figure remembered by the author of the Gospel and by his community as the guarantor and eyewitness of the stories contained there (cf. 13:23-25; 19:35; 21:24). For this community, their guarantor is in some tension with Peter and has slightly more authority. What is doubtless reflected in this text are tensions between several different late first-century or early second-century churches. It is then fascinating to note that here the beloved disciple believes first, even without seeing Jesus, as Mary does, and even without knowing the Scriptures that tell of his rising (20:9), the Scriptures to which Paul testifies (1 Cor. 15:4). But then, the Gospel book itself finally becomes one of those Scriptures: it is written so that we may believe (20:31).

For us, like the beloved disciple and Mary and Peter and the rest, we come to believe in the resurrection together, in company, huddling together against death, calling to each other to come and see, sent again and again to be with each other, no matter what the tensions are. But for us, unlike what is reported of the beloved disciple, the Scriptures themselves, including this text, are one basic place where we may hear the voice of the shepherd calling us by name. That "calling by name" may be there for us, especially, as we recognize that the Scriptures, in their accounts of human sorrows and losses, and in their way of gathering those sorrows into the story of the death of Jesus, speak powerfully of our own lives. Then the word of the resurrection pulls us up to life, as Mary was so pulled.

The sermon today should aim to use the Scriptures to call those in the assembly by name.

Mark 16:1-8 (RCL)

For commentary on this text, see the Gospel for Easter Vigil, above.

First Reading
Acts 10:34-43 or Isaiah 25:6-9 (RCL)
Acts 10:34a, 37-43 (LFM)

The lectionaries begin today to read from the book of Acts for the first reading, doing so for all of the Sundays of Easter. It is an interesting decision, based on the idea that this second volume of Luke-Acts is, in fact, a book of the acts of the risen Christ in the churches. But on this Sunday, the RCL also provides a reading from the Hebrew Scriptures as an alternative. If you have the choice, I would urge you to follow this option and use the Isaiah text. Here is one of those ancient Scriptures that the earliest Christians understood to be speaking of the resurrection of Jesus. Here is yet another magnificent image, like the images of the readings of the Vigil. Here is a text that truthfully evokes our sorrows and the shared lot of human death, while also speaking of God's life-giving mercy.

For Christians, the eschatological feast promised by the prophet has already begun. The supper of the Lord, wherever it is celebrated, is already gathering the nations onto the mountain of the feast. And, in the gospel of the death and resurrection of Jesus, God is already beginning to wipe away tears and announce the end of death.

The reading from Acts, the narrative of a sermon presented as given by Peter, presents a straightforward Lukan summary of the ministry, death, and resurrection of Jesus and their consequences. Also here, the meal of the church makes an appearance. We have come to believe that the one who ate and drank with the first witnesses, after he rose from the dead, also eats and drinks with us now, making us, too, witnesses to the forgiveness of sins through his name.

Psalmody
Psalm 118:1-2, 14-24 (RCL)
Psalm 118:1-2, 16-17, 22-23 (LFM)

Psalm 118 has played an important role in the formation of Christian imagery. It was used in several places in New Testament writings (cf. Mark 11:9; 12:10-11; 1 Pet. 2:7). Its imagery recurs in every use of the *Sanctus* around the Lord's table (vv. 25-26) as also in every Palm Sunday procession (vv. 25, 27) and every Easter proclamation: "This is the day that the LORD has made" (v. 24). Christians take the "I" of the psalm to be Jesus Christ himself, who was "pressed and pressed" (v. 13, ELW) but who lives (v. 17) and becomes the chief cornerstone (v. 22), and the "we" toward the end of the psalm (vv. 23-27) to be the Christian assembly, gathered in praise. That very assembly gifts us with the possibility of singing along with our risen Lord, "I shall not die but live, and declare the works of the Lord" (v. 17, ELW). It is exactly the right psalm for Easter.

Second Reading
1 Corinthians 15:1-11 or Acts 10:34-43 (RCL)
Colossians 3:1-4 or 1 Corinthians 5:6b-8 (LFM)

Easter Day is so important and so rich that the lectionaries have some trouble deciding between many options. (For commentary on Acts 10:34-43, see the first reading, above.)

The passage from 1 Corinthians 5 is a remarkable extended metaphor; Jesus Christ, in his death, is the new paschal lamb, and Christian life is to celebrate the new feast of his saving death continually. Paul urges that as the old Passover was observed with a week in which only unleavened bread was eaten, this new Passover is to be observed by Christians all the time, ridding their lives of malice, as if it were the leaven to be swept away, and instead filling the metaphoric tables and houses of their lives with the "unleavened bread of sincerity and truth." The passage from Colossians 3 is yet another brief exhortation for Christian living, rooted in the death and resurrection of Jesus. For this Deutero–Pauline writer, if we are baptized into Christ, we have already died in him. Our life is where he is: hidden in God and with the poor. If one is careful about interpreting the "things that are above" to be genuinely the things that are in God, then this way of reading Easter gives us both astonishing freedom from fear and a new way to live toward others. Either of these texts can call Christians into a kind of daily celebration of the meaning of Easter in our lives.

The passage from 1 Corinthians 15, however, is the yet more basic Easter text. It contains Paul's use of what is very likely one of the oldest summaries of the Christian faith, the testimony to Jesus' death and resurrection as occurring "according to the scriptures" and as witnessed by Peter, by James, and by a whole assembly of people. Paul says that he has both received and passed on this summary, and he then adds himself to the list of witnesses. Paul has seen the Risen One in just the same way as did the others, though he is a great sinner. Such a testimony presents a very different idea of the resurrection of Jesus than that contained in the much later accounts of the empty tomb. For one thing, there is no mention of the empty tomb. What is crucial is that Jesus was encountered, that he appeared. Furthermore, Paul's vision of the Lord (cf. Gal. 1:12, 15-16) is held to be of exactly the same sort as the earlier appearances of the Risen One. Such statements help us to see that resurrection of Jesus is not to be regarded as an old and odd—and to us inaccessible—resuscitation of one corpse, but as the very "ascension" of Jesus to which the Johannine Gospel seeks to give another kind of narrative shape. The Risen One, seen by several witnesses in the ancient church, is now accessible by us all in the Christian meeting, in the word of those witnesses, in the Scriptures and in the sacraments, in the body which is the assembly, and in the body of the wretched poor.

The passages from the LFM are set, with the choice between 1 Corinthians 5 and Colossians 3 a simple decision between two similar Easter instructions for Christian living. If I were serving a community that uses the RCL, however, and choosing among the options for reading at this liturgy, I would select John 20 as the Gospel, Isaiah 25 as the first reading, and this passage from 1 Corinthians 15 as the second reading. Isaiah gives one of the voices of the ancient Scriptures that help us to encounter the resurrection of Jesus, and John and 1 Corinthians both refer to those Scriptures. Then I would seek to preach in such a way that my hearers in the assembly could hear themselves called by name in these very passages. In a way, our assembly would then join Peter and Mary, James and Paul, and all those five hundred brothers and sisters in seeing the Lord, but now the seeing would be with our ears.

In these same Scriptures—but also in the holy supper and in the very assembly you serve—may you hear your name called as well.